Praise for Frederick Barthelme's *The Brothers*

"Barthelme has managed to reinvest highly familiar material with new vigor and insight. . . . In *The Brothers*, [he] has split his archetypal middle-aged hero into two characters . . . and we come to understand both their shifting balance of power and the circumstances that have brought them to their current emotional impasse." —Michiko Kakutani, *The New York Times*

"Barthelme writes with exceptional beauty about what Biloxi looks, smells, tastes, and sounds like—its tawdry but lovely gulfside edge—and there is to the characters' confusions and shamblings a new fine melancholy never before quite as codified in Barthelme's fictional world." —*Kirkus Reviews*

"A funny book, full of odd, lingering warmth" —*The New Yorker*

"*The Brothers* is rich with implication and full of delightful images. It takes the virtues of minimalism and builds on them to produce a story that resonates long after the last page has been turned." —Robert Boyd, *St. Louis Post-Dispatch*

"Barthelme's strength as a writer [lies] in his insights about ordinary lives in the contemporary deep South. His observations and descriptions are wry and pungent . . . he wins the reader over by a steady array of quirky characters and visual detail." —James Naiden, *Minneapolis Star Tribune*

"In such wonderful books as the short story collection *Moon Deluxe* and the novel *Natural Selection*, Frederick Barthelme emerged as the voice of the new Southern suburbanite, more yuppie than cracker. He still is, more or less, but the voice is altered in this new and thoroughly delightful novel." —Roger Harris, *Newark Star-Ledger*

"His eye for the weary tackiness of coastal Mississippi and its inhabitants is as sharp as always, his ear for American speech as accurate as ever." —Fredric Koeppel, *Memphis Commercial Appeal*

THE
BROTHERS

a novel by

Frederick
Barthelme

COUNTERPOINT
WASHINGTON, D.C.

Library of Congress Cataloging-in-Publication Data

    Barthelme, Frederick, 1943-
      The brothers: a novel / by Frederick Barthelme.—
      1st Counterpoint pbk. ed.
        p. cm.
      ISBN 1-58243-130-2 (pbk.: alk.paper)
      1. Brothers—Fiction. 2. Biloxi (Miss.)—Fiction. I. Title.

PS3552.A763 B74 2001

813'.54—dc21   00-065949

FIRST PRINTING

COUNTERPOINT
P.O. Box 65793
Washington, D.C. 20035-5793

Counterpoint is a member of the Perseus Books Group

10 9 8 7 6 5 4 3 2 1

For Rie

THE
BROTHERS

1

AT FIVE-THIRTY on Friday afternoon the eight-block crescent of downtown Bay St. Louis, Mississippi, looked like an airport postcard of a Mediterranean seaside village, one of those bathed-in-light towns, high off the sparkling water, trees bent with wind, everything going red against a swelling sky. Del Tribute, driving from Houston to Biloxi, cut through just to take a look, then went back out to the highway for the drive down the coast, riding high in the Vibra-Matic cabin of a sixteen-foot Ryder rent-a-truck with his car and everything he owned or wanted to own, just about, in back of him and the rest of his life somewhere out front. It'd quit raining, and the sunlight was glittery as he crossed the bridge over the bay, but his fellow travelers didn't seem to notice the light. They were busy jerking past him, spitting from their car windows, dodging between lanes, sucking beer out of cans in brown sacks, tossing hunks of sandwich into the road, popping the grimy kids, and wringing back their stringy blond hair. There were lots of Ford Pintos out there on Highway 90, and they came in all colors, but it seemed as if most of them were blue. There were dogs too, dirt-yellow dogs and brown-spotted dogs, black mud-caked dogs, most of them in the beds of pick-ups or the back seats of Pintos. There were a few low-riders and custom cab-overs, plenty of big black sedan-style motor-cycles ridden by old tattooed men with their women in cup seats up over the back wheels, and there were lots of rusty fenders, pitted bumpers, taillights scabbed over with red-orange plastic and silver duct tape. All along the water, cars were stacked up anglewise and kids in swimgear loitered, girls walking in that prance bikinis seem to magnify.

At a gas station in Henderson Point, just across the bridge, he bought a diet Coke, and the guy behind the counter wanted to talk shoes. "Where'd you get them sneaks?" the guy said, pointing down over the counter, without looking, at the high-top you-pump-'em sneakers Del bought right after the divorce because he thought his regular shoes were uncool. By now he hated them so much that it was all he could do to wear them for moving.

"They're for sale," he said. "Make me an offer."

"I didn't say I wanted to buy 'em," the counter guy said. He was straightening a jar of short rubber snakes that were painted Aztec patterns in Day-Glo colors. "I was thinking they looked kind of dumb on you. No offense, of course."

"That's why I'm selling them," Del said, as he thumbed through a stack of handouts on the counter. One of them was a single sheet that looked like a local newsletter, something for the alien-life-forms crowd, featuring a headline about a guy barbecuing his neighbor's dog.

"Yeah," the counter guy said. "This looks to me about like you made a serious fashion error."

"They were a gift," Del said.

"I can get you a sawbuck, maybe," the guy said, using a snake tail to weed a fleck of tobacco out of his teeth.

"Hey, look," Del said. "I'll take them out here in the drive-way and set them on fire before I'll sell them to you for ten." He was grinning to be sure the guy wouldn't take it wrong.

"You set 'em on fire and I'll give you twenty," the man said. He was grinning too.

Del got outside, up in the truck, and out on Highway 90, which ran from one end of the Mississippi coast to the other. He still had thirty miles to go before Biloxi. He was thinking about being fifty years old. He wished he was fifty and settled somewhere with a happy wife, a nice lawn, a pair of attractive and loving children doing well at Emory. There was something magic about fifty, something potent. Maybe it just seemed that way to him because in the home movies and photo albums, his mother and father always looked fresh and vigorous and healthy when they were fifty. They looked satisfied, they looked like they had the world by the tail. It wasn't nearly so good, of course, in real life. There had been fighting, there were arguments over fish sticks that ended with his father hurling a fish-stick-portion impaled on a fork across the dining room to prove some point, fork and fish end over end through the air and into the kitchen. But in the snapshots his parents looked above the fray. That's how he thought of them when he thought of them in their prime. Fifty was wonderful for them—they looked great, they acted cool, they seemed bemused by everything—and that was how he imagined it would be for him.

Now, as his parents neared eighty, they were still sprightly, still fully functional, but nobody would accuse them of being in their prime, looking great, or being bemused by anything.

He checked his mirrors and stuffed the plastic screw-top Coke between his thighs. The sky swelled up into a smooth and lovely gray, showing a weather head. Light on the blacktop seemed to glow slightly—it wasn't just sunlight on the ground; it had thickness. A white heron winged up against the gray sky, its yellow feet dangling. Straight ahead, there was a red-and-white-striped microwave relay tower, maybe two hundred feet high, each stripe forty feet tall, its girders a delicate sketch against the gray in the sky. Rain started snapping against the truck, popping the glass and running up toward the top of the windshield. A guy swerved by with three big cardboard boxes of Hanes Activewear in the back of his Blazer. The rain came in little tufts, enough just to wet the windshield before it would stop, then start again. The wipers cleaned the glass in two passes, then started screeching.

He was moving to Biloxi because he'd been given a condominium, outright, by his ex-wife's rich father, a going-away present. It was less than a month since the divorce papers were final, and he was driving straight through from Houston.

Del was about forty-four and figured that was near enough to start thinking about fifty. Early retirement. Maybe he would become a tiny gambler, slip by on blackjack winnings from the new casinos—nothing big, just a few hundred here and there, enough to buy fish dinners at the shack restaurants and dodge back to the new condo he hadn't even seen yet on the fourth floor of Tropic Breeze, a concrete-and-brown-glass pyramid building from the seventies, overlooking the Gulf. He'd seen photos, but not the thing itself. Whatever else, he was ready to quit worrying and start getting the relief that played on his parents' faces in all those family photos.

His older brother, Bud, who was fifty and a little more, had been living in Biloxi with his wife, Margaret, for eight years. They taught communications and tech writing at one of the half-dozen Gulf Coast junior colleges, sometimes at two of them. Del had visited them occasionally, but it had been a while.

He and Karen had been married twelve years. They met in graduate school when Del was in his late twenties and later he asked her to marry him, and she accepted when she figured out he was serious, so they got it done at City Hall and honeymooned in Galveston. He took her out to eat at a brand-new modernized Shell Food Mart down there—she thought that was pretty funny. They had Rainbo cinnamon rolls and Borden's chocolate milk and some crispy things that looked like little ants. They sat out in the parking lot in his car with the doors propped open, listening to the Gulf and watching the sky. When the honeymoon was over they went right back to school. Later they went to Oklahoma State, where he got a doctorate in communications. Then they moved back to Houston. He got on doing PR for the city council, then the mayor, but he lost interest too quickly, so screwed up some stuff, and didn't move up in the firm. In fact, he moved down, then out. He dodged around from job to job. His employers always said he was a hard worker and a good sport, and they always sent him along with their very highest recommendations.

Eventually Karen turned up in love with a horse trainer, the oldest son of a friend of her father's from up in the Panhandle, so they separated.

In the family, her father was always the Doctor. He'd bought just the right hundred acres of empty farmland in southwest Houston in 1939, and the land made him rich, and being rich made him stupid. He always seemed to have some white stuff on his lip, at the corner of his mouth, and he never seemed to know it. Karen always wiped it off for him. The Doctor was so glad Del hadn't gone after money in the divorce that he messengered over the condominium deed the day after. He'd had four units once; three sold at profit, and he hadn't much use for this last one, so giving it to the departing son-in-law wasn't a big deal, just easy generosity. And if there was a hint that Del might want to relocate to Mississippi, where was the harm?

2

BUD AND MARGARET were supposed to be waiting for him at their house, but when he got there, Bud had taken off for California, and Margaret was upset. "It's a movie thing. All he does is rent movies, hundreds of them, watches them day and night. Every crazy movie you ever heard of. His big favorite is this thing called *Santa Sangre*. Very strange. He wants into the business, and this ex-student has a deal, so he's out there."

They were on the glass-enclosed sun porch of the old white house she and Bud had a few blocks off the highway in a hundred-year-old residential section, one of those neighborhoods where people fix the houses up. They hadn't done much, so the place had a pleasantly worn feeling. Bud's cat, Walter, was stretched out on one of the windowsills.

Margaret was tall, athletic, lots of tone, late thirties but could pass for mid. She'd always been sexy, that loose kind of comfort with her body that ended up with showing it around a bit, accidentally or otherwise. Del wasn't above taking advantage.

"He just drove off?" Del said. "He knew I was coming, right? And he just left?"

"Yep. Yesterday. You could have passed him on the road. He said he'd call you tonight."

They had a beer together, sitting on the porch, she on the cane sofa and Del in one of the wicker armchairs. She was all in black, jeans and a tank top. He was having trouble keeping his gaze out of the red zone, and she could tell.

"It's going to be you and me for a while," she said, spreading her arms across the back of the sofa. "He could be gone weeks, or even months, I guess. All summer. You don't mind just me, do you?"

Del smiled tight at her. "No, I don't," he said.

"I'm sorry about Karen," Margaret said. "I liked her."

"So did I," he said. He was cracking his beer can, making a noise like the clickers kids used to get for parties.

"You want another one of those?" she said, meaning the beer.

"I need to check out the condo," he said.

"After dinner," Margaret said. "Why don't we take a look inside?" She was up and moving, reaching for Del's hand, pulling him to his feet.

"O.K.," he said. "Where should I put my truck?" He waved toward the front of the house, where they could just see the tail of the rented truck almost covering her shallow yard.

"It's fine right there," she said. She pressed her cheek against his shoulder. "I'm glad you're here, really. We'll be good for each other right about now."

She started to show him around the house, beginning with the porch they were leaving. "The realtor made a big deal out of it, the porch. She kept calling it the Florida Room," Margaret said, "like it was something special, something from a grander moment in the history of real estate, no doubt. She'd come in and sweep her hand back and forth and tell us about the rare pleasures of the Florida Room, like they were all about appetites of the flesh. It's been a house gag since."

Del had seen the place before, but it had been years. As they went through, he was pleased that it still looked unfinished, undecorated, in progress, as if Margaret and Bud were everywhere evident in the mismatched furnishings, the peculiar rugs, the framed pictures on the walls, the oddly-tossed-together quality of things. This was an aspect of them that was at once appealing and a little scary—like him, they weren't quite grown up. Though Bud was older, they lived like thirty-something, not the TV-show style, where everybody was busting a gut to get with the program, but the too-early-to-start-worrying style, the What? Me worry? arrested-development style. The taste, where there was taste, was reserved—reissued Aalto chairs from the thirties, a couple of antique and rather odd-looking side chairs, a plain modern sofa, Palladio prints. The restraint was cheek by jowl with virtue-out-of-plainness Storehouse furniture and with things that were ridiculous and grotesque, like the green imitation-lizard plastic, padded stools from Wal-Mart that Margaret seemed too fond of. Nothing fit together very well, and that was refreshing.

"It's really clean in here," he said, finally.

Margaret turned around and smiled at him, her head tilted just a bit so that he'd know that she knew what he meant. "It's not that peculiar, Del. Won't hurt you."

He liked the sound of her hardwood floors, the way the wood echoed his footsteps and Margaret's when they walked through the rooms.

Over sandwiches, she told Del she'd fixed him up with a temporary job at Audio Instincts, a stereo and TV joint on Highway 90, owned by somebody in her sister's husband's family.

"I told the guy you were a wizard with electronics," she said. "You are, aren't you?"

"Sure," he said.

"So there you go," she said. "This'll break you right on out of that PR death spiral. Let's finish eating, and I'll take you out and show you the place."

AUDIO INSTINCTS faced the water through a maze of giant plaster-and-lath animals that were part of the tourist business, which was about eighty percent of what Biloxi, and the rest of the Mississippi coast, seemed to be about. That and dock-side gambling, a new enterprise that had just come in the year before and taken the whole coast by storm. Several casinos were already built—they were actually paddleboats, Missis-sippi riverboats, anchored to the beach—and there were more to come. But for the entrepreneur the best deal hands down was a Wet Willy's franchise, or even some no-name knock-off half-as-good water slide, or a bungee crane, or the thirty-foot-tall-monster-painted-like-a-giraffe business. Del liked the plaster-and-lath creatures right away. A bunch were in the minigolf trade—the course across from the Audio Instincts store had a giant condor hole, a giant orangutan hole, a giant pole-vaulting ostrich hole, and a few holes Del didn't recog-nize. Other big animals were advertising gasoline and charter boats and trampoline parks and souvenir shops, and even the Triple XXX Video shop, that one a white-chested skunk up on back legs, a messy grin on its face and a bright pitchfork in its forepaw.

Del and Margaret looked in the window at AI, pressing against the glass like kids. It didn't look too bad. There were two listening rooms; the place was arranged in a sensible way; the equipment wasn't the best, but it wasn't the worst, either. He took a certain satisfaction in that. "I'm glad they don't sell junk," he said. "I can sell it without feeling I'm taking advantage."

"You're going to be the salesman with a heart of gold," Margaret said. "The first one."

They went by the condominium, which looked better than it had in the picture he remembered seeing. It was well maintained and had a nice view of the Gulf. Across the highway, running out from the beach, there was a smallish marina-like set of boat slips. The face of the building tilted back pyramid style, so every condo had an open balcony with a sun screen over it.

They buzzed the manager, and Del introduced himself and Margaret, and then the manager called up to see if Del's tenant, a woman named Pixie, was in. She was, so Del and Margaret went up. Pixie kept her "product" all over the place, and she wasn't quite organized. She was a Hi & Dri Hair Services salesperson, a miniature pink-haired woman of thirty-five, and she seemed to be moving her belongings out one tiny white box at a time.

"You got my letters, didn't you?" Del asked.

"I'm slow-moving here," Pixie said. "But I'm getting it done. Maybe a week, and I'm gone."

"Don't you worry," Margaret said. "He'll be staying with me a few days, anyway." She looped Del's arm and pulled him over to the glass wall that looked out on the Gulf. "Pretty," she said.

"Birds hit that glass sometimes," Pixie said. "Splack! Right into it. You have to call Tommy, from downstairs, to clean 'em up. They flap and flap out there, sometimes flap themselves right off the edge down to the apartment below."

"No kidding," Del said.

"They come in here like smart bombs," Pixie said, doing a missile glide pattern with her hand, making a flight whine, finally banging the points of her cherry-red nails into the palm of her other hand.

Margaret guided Del toward the door. They were stepping

over sample cases full of wigs, hairpieces, twists, and thatch, hundreds of tiny sample bottles of hair care products, even some of that new spray-on hair that changes ambient body hair into full-grown head hair instantly.

"We gotta scat," Margaret said.

BUD CALLED that night and said he knew California was the perfect place for a guy like him, and he wasn't even there yet, he was in Las Vegas. "I got the California rash," he said. "Big lips, bad actresses, sex all over everybody, galactic ideas, top money—it's a wonderland."

"That's good, Bud," he said. "But what is the plan? What are you going to, like, do? I just got here, and I figured you'd be here, and I don't know if I can do this without you."

"Do what without me? You're fine," Bud said. "And now that you're there, I can really take my time and check this movie program out."

Margaret tagged Del's arm and whispered, "Ask him where he is. Get a number."

Del asked and got the number. Bud was calling from the Firelight Tonight Motel. "But what is the point of this trip, really? You're going to hang out a week and then you're back here like nothing ever happened? I don't get it," Del said.

"No," Bud said. "I can't really explain it, can't make it clear. It's not even clear to me. I'm going on empty here. Instinct. It's just one of those things. You know it when it hits you. Need."

"What need? Travel? Get away? Be alone? Be stupid? What? What about Margaret? What's happening with her, with the two of you? Have you been getting along?"

"We're doing good," Bud said. "Or maybe not good—who ever knows? You take a bath with Margaret, and you don't know. Is she standing right there? Don't tell her I said that. You just keep an eye on her for me. That's your job. That's your assignment." He coughed, and Del heard a siren go by a thousand miles away on some street out there in Las Vegas. "I'm sorry about the divorce and all that. With Karen," Bud said. "Are you all right?"

"I guess," Del said, sighing artificially. He felt on the spot for an answer that didn't require discussion. "Partly I'm relieved. It's odd, though, to be unmarried. I sort of like it."

"That's what you tell yourself," Bud said.

Del waited, then said, "I'm not saying I'm giddy, just that we burned it out a while ago. It was over way before. I miss *her* now and then, but not marriage. Mostly I miss the way I felt ten years ago."

"There's no news there," Bud said.

"I didn't know things would slow down this much as you go along, but they do get dry, don't they? Still, that's not the divorce."

"No, that's normal shrinkage," Bud said. "That's the law of diminished pleasures." Bud sounded as if he wanted off the phone. "You seem all right to me. You'd like this place out here. It's different, everything's alive, everything's moving— I've got a Corvair already. A good one. Brown. Traded the old van for it. I'm headed out across the big yellow sand, running for the promise."

"You got a brown Corvair," Del said, shrugging at Margaret, who was leaning against the kitchen wall, listening.

"It's a great brown, Del. Jesus, you wouldn't believe it. It's so brown it makes my legs weak, makes my heart sing. It's *deeply* brown."

"Uh-huh. So when are you coming back?"

"I don't know. I can't say. These things take time. I may get out here and get hooked into something, you know, have to tailor my schedule around something, God knows when I'll be able to cut free. Meetings and all that. Could go that way.

For the time being, you have to figure I'm out of pocket. Things are on the flux."

Del rubbed the heel of his hand into his eye and wiggled the phone at Margaret, asking if she wanted to talk. She nodded.

Bud said, "Hey! You there? You guys loosen up, O.K.? Maybe I'll get you a Corvair while I'm out here. A Studebaker Hawk. A Pacer, huh? You name it. This is a living graveyard, vision of the future. You don't want to sit down out here, because you never know if you're sitting on a ride."

Listening to his brother on the telephone, what Del thought was that Bud was a little too excited. He gave the handset to Margaret.

THE IDEA WAS that his staying with Margaret was supposed to be friendly and familial—they were supposed to be pals. Instead, it went wrong right away. She was worried and nervous, and he was happy to have somebody all to himself again, and they started horsing around, having fun together, and one thing just naturally led to another. Pretty soon they were out in the Florida Room, aiming at a little too much intimacy. Margaret was more forward, ready to go a little farther, to stretch propriety, but at the same time, she kept the boundaries clear. He observed the limits without argument.

"What's the answer with this?" he asked one night, the dark glass around them shoaled with raindrops. "Margaret? This is crazy."

"It's not," she said.

He waited for her to say something else, to elaborate, to explain, but nothing came next.

"I've always liked you," he said, "but this *is* crazy. We've got to stop. I can go to a hotel."

"We will stop at the proper moment," she said. She was

crosswise on the couch, her head in his lap. He was splitting her hair into sections.

"I think this is it," he said, rocking back to boost her off his lap. "C'mon. Let's get straightened out. Sit up, will you?"

"We haven't done anything terrible," Margaret said, getting up. She crossed to the television and snapped it on, tuning in the Weather Channel and muting the sound. "Anyway, we have an understanding, your brother and I."

"Thank God I don't know anything about that," Del said, raising and shaking his hands as if to declare himself happily out of that business. "But I'm betting Bud doesn't want this, and you don't either, really. And I don't. Hey, this is the unwanted."

"Oh," she said, coming back and sitting on the coffee table facing him, her knees straddling his. "I'm not your kind of girl, that it?"

"That's not what I said," he said.

She leaned forward and kissed his cheek, then twisted his head with both hands and got his lips. It took a few minutes before he was up and out of the room.

SO THE FIRST FEW WEEKS Del was in town were weeks with his brother Bud as a kind of shadow figure, somebody just in the walls, in the medicine cabinet, off the page. Del and Margaret had this time together, the sexual play becoming more open, longer-lasting, increasingly intimate. Sometimes they talked about it as if they were just friends and maybe a little bit more. Sometimes they said how creepy it was to be doing what they were doing, how creepy and exciting. He couldn't tell what her satisfaction in their play was—pleasure, need, retribution, havoc, chaos, or all of that. Or something else. Some days they pretended nothing was happening, as if skirting sex with your brother's wife, on the porch of your brother's house, was as normal as anything could be, wouldn't raise an eyebrow anywhere on the planet. Sometimes they would decide they needed to "talk things out," and there would follow lengthy, tiring discussions of what they were doing and why, full of drugstore psychology and acknowledgments of guilt. After those sessions, she sometimes sulked, and sometimes he did, and sometimes they just let it alone for a while.

"What're we going to do when Bud comes back?" Del said one night on the porch.

"We're not doing anything," she said. "What do you mean, what're we going to do? We're going to stop."

She was much too patronizing, as if he was childish to imagine otherwise. It hurt. "Things are getting good, though," he said. "It's like having a new girlfriend with a hot edge—somebody who's smarter, and tougher, and who's been deeply screwed by my brother."

"That's not pretty," she said.

TWO WEEKS AFTER Del got to Biloxi, the UPS overnight woman came to the door with a package from Bud. Del had to sign for it, because Margaret wasn't home. He made a kind of sawtooth signature in the little LCD space on the UPS woman's electronic tablet. He thought about opening the package, but didn't, finally. Later, when Margaret got home from work, she opened it. It was a videocassette, marked "Bud Working" in bold letters on the edge.

"You want me to go to my room?" Del asked. "Leave you alone?"

She looked at the tape, then at Del, and then said, "Maybe that's not a bad idea. Let me just look at it a bit, and then I'll call you. That O.K.?"

"Fine," he said. He headed off to the room he'd been sleeping in, the spare bedroom, which was down the back hall from the sun porch.

He stayed there an hour, resting on top of the bed, his arms folded across his chest, crossing and recrossing his feet. Eventually he got up and went to the door, opened it a slit. He couldn't hear any TV sound, so he didn't know what was going on, whether she'd stopped watching, or muted it, or what. Or whether she'd changed to MTV or the Prevue Guide channel, which she watched all the time.

He crept down the hall, telling himself he shouldn't sneak up on her, and leaned around the corner into the sunroom, trying to get a look at the reflection of the TV in the late-afternoon glass without alerting Margaret.

Bud was on the TV. He was sitting there on the screen. Margaret was on the sofa, staring at Bud on television. Del watched from the hall for a minute. Bud wasn't talking; he wasn't even looking at the camera—he was working, or that's what it seemed like in the reflection in the window. It was hard to see what was on the screen because Del was looking at it backward, reflected in the porch glass. Bud had papers, his briefcase, up there on the desk beside him, and he was writing things on one of his famous yellow pads, periodically moving the stuff he had on the desk as if he was looking for some paper he'd misplaced.

After a while Margaret caught Del watching and signaled for him to come over and sit with her on the sofa. She patted the seat beside her.

"Sorry," he said. "I got too curious."

"Just come watch," she said.

So he did that, he sat next to her, and together they watched Bud on the screen. It was clear there wasn't anyone running the camera—he'd just put it there, pointed it at himself while he was sitting at this desk in what looked like a hotel. Bud had gotten his head and shoulders in the picture, and a little of the desk. On the wall over the desk there was an oil painting, the one with the orange ball and the seagull.

Sometimes Bud was whispering on this tape, but Del couldn't make out what he was saying, mostly curses and the kind of sounds a person makes when he gets an idea or remembers something suddenly. There were also lots of breathing noises, and paper-shuffling noises, and chair creaks.

Margaret put her arm around Del, pulled him close, and leaned her head on his shoulder. It was getting dark outside, getting to that kind of half-light that changes the way things look inside, that makes everything in the room look filtered. He smelled Margaret's shampoo. They hadn't turned on any lamps yet, so they were sitting there in this slanted light watching Bud on TV.

They watched for two hours. Not once did Bud say a thing to the camera, although he did glance out at them a couple of times. Those were startling moments. He smiled, or tried to smile. He did this thing he did with his face when he wanted to smile, anyway. Del recognized it. He'd seen it since they were kids. Bud seemed to be looking right through the camera, right across time and space, right at them.

Later that night Del found Margaret watching the tape again, and he sat with her, and they looked at the whole thing all the way through a second time.

This became a regular event for them during the time Bud was gone—almost every night they'd sit together on the sofa and hold hands and watch Bud work. They'd started taking their dinner out to the porch so they could eat with Bud. Then they'd do the dishes and clean up the kitchen, and then they'd go back out to the sun porch and talk. The sexual stuff had cooled off some, so most of the time they just touched each other lightly, stroking forearms or shoulders or cheeks, or leaned against each other, or intertwined arms and legs reassuringly. A couple of times they did get into the heavy trucking, with Bud looking on, though more often they just sat there with Bud's big face shining down on them, enjoying each other, and him too.

A MONTH AFTER Bud left for California he telephoned from the Los Angeles airport and asked Margaret to pick him up in New Orleans. The call came without warning on a Saturday at noon. Del and Margaret had been planning a drive over to Bay St. Louis, to an oyster place she'd heard about.

Before she'd even hung up the handset Del was moving around the room. He said, "Shit. I don't know. I gotta get out of here."

"It's fine," she said, trying to slow him down, steady him by catching his wrist. "It's going to be O.K. I don't want you running out on me now. We don't know what we're looking at here with Bud. Take it easy, don't worry. Let's wait and see what he says."

"Great idea," Del said. "He walks in and what, I tell him I really like your tits? That'll be fun. I can imagine what he's going to say to that."

"Don't be a jerk," she said.

"It feels really shitty, doesn't it? I'm a half-order of some leftover, yesterday's takeout."

"What?" Margaret said.

"The way he calls and you jump for the keys."

"What do you expect me to do? He's my husband. You want me to tell him take another month?"

"Yeah, well. Never mind. You go get him, and I'll be fine. Maybe I'll check on Pixie, just as a precaution."

"You're being silly," Margaret said. "But it's O.K. Go ahead and check her, but come here first and give me a hug." She opened her arms. Del went to her and they kissed, held each other for a while, rocking slowly side to side. Feeling the warmth of her against him, he thought it might be the last time he would hold her in that particular way.

IT TOOK MARGARET and Bud longer than necessary to get back from New Orleans. She'd left Biloxi at three to get him coming in on a four forty-five flight, and they finally got back to the house around eight.

Bud was in the shower, cleaning up, when Del caught Margaret in the kitchen and asked why the drive back had taken three hours. She said, "We were talking a lot."

"Oh, good," Del said. "Good. Is everything O.K. so far?"

"Seems to be O.K.," she said. "Everything's being talked about. Everything about Bud running off to California, anyway."

Del nodded. "Pixie's fine too. She's almost out. Her brother died of cancer and she had to slow down the move, but she's back on track now. Those little white boxes are blowing out of that condo."

"What boxes?" Bud said, coming into the kitchen toweling his hair. He was slighter than Del, but broad-shouldered, with sharp eyes and a smile that seemed to go on and off very quick. Both of them were better than six feet, and though neither was athletic or inclined to exercise, both seemed fit.

"My tenant is packing all her things in white cardboard," Del said. "Special white cardboard."

"Huh," Bud said. He crowded Margaret from behind, kissed her neck as she rinsed a plate. "We having food next?"

"Sandwich," Margaret said. "You reappear suddenly, you get a sandwich. Give notice, get a roast."

"What happens if I never leave?" Bud said.

"Fed through a tube," Del said. "Delicious stuff—Grape-Nuts, everything."

Margaret gave him a cockeyed look, and he shrugged. "You hungry?" she asked.

"I guess," Del said. "I don't know."

He made himself a quick sandwich and went out to the porch to watch TV. Bud and Margaret moved through the house as if they were the only ones there, back and forth in the kitchen, to the bedroom, and back. Del stayed on the porch and watched the way their arms and legs moved when he could see them out in the kitchen, watched their heads cock and twist as they talked, their bodies lean toward and away from each other—after a while it was like watching pipe-cleaner people taking positions in a shoe box.

They were getting along too well. To Del that suggested she wasn't telling Bud about them, though they hadn't decided whether or not she would. It had come up, of course, but they'd skipped the decision part. He wondered if Bud had ever intended to do anything in California in the first place, or if he'd just been making up some kind of gyp crisis so he could spend a couple of months piddling around out there with the girls of summer, feeling his so-called oats.

After Bud and Margaret had finished off their sandwiches in the kitchen, Bud came out and sat with Del. "So I hear you guys have been spending lots of time out here, enjoying the timeless pleasures of the Florida Room?"

"We watched you on TV a lot," Del said.

"I heard that," Bud said.

"So what happened? How come you're back so soon? This was your escape into the new world."

"I've been gone a month," Bud snorted. "Besides, where'd you get the idea I was escaping? I was just checking it out, looking around. Things didn't go the way they were supposed to, is all that happened. This kid I taught is a hero among the studio suits, but he doesn't remember my name too well."

"That's too bad. So where's this Corvair you got? How come you're flying back?"

"It burned up," Bud said. "I had a big freeway fire. I was lucky to get out alive."

"Sure," Del said. "Sure you were."

"No, it's true," Bud said. "The first part is true, anyway. Only I wasn't in the car when it was hit. I was off in the bushes, taking a double dip, and I looked up and this giant Black Hawk Bacon tractor-trailer jackknifed into my Corvair at about eighty miles an hour and *ka-blam!* The goddamned car exploded." He shook his head.

"Are you serious?" Del said.

"Yep," Bud said. "Fire sailing through the midnight sky. It was really gorgeous, in that horrible way." He shivered, shaking off the recollection. "The guy died."

"Christ."

"I guess I *was* lucky, wasn't I? You and Margaret had a good time, though. She says you're closer than ever."

"She said that?"

"Sure she did. She tells me stuff." Bud gave Del a forced smile and a pat on the shoulder. "Don't you worry, though," he said, flapping his hand like a bird's wing alongside his head. "It all floats away eventually."

Del wasn't sure what that meant, or if it meant anything at all, so he nodded as though he understood what Bud was saying, thinking he needed to get Margaret and square their stories.

That first night Bud started designing the new couch, a tufted thing with no arms or back—he called it a "divan." It was the only thing he'd ever designed in his entire life. He designed it for about three hours that night, did drawing after drawing out there on the floor of the glass-enclosed porch, working on a roll of shelf paper that had faint bluebells on it.

The next day he and Del went out on the other side of Ocean Springs to a highway lumber store called Necessary Wood. It was the only lumber place open on Sunday. When they got back to the house they started building the divan. All three of them had to pitch in and help. That's the way it always was with Bud's projects—they were Bud's *and* everybody else's. It took four days to complete the divan. When it was finished it was plenty uncomfortable, but Bud put it out on the sun porch and said it was exactly the kind of thing he'd always wanted.

THINGS TURNED a little nasty when Margaret decided to talk to Bud about his drinking a couple of days after he got back. He wasn't drinking that much, anymore, and Margaret acknowledged that, but seemed to want to be sure he wasn't going back to it. She wanted Del's help, so the three of them sat down at the kitchen table. "To begin with, Bud, if you start the drinking again you're going to kill yourself. I don't want to let it happen. I think that's one of the things we have to work on first."

"Yeah," Bud said. "Let's work on me first." He looked at Del as if to see what Del was going to do in this conversation. "You want to work on me too?"

"Not on your life," Del said, watching some phony congressman on C-SPAN on the six-inch TV mounted under the kitchen cabinet. "But sometimes you do drink too much, or you used to."

Bud gave him a nasty smile. "I guess if I was *still* drinking like I used to drink I would be killing all three of us, right?"

"You already cut back—is that the point?" Del asked. Bud stared at him, and Del said, "He's already cut way back, Margaret. I think that's his position."

"So maybe he changed while he was out on the coast," she said. "But I'm not sure. When he was drinking before, he reminded me of Bobo. You kind of lose something, you know, Bud?"

Bobo was the neighbor Hilary Jakes's almost-adopted son, a kid who came from a home and was apparently the son of alcoholic parents. Bobo had brain trouble.

"God gave us Bobo," Bud said. "Or gave *them* Bobo. He's all right."

"I know that," Margaret said. "But if we ever wanted a child or anything, right? Know what I'm saying? I need *you*, not some half-there version of you."

Though Del had known Bud to drink plenty, it seemed as if that was over, had been over for a while, so he wondered why Margaret had brought it up. Maybe she was nervous about things, maybe she felt more guilt than she said.

Years before, when Del had come to visit them from Texas, Bud would sometimes get drunk and be ugly about the school, the people who worked there, and other people too, like TV news jocks, politicians, sports guys—anybody who stood up and made a jerk out of himself or herself for no good reason. When he was drinking, Bud thought a lot of things were wrong, more things than not. So they'd sit together on the porch, and Bud would tell Del what those things were, in endless detail, just the way their father had done years before, at the dinner table.

Every once in a while Del would say, "Jesus, you sound just like Father, don't you?" And Bud would tell him how everybody becomes more like his father or her mother as he or she gets older, how you watch it happen, powerless to stop it, how it sneaks up and you find yourself saying things your father said, or laughing some way he did at a point in conversation, or even smelling like him, rolling over on the bed in the afternoon and noticing that the pillow has that unmistakable scent of your father in it, that scent from another time, back to confuse you.

On those visits, when Bud was drinking, he would eventually fall asleep; when that happened Del and Margaret would spend their evenings together, talking about Bud, watching movies on television, reading, leafing through magazines and newspapers. But now that Bud wasn't drinking so much, Del almost wished he were, so he wouldn't go off with Margaret every night, taking her to bed with him, leaving Del alone in the rest of the empty house.

"So what's the deal over there?" Bud said, pointing toward the neighbor's. "What's the latest?"

"Bobo's having trouble with his girlfriend. Her name's Lollie," Margaret said. "They're too far along for kids their age, is what Hilary says. Lollie's older than he is, anyway."

"He could be twenty, for all we know," Bud said. "Veteran of some foreign war. Maybe he was out there in that sinkhole by choice."

"It wasn't a sinkhole he was in," Margaret said. "It was a piece of giant concrete pipe. And he was living there because his parents were drunks."

The people from Roads and Highways found Bobo living in a section of drainage pipe out near a dead-end spur off I-10. He was put in a state school, and it turned out Hilary Jakes knew one of the teachers there, and this teacher started talking about the new kid a bulldozer driver found living like a wild animal in a pipe near this settlement called Bobo Line, Mississippi. That's how Bobo got the name. Pretty soon Bobo was coming over to the Jakeses' for visits and cookouts and movies at the mall. He was becoming a regular part of the family.

"Hilary says Bobo's the conscience of their marriage," Margaret said.

"What does that mean?" Bud said.

"It's about keeping them together," she said. "Now she's afraid he'll go too far with Lollie. I don't know why they have to do it at thirteen—we waited, didn't we? We found all kinds of things to do while we waited."

"Underwear," Del said. "We did underwear."

"Well?" she said. "That made it better, didn't it?"

"They don't wear underwear," Bud said. "And there's a Condom Tree at the junior high. They get samples in the mail."

"I guess it's not the same, is it?" she said.

"No," Bud said. "Now it's: Hurry up, kid, get it over with so we don't have to worry about you. And here, let me hold your trousers."

"Oh, it's not that bad," she said.

"I think it probably is," Del said. "Bud's right. It's our fault too."

"It's not my fault," Bud said. "I discourage it at every op-portunity. I think we should bind their little sex parts." His eyes narrowed into tiny slits, and he smiled.

"Careful," she said.

"Make them wear steel pants," Bud said.

"Bud's always saying horrible stuff about Bobo," she said. "It's supposed to be funny."

"I said he came in a can," Bud said, waving her off. "That's the kind of terrible thing I say. My compassionate wife objects. The kid's brain damaged."

"How would you know?" she said.

"I talked to him," Bud said, doing a big, slow-moving fish mouth. "You've got to use tiny words and talk real slow. And get a mouse squeaker to squeeze to keep his attention."

"You never will get it right, Bud," Margaret said.

———

NEXT DAY Bud went out to the college around noon to check his mail, which Margaret said had been stacking up out there since his trip. Del and Margaret were left alone at the house. They were in the kitchen having sandwiches when Bud left. At first neither of them said anything, but then Del asked. "So what did you say?" he said. "He brought it up, but I didn't know what he knew. He didn't seem upset."

"I didn't say anything, just gave him the baseline," she said. "We're friends, and I've always liked you, that kind of thing. I like you more now, so on. You don't think I ought to give the details, do you?"

"I guess not," Del said. "I don't know."

"It's not that bad," she said. "It's not like *The Young and the Restless,* or whatever. The rest of that. I don't think we should worry. He'll get it eventually. We were here together, he was gone, we were worried, you were just divorced, nobody knew what the deal was, when he was coming back, or even *if* he was coming back—you can't control all of that, what happens. We like each other, we're here alone, you know. You touch me, I touch you, we hug, kiss—what's the big deal? We got caught up in some involuntary fondling."

"That would be a great explanation if we were in junior high," Del said. "But we aren't, exactly. Except insofar as all of life is now remarkably like junior high. Let's just let it go and hope he doesn't ask too many questions. That O.K.?"

"Perfect with me," she said, wiping down the countertop with a square of yellow paper towel.

"I miss you, though," Del said. "He gets back, and he's only here a couple of days, and I already miss spending time with you."

"The feeling is mutual," she said, running a forefinger across the back of his neck. "But we'll get over it."

"I guess I should move over to the condo," he said. "I don't want to, really. I've got to check on that woman."

"You ought to stay here for a while, anyway," she said. "Until things settle out."

Del had started working afternoons and evenings until ten or ten-thirty, so when he came in from the store he spent a lot of time out on the porch watching TV—repeated news and interview shows, the hour-long "three actors help you with your hair" commercials. He liked to record the overdone women newscasters so he could stare at their lips in slow motion. He recorded just the extra-close shots, popping the buttons on the remote, then played his jump-cut tapes back in frame-advance mode. One night he was sitting there going in frame-by-frame on some woman's lips, watching her tongue snake forward, or up under the roof of her mouth, watching the way her lips loosened and got fuller on certain words, tighter and drawn on others, noting that her lips were three completely different colors, four if you counted the line around them, when Margaret came out onto the porch and started laughing.

"Who does *those?*" she said. "Jesus, that's amazing."

"They look like the work of the famous car painter von Dutch Holland," Del said. "The trouble is that when they do a side view of this woman she looks like a piglet."

"And she's a dip," Margaret said. "I've seen her."

"That too. But at least she upset Bernie, getting hired. Anything that upsets Bernie is O.K. by me."

"Did Bernie come down in his robe when they hired her?"

"Had to," Del said.

Bernie Shaw, the CNN anchor, had gone on the air live in his bathrobe during the Tiananmen Square crisis. Having done it, he couldn't stop talking about it, saying over and over how he'd "come down in his robe" to meet the crisis. It wasn't that he'd done it, but that it had so impressed him, that made him the butt of the joke. Which was risky because he was African-American, but he earned it—he was exactly like Ted Baxter on *The Mary Tyler Moore Show,* only he was black and he was real.

BUD TALKED to Rudy Glass, the department chair at the college, about working the second summer semester, but Rudy told him he'd better take the time off to get straightened away after his episode. That infuriated Bud, who didn't think it was the chairman's job to look after his personal life.

"He probably doesn't have any courses," Margaret said. "He's probably trying to be nice, the way he's saying it."

"He's a bottle brush," Bud said. "He's debris and offal."

The three of them were in the front yard while Margaret washed the car.

"I was sitting right here yesterday," Bud said, "and that Lollie girl came by wearing nothing but black tights, a smoky-colored tie-dyed T-shirt ripped off about rib-high, with 'Buy One Get One Free' printed across the tits. She had some very big shoes, and she was driving a motorcycle."

"You the neighborhood watch?" Del said.

"Were we like that at thirteen?" Margaret asked.

"I wasn't," Bud said. "I was fond of chemistry sets. Production of gases by application of heat was one of my big faves."

"Yeah," Del said. "And you had the big red set with the double foldout—four sections, sixty-four chemicals. I had the little one—two sections, thirty-two."

"The blue ones were best," Bud said. "I think our parents didn't get the brand-name deal too well. We were always on the bottom end, like Marx and Lionel. Same thing. I've never forgiven them."

"Jesus, forget chemistry and think about Bobo," Margaret said, shaking her head and then resting it against the car top.

"He's a lucky little prick," Bud said.

"You should be so lucky, Bud," Margaret said. "You should live in hope. You should get somebody to stuff a wad of Borax in your face." She swished the hose in his direction, splattering him.

BUD SEEMED to be performing for Del, showing off, being more off-the-wall and harebrained than usual, and doing it in order to prove something. It was as if he wanted Del to watch him live his life, watch the way he talked to and signaled Margaret, the way he touched her when they talked. Del hated it.

Bud did this thing with his hand, making it into a gun finger and firing it at Margaret whenever she figured out what he was going to say before he said it. He was always shooting somebody with that gun finger, and when something he agreed with was on television, he shot the screen.

When Del and Bud were kids, they weren't friends. Bud was seven years older and had different friends, music, clothes—they didn't have anything in common. Bud was like an extra half-parent. It was that way until Del was finishing college and they started talking. He talked to Bud on the phone all the time. They'd talk about advertising and teaching. They planned things: not the usual holidays or trips, but new businesses they could start together—Little Thighs was one. It was a fast-food idea for these chicken thighs that Margaret cooked and that Bud thought would make their own market. He was going to go mail order on that idea.

Back then Bud wasn't comfortable teaching, because it slowed him down. "We're supposed to be out here working magic," Bud said during one late-night call. "But magic is magic stuff, made at night. Magic needs a receiver."

"As they say," Del said. "I don't know what you're complaining about. They only make you work twice a week, right?"

"Yeah, but it's a gas station," Bud had said. "We pump low lead into the brain cavities of these kids. It's disaster, it's killing them slow. It's shameful."

"You may be overstating it," Del said.

"Maybe," Bud said.

Bud had always wanted to be a shape shifter, it turned out, a rainmaker, something fancy, somebody who made the ground he'd walked on better than the ground he hadn't. He'd done a stint as artist and musician right out of college, done psychedelic stuff, then concept art, earth art, bag art, roto art—all the kinds of art that were being done in those days—but that blew over, and he settled for the dinky job at the dinky college. That hurt just as the cliché says, but he still shot to California, or someplace similar, once in a while, hoping to break out. He hadn't given up, but he was hit and limping, beginning to content himself with the smaller adventures.

Their father never quite got Bud, never understood what Bud's problem was. He used to say that at dinner a lot. "What's Bud's problem?" he would say, pointing to Bud with his fork, a piece of beef hanging off the end of it, and their mother would say, "Oh, Phil, don't start up." And she would give him a look across the table, and the conversation would shift to something else, some bit of political wisdom their father wished to impart, some bit of discernment about the engineering trade. He was a structural engineer, their father. He specified what kinds of steel were needed in buildings, how thick the concrete piers had to be and how deep they had to go into the ground. He was a foundation man, in a certain way, committed to the basics. Bud's fanciful interests left him speechless.

Their mother, by contrast, thought Bud charming without exception. No matter what Bud did or said, their mother invariably thought it was wonderful, terribly funny, heartbreakingly true. She became his best audience. She was too easy. He could make her laugh anytime. He could crack her up. Whatever he said, whatever he did—he'd do a little sketch, a little drawing, play a little something on the piano—no matter what, she loved it.

There was a short time toward the end of Del's high school career when everything was going right, everything in his life and in their lives was flawless. It was a time he'd never forgotten, a matter of a year or two when all things were in balance, when people got along, when even his father was civil and understanding and responsive and lighthearted, when all in the family had enough of what they needed and what they wanted.

At that time Bud was just out of college, being a hip young thing with loads of talent, going in every direction at once. Their mother and father seemed happy together, in their admirable fifties. They had a house in Houston with a hugely green lawn, and things made sense in a way that they hadn't since. Everything seemed perfectly tuned—what people knew and didn't know, what they believed and how they acted, what they said to each other and what they would not say, what things cost, looked like, how the values were derived and distributed and held, what people were willing to do to and for each other, which motivations were honorable and which were not. It seemed in memory a remarkable time, a time not at all like Del's adulthood, a time when the world was trustworthy, gentle, true.

Sometimes Del wondered if that memory wasn't just foolishness, if the world had been no more trustworthy then than now, if at a certain age you don't simply assume the world, and its people, and its ideas are in your own image of them, later to learn that it isn't that way at all.

When Del noticed his life getting out of balance and so

recalled the moment when it was perfectly in balance, he mentioned this to Bud in a telephone call, and Bud sighed and said, "Well, nothing ever was, anyway."

Del found out much later that the line, which he found so evocative, was the title of a tune written by a jazz bass player on a Verve LP. He found that out because years after Bud said it, Del happened to buy the album too.

MARGARET WANTED to go to the store to pick up her glasses, and Bud wanted his shirts from the laundry.

"Then we'll go to the pool," Bud said.

"I'm not going to the pool," Margaret said. "You and Del can go if you want to."

"Yeah," Del told him. "That's where I draw the line. The pool."

The place Bud was talking about was one of those community pools surrounded with chain-link fence. The city built it in the fifties, when just a few people lived in that part of Biloxi, but now people came from everywhere and used it.

"Too many bodies in there," Margaret said. "All kinds of people doing their junk in the water. And when they're gone the water just sits there and stews. I'm not going in there for anything."

Still, she got on her new bathing suit, trying it out, showing it off for Bud. She'd already modeled it for Del, who didn't like it particularly. It was trying too hard, was what he'd thought. It was aquamarine with a V-shape down the front; she called it a "revival affair."

"C'mon," she hollered from outside at Bud and Del, who were watching her from the sun porch. "Get that hose and let's go. Let's get into some heavy squirting."

She had a white towel wrapped around her waist, so it looked as if she were dressed, but when Bud went out in the backyard he stripped down to his Jockey shorts. Del stayed inside, watching Bud and Margaret hose each other around in the yard. They were laughing and getting along great again, grabbing at each other like kids, hose wrestling, giggling as though they were telling jokes nonstop. When Del saw them together like that, just the two of them, Bud and Margaret through a window, or way off in another room, they seemed made for each other.

Some nights, after Bud and Margaret were sleeping, Del swiped the little emergency portable radio she kept in the kitchen cabinet and listened in bed until he fell asleep. He'd close his eyes and try to see himself a kid again, outside, sitting on the hood of a car somewhere, back when the metal hoods of cars were thick enough so you could sit on them, sitting and smoking and hanging out with a bunch of kids at the drive-in. And when the radio played a song he really felt, one he could *remember* feeling, he wondered why he wasn't someplace where he could hear it right, like at the beach with a woman of his own just like Margaret, walking the crusty sand at night, foam rolling up on the shells, wind bringing up bumps on her skin, or why he wasn't at some country club with her, sitting at one of those white metal tables by *that* pool, drinking something silly from an awkward glass and noticing what pretty hair she had, the way it held the swimming light.

He'd fall asleep listening to the radio and wake up the next day around noon and look out and the sun would be high and round as in some movie. Out the window, the yard would be a burning green desert, like another planet. Margaret always said the yard was important to her, but Del never figured that out. To him it was just some hot grass.

A COUPLE OF DAYS before he moved to the condo, Margaret took him to the doctor so he could get a checkup. The doctor had a tiny office, cheesy furniture, bad lamps, plastic plants. His magazines looked as though he got them from a paper drive. There were copies of *Ding Dong* magazine and assorted trade magazines from the veal industry. The doctor apparently had holdings in veal.

"How long has it been since you've had that tetanus booster?" the doctor asked.

"About thirty years," Del said.

"We'll give you one, anyway," the doctor said, patting Del's forearm. He gave Del the shot. The doctor had long hairs on the backs of his hands, just two or three hairs on each hand, each several inches long, so that it seemed he must have cultivated them. He had to be careful just to be sure they didn't get caught in a shirt cuff.

Afterward Margaret and Del went to have ice cream at the food court in the mall down Highway 90. She seemed to have a lot of fun watching the fountains there. But then, when they got home, Bud wanted to have a private talk.

"You don't mind, do you, Del?" Bud asked. "It's a marriage thing."

"It's O.K.," Del said. "I understand. I need to get out of here, anyway. I don't want to run into Pixie, but surely she's gone by now."

"No rush," Margaret said. "You can stay here forever, far as I'm concerned. You're no bother."

He smiled at her, wondering what she meant and what Bud thought about her saying it. He guessed life with Margaret wasn't all that perfect once you got used to it, but he was sorry his time at it was over. It had gone by too fast, he hadn't been paying enough attention, and the moment had sort of lost him, leaving him spinning, untethered, a head-wagger. And now things were leaning back toward normal—Bud was going back to work, Margaret was a wife again, Del was a new boy in town, with a job selling stereos.

He went out for a walk, thinking maybe he'd go over to the condo on foot and check out the slow-vanishing tenant, but then decided that was far too energetic, so he stayed on the block. There were no dogs around and the birds were too high up in the air to be interesting to watch. He didn't know how long he ought to stay outside, or if Bud or Margaret would call when it was time to go in. He picked up a few twigs from the street and thought about making twigs a hobby, starting a twig collection, or maybe making twig furniture or twig art. He'd seen some of that, and it was pretty interesting. There was a long twig stuck in the fence between Bud's yard and the neighbor's yard, and he broke off some of the bark. He thought he'd sandpaper that twig until the little knots on it were like hard bites under the skin, the kind you never stop scratching.

There was something about the way Bud looked at him, something about Bud's way of acting when the three of them were together, that meant Bud had a good idea of what had gone on while he was in California. Bud didn't come out and ask, though, and Del didn't volunteer. Margaret would tell him sooner or later. She'd said as much. Bud seemed sad about being back and spent time sitting in the sunroom, watching the tape he'd sent from California, but Del figured his melancholy had more to do with what he knew or did not know than with the collapse of his career in film.

DEL MOVED to the condo. Pixie was fully removed, but he lived out of suitcases and cardboard boxes, anyway. He didn't like the scars and indecipherable marks on the walls, the look of the closets and the shelves, and he didn't want to put his shirts and things away. For the first weeks after he'd moved he didn't see very much of Bud and Margaret. He called them every couple of days; sometimes they called him. Sometimes

Margaret called when Bud was gone, so she could talk more freely. Neither of them came to see him.

"I'm antsy," she told him on the phone the weekend before his birthday.

"No you're not," Del said. "Take it easy."

"Really," she said. "Something's about to happen. I don't know what. School's starting. He already hates it; he's complaining about the people over there, about the self-serving crap, the smugness, the ritual stupidity—the regular stuff he always complains about. He's not wrong; it's just that I've had years of it. And it's worse this time. It's worse than before you left—he puts on a show for you, cleans it up. Yesterday he hit the wall so hard his fist just went right through. This was because Rudy Glass hired some twit Bud didn't want hired, some giddy woman who Bud says ought to run a high school newspaper."

"And he knocked a hole in the wall?"

"Just one side of it," she said. "He takes the stuff way too seriously. It's crazy." Margaret sounded much more frazzled than he'd have expected her to sound or than he'd heard her sound. "I miss you," she said, then she laughed. "I don't mean anything by that, though. I didn't mean what it sounded like."

"It's fine. It's O.K.," Del said. He was fiddling with a spice bottle in his small kitchen, screwing and unscrewing the top.

"I may get out," she said. "Get a place of my own for a while. Or tell Bud to."

"You should just settle down," Del said. "He's just going through stuff—it'll be fine. Did you ever, like, say any more about us?"

"Some," she said. "Enough. He knows as much as he wants to know. I told him things got a bit out of hand. I said things got carried away a few times; that's really all I said. He got the idea."

"I hate this part. Really," Del said. "He hasn't said a word to me. How did he take it? What's he say now?"

"It didn't upset him that much. The worst was when I said I was attracted to you. He said some nasty stuff then, but that was it. I was looking for more trouble. After a while he shrugged and said he could understand it. Then he wanted to know which of you I liked better."

"Oh, shit," Del said.

"I think he knew already," she said. "I think when he got back he knew things had gone some haywire. He may have been relieved at how little it was."

"Sure," Del said. "We were monuments of restraint and responsibility. Kiss me here, kiss me there."

"I think you worry too much. He loves you, really. And he's not doing so well," she said. "Are you going to call him?"

"Yeah," Del said. "I'm calling him soon."

3

Two days before his forty-fourth birthday, Del stopped
for dinner at Bob's Fish Town, a beachfront restaurant
that had been a gas station once but was restyled in hard plastic seats, shiny-vinyl booths, and bright tabletops, all in an
effort to make it seem like a regional fast-food stop, in hopes
that would trick tourists into thinking it was someplace safe.
The owner always greeted people by saying, "Hi, I'm Bob, the
owner," so everybody called him Bob the Owner. He was bit-
ter about fast food: he had IT MIGHT AS WELL BE POPEYE'S
stenciled on the front window, but the first five words were in
a tiny white script and the last was in giant red-and-gold letters
that looked awfully familiar.

Fish Town had fish and chicken specialties, sharp sauces,
and Bob the Owner's legendary whole-fried potatoes, which
were whole and fried in cheap grease. Bob was a Minnesota
native, educated nine years at Boston and Florida State, with
a couple of advanced degrees that he didn't hold in such high
regard because he said these days the schools were giving away
doctorates as if they were invitations to get pizza delivered two
for one. He was big, powerful, slow-moving. His father had
been a chef at a hotel in Minnesota, and after graduate school

Bob got back into food because he never wanted anything else enough.

Del had become a regular customer at Bob's Fish Town. Margaret had taken him there when she was showing him around, and he'd been going there a couple of nights a week since, always taking the same booth by the front window, overlooking the Gulf.

He was in the booth, flirting with a plate of chicken livers, when he heard Bob the Owner go into his new-customer greeting. Del looked over his shoulder and saw a slightly gangly young woman with light straight hair and exquisitely cut facial features—great eyes, wide perfect lips. What was startling was that this girl looked something like a younger, thinner, pastier Margaret. She was wearing yellow glitter pants, black socks, high black shoes, and a Burger King uniform shirt with CANDY stitched over the breast. She had a few fluorescent sheets of the kind that always advertised lost dogs or garage sales, and she was showing them to Bob and pointing at his bulletin board. They talked for a minute, got it worked out, and then she brought her big quart glass of iced tea to the booth next to Del's. He smelled her when she went by, a summery, Sea & Ski smell.

There were other people in the restaurant, parts of families, soldiers from the air base, people who'd been sent to pick up food while less energetic mates sat at home in front of TVs. Not many people, but a few. When the girl got settled in the booth next to his, Del pushed his fried chicken livers aside and banged his salt shaker on the table, then turned and said, "Will you lend me your salt? Mine isn't working."

She gave him the salt but didn't speak. When he returned it, Del said he'd seen her talking to Bob the Owner and asked if Bob was a friend of hers.

"This is Bob?" she said, pointing across the restaurant to Bob the Owner.

"That one," Del said.

"Yeah; I guess he is now," she said. "He's going to let me put some of my stuff on his bulletin board."

"What stuff? What is it?"

"They're poster things," she said. "It's really this magazine I make up, but it's only one page, so it's like a poster. That's the way I want it, just one page. More than that and who cares, is what I say."

"Will you let me see one?" he said. "Have you got an extra one?"

She slipped a free hand into her knapsack and pulled out a bright lime-colored sheet. "Here's your own personal copy of the current issue," she said, handing it over. "My name's Jen."

They shook hands over the back of the booth and he took a minute to read her one-page magazine, which was arranged like a newspaper on an eight-and-a-half-by-eleven-inch sheet. The name of it was *Blood & Slime Weekly*—that was at the top—and it was subtitled "The Hi-Speed Terrorzine." The first headline was MOTHER FOUND SHOT AFTER TODDLER ANSWERS PHONE, followed by this sentence: "A 21-year-old woman was found fatally shot in her home after her 3-year-old son told relatives who telephoned that his mother couldn't come to the phone because she was dead."

"Yikes," Del said.

"Which one?" she said.

"The dead mother," he said.

"Oh, yeah—this is my special all-mother issue," she said.

He skipped the rest of that one and went on to "An Australian pie salesman has confessed to police that he killed five elderly women who he said bore an uncanny likeness to his mother." This was a Reuters wire story about Corsair Pole, fifty-eight, a pie salesman and father of four teenage daughters, who pleaded guilty to murdering five women who were beaten or strangled in 1993.

Pole admitted that his victims, aged between sixty and ninety-two, bore an almost unnatural resemblance to his mother. He was described by police as calm and composed when admitting the killings, but he broke down when the jury heard a tape of his confession, in which he said, "One side of me is good, but the other is dark and evil—I am not a free man."

Prosecutor Robin Juliet said Pole knew the fifth victim, a friend with whom he arranged to have lunch before killing her. When she was discovered, her body was smeared all over with butter and gravy, apparently from the dish she had prepared for her attacker. A pork chop was discovered wedged in her rectum. Police subsequently found Pole semiconscious in the victim's bath after he had consumed a bottle of Scotch and a quantity of prescription drugs.

Del listened to Jen eat as he read—her jaw sometimes cracked in its socket when she chewed. He said, "This one's not so interesting, is it? The pie story."

"It's not? I probably should have doctored it," she said, patting her knapsack. "I have my computer, so I can do that. I go for slash and burn, but sometimes I have to add the really abnormal stuff, the details—people on fire and stuff. I don't know, I just like that. Don't you love the way this guy says part of him is good and part bad? Did you read that? That's great stuff."

"He killed these women, though," Del said.

"It's everywhere," she said. "No getting away from it. It's a horrible world."

"Maybe so, but you don't have to encourage it."

"I'm not encouraging it, pal," she said, snapping the sheet out of his hand. "I'm just noticing it, helping other people to notice it."

"O.K.," he said. "I can see that. So what you do is go out and put these around all the time?"

"Whenever I make them. I don't do it all the time, just sometimes. When I feel like it. The stories never stop, though."

"Hey—did you do a barbecued-dog story once? Like, back at the first of the summer? I saw one of those at this gas station in Henderson Point. Looked like this," he said, pointing to the green issue she'd taken back from him.

"No kidding? Yeah, I did that one. That's a great story— a guy who hates his horrible yuppie neighbor, so he gets the guy's dog and cooks it. That's one of mine."

She showed him some old issues of her one-page magazine, and they sat there in the two booths while the sun went down. He liked talking to her that way, each of them safe in a booth, so he was looking for things to talk about. He told her about Bud and Margaret, and moving from Houston, and then, when he was running out of stuff, he told her about this jazz piano player he'd heard about a couple of years earlier who wasn't allowed to enter the country because he was Cuban but was so good that musicians went to foreign festivals just to be able to play with him.

"What kind of musicians?" she said.

"Well," he said, "people like Charlie Haden, Paul Motian. Regular jazz guys."

"Never heard of them," she said.

He told her he was selling stereo equipment at AI, just as a temporary thing, and that he had some pretty good stuff if she was interested.

"Nah," she said. "No cash. Besides, I don't listen to anything I can't carry."

"We've got Miniaise portables, some new tape deals."

"You want me to buy something from you?" she said.

"No. Well," he said, shaking his head and waving his hands around. "I don't know." He was thinking it was a big mistake to have brought up the equipment, because it made it seem as though he was trying to sell her something. "I meant maybe I can sort of lend you some equipment," Del said. "You know, demo stuff. No, I don't want you to buy anything."

"Oh, sure," she said, giving him an I-wasn't-born-yesterday look. "So what's in it for you?"

"Well," Del said, "I thought maybe we could go look around at the store, and you'd feel O.K. about that, safe, and we'd be together for a little while, just to see what happened."

"Are you expecting something to happen?"

"No. I just want to spend a little time with you."

"You want to go out with somebody your daughter's age, is that it?" she said.

"I don't have a daughter," Del said. "But if you're that age—then yes."

She smiled at that, an odd and confident smile that was really just a slight drawing back of her lip, showing her pretty teeth, and a sideways glance. "Sure," she finally said. "Why not."

They left together and went to the store and he ended up letting her have a fourteen-hundred-dollar Denon system on extended loan. They took it over to an apartment that she said wasn't really hers, or that she didn't spend much time in, and he helped her set up the components, then produced the Rubalcaba CD that he'd been talking about earlier, so she'd have something of his to listen to. Then he left.

For the next couple of days, he watched the apartment nonstop, watched Jen come and go at odd hours of the day and night, sat in his car parked in the street under the huge live oak tree and watched her move like an open invitation across the lighted windows of the apartment.

She was on the first floor of a two-story house, an old place with new white paint and elephant-gray trim, all the shutters

and spouts and the rest carefully prissed up, probably by the
landlord, who was a barely bearded guy Del saw several times
in his vigil—once going upstairs with carpet samples, once
standing on the concrete porch downstairs talking earnestly
with Jen, while she looked friendly if just a bit cool to his
attentions.

Late on the afternoon of his birthday, he drove to Jen's
apartment, parked under the tree, and settled in for some
watching, a new diet Coke fresh and sweating in the foam
rubber can carrier he'd bought at the car wash and never used
before. After thirty minutes of staring at her house, waiting
for her to come home, reading snatches of stories in the *New
Republic* he'd found in Listening Room A at the store, he decided that maybe he'd take a closer look at the apartment,
maybe look in a window, walk the grounds. He figured if
anybody said anything, he'd say he was interested in the property as an investment, that the owner had sent him to look the
place over. He thought that would get him back out to the car
in case of an emergency.

The afternoon was hot but turning dark from low clouds
that were sweeping in off the water, bringing rain. He circled
the house and noticed that a back window was open in what
he guessed was Jen's bedroom. There was a screen, but the
window was up a good six inches. He chinned for a look, but
he couldn't really see in. It just looked black in there. He was
hit by cold air from the air conditioner and the beachy Sea &
Ski scent, and that did it for him. He stuck a hole in the screen
with his Audio Instincts mechanical pencil and snapped aside
the hook and eye. Then he lifted the screen, raised the sash,
and climbed into Jen's bedroom.

She was sitting cross-legged on the floor alongside the bed,
messing with some magazines and her portable computer. She
turned and jumped up and let out a short, harsh scream, but
then she recognized him. That relaxed her, and she settled

down, scrubbing back her hair, and said, "Hey, what the fuck is with you? What're you doing?"

"Hello," Del said. "My name is Dick."

"You changed your name since yesterday?"

"I came in the window," Del said. "I smashed the glass, ripped the screen, broke the sash lock, crawled in. I know I shouldn't have. I scratched myself. Besides, it was the day before yesterday."

"The window was open, I thought," she said, turning to look at it. It was wide open, the screen akimbo. "Besides, this isn't funny. Do you want to just get out of here now?"

"I don't, but I will," he said. "I was prepared to do all that stuff."

"Uh-huh. And why? You were going to break in and steal stuff, or did you just want to come see me again? Am I that alluring? Should I be flattered? You could have asked, yes? That would have been easier. Where's the scratch?" She looked him up and down.

"I got my arm and my leg," Del said. "It's nothing. Forget it."

"Did you want me to fetch the peroxide?"

"I don't necessarily mean you any harm at this time. The truth is I'm almost fifty years old and this is my birthday, and on my birthday every year I do something I want to do, and since I brought you the stereo, what I've wanted to do is break in here and hide and then maybe watch you undress."

"Oh," she said, stacking the magazines she'd been looking at. Her computer was open on the bed, text scrolling up its screen. "I could call the police, couldn't I?" she said.

"That'd knock you off the computer," he said.

"Yeah, well, that's true. I'm downloading some new things from Compuserve."

"Maybe we can forget the undress part," Del said. "I think I said that just to point us in the right direction."

"We might be able to arrange it," she said, her eyebrows going up in perfect symmetry. "It's not a giant big deal. You don't want to see my ankles, though. They're covered with bites and bruises. They're a mess."

"I'd die to see them," Del said. "I'm afraid you've smitten me. I've been watching you."

"I thought you said you were forty-four."

"I am," Del said. "But I think a lot about fifty."

"Today's your birthday?" She gave him a smile and headed for the bathroom. In a minute she was back with a brown plastic jug of peroxide, a wet washcloth, some tissue, a tube of Polysporin, and a heating pad.

"Let's see the damage," she said.

He showed her his elbow and his calf. The scrapes were like red roller-ball pen lines, fast-scabbing. She poured peroxide on his leg and on his arm, rubbed the wet washcloth on his face and hands, then dried him off with the tail of a shirt hanging on the doorknob of her closet, an Exxon shirt, gray cotton. She plugged the heating pad's cord into an outlet on the wall and handed the pad to him. "You're not sitting on my shoes, are you?" she said.

"No," Del said. "Not at all."

She took everything back to the bathroom. He sat there and listened to her shake a towel, rinse the sink, wring the washcloth. He felt the warm pad warming him.

THAT WAS their first night together. Nothing happened. They listened to the CD he'd left her, and to one she had, and after a time he went home. The next night they went to his condo, brought in Chinese food from Mandarin House, ate some of it and saved the rest, talked for a while, watched the water and the sunset, and then started making out on the couch. She was so gorgeous he was surprised she was there with him, but he tried not to be too obvious about just how much good fortune he felt he was having. The only light in the room was reflected street light, and she looked lovely in that. They went over each other in great detail, touching and examining, and he got more excited every minute, with every kiss, every brush of her lips, every trace of her sharp fingernails, until, not long later, she was in his lap, facing him, her thin legs straddling him, her knees driven into the sofa cushions on either side of his hips, and he was inside her.

After a few minutes of this, she suddenly stopped moving and said, "I'm not moving. Not another muscle. I'm going to be completely still. It's like I'm dead here, it's like you're making it with the deadest girl in Mississippi."

"You're so exquisite," Del said, caressing her shoulders and her neck with his face. "Just keep it up, stay perfectly dead. Don't move an inch. I just want to feel you here." He smelled her hair, felt her small breasts flatten into his chest as she inhaled, then stick to his skin before pulling almost free. She was panting slowly because she'd been doing the work. He loved the way they locked together, necks cocked, her thighs slipped into the notch just at his waist, chins tucked, arms latched each behind the other.

Finally, without moving, she said, "Screwing kind of sucks, doesn't it? I hate it sometimes. It doesn't matter who you screw anymore. Sometimes I really do think we want abstinence, but whoever heard of that? Bing Crosby? But it's right too. Screwing doesn't do anything; I don't care about it. Are you having a good time? I guess I am, but I don't care, really. I could be screwing you or some other bumpkin, and it wouldn't matter to me."

He looked out the window, over her bare shoulder, his interest in a nosedive. "This is great. You're a real romantic, aren't you?"

"Well, so what? That's the truth. Things change. Summer's almost over."

"Are you moving? I thought you weren't going to move," Del said. "You're starting to move—I can feel you. Stop. You're thinking about moving, I can tell."

"I'm in a box," she said. "In a crypt. I'm Madonna in a meat locker. Hanging here cold, twisting slow, slow. I'm strapped in. Restrained. Wrapped up. Nothing's moving anywhere. It's silent night. I'm a fist here. Your fist."

"Oh," Del said.

"You want to get it over with?" she said.

He was thinking that she could not be more beautiful. It was only their second night together. She was twenty-four, a few years out of school, so soft it surprised him to remember when he'd last liked sex as much as he liked it with her—the way she made herself open, savorable, as if she had a lifetime of sex play in front of her, plenty to waste on him. He liked the way she insisted they try small pleasures: nips, and squeezes, and scratches, and slides. He was amazed at her newness, her skin like a fine, light leather glove—it gave him goose bumps. She was a gift. It was too easy.

Jen was shiny and smooth all over—the cheeks of her buttocks as clear and radiant as a baby's, her hair a shower of lake light, her whole bearing a suggestion of things still very much possible, the time to do all those things written in absent flaws, in perfect skin, in sympathetic years.

He was holding her steady, thumbs and forefingers almost circling her tiny bare waist, around which she wore a wire, a thin red copper wire, a piece of personal jewelry, he imagined, or just something she'd happened upon, put on, and forgotten. His palms splayed out over her hips. He was looking past her shoulder out the window, his stare resting on the horizon where the sky met the water, gray to gray. Kids have it all, was what he thought, feeling the way she held him inside her, the way her thighs hooked his hipbones, the scarce weight of her, feeling her sharp hair tracing his shoulder, his ear. They get everything, and suddenly comes adulthood and they don't know what hits them, so they slink off into the Neverland of silly dresses and fat-man trousers. That's where he was. Maybe it was still easy at twenty-four to be beautiful, but he hadn't seen it in a while.

She twisted a little over him, taunting, enjoying her power. "I'm sorry," she said. "I couldn't help it. I'm not as dead as I wanted to be, I guess." Her smile curved toward a leer. She was having a good time, it looked like, amusing herself as much as she was making love to him, and she was proficient in just the way he imagined everybody was by now. Horizontal shadows and strips of light caught her face and made war paint. Her breasts were razor sharp and perfect and new, and she used them like weapons. She was pumped up straight on her hands, leaning on knuckles stuck into the back of the couch, facing him, in his lap. He guessed that she knew he was watching her reflection in the glass and watching her at the same time, and that she knew what she looked like to him. She did a snake act for a minute, slow spoon-digs with her pelvis, drawing away, letting him slip a little, stopping short of releasing him.

They were doing what had seemed silly even to imagine when she walked into Fish Town and stopped to talk to Bob. "I love you," Del said. "I know it's crazy."

"I don't like that," she said, twisting suddenly off him, flattening herself on her back diagonally on the sofa, her head on the arm, her feet perched out on his knee. "It's not about you, O.K.? It's that it's a film thing now, screwing without moving so we can *really feel* the sex. It's boring. I saw it on the late show a hundred times."

"You did not see it on the late show," Del said. He was startled by her quick change of mood, but he didn't feel desperate about it. There was something in her that reassured him, made him know he really wasn't what backed her off.

"That film stuff ruins it for me, disauthenticates it," she said. "Before, it was great, but sooner or later somebody notices and puts it in a movie, and that gets on TV, and then it creeps back into our lives as the TV version of the real thing it really was before."

"This was pretty real for me," he said.

She grinned at him, obviously pleased. "But every time I screw somebody it's like being in the movies fucking, up there on the screen. I can't wrap my legs around somebody without seeing some actress do it—Susan Sarandon, or Theresa Russell, or that idiot blond woman with the tortured mouth who always seems to be screwing Andy Garcia. It's a living hell—here's the wide shot, and here we come in on me, my stomach taut and tanned, the curve of my flattened breast, the permanently stiffened nipple, the trace of golden hair and the drops of spray-on perspiration, here are my hips rotating, rocking-horse style, here are my teeth nipping the lobe of your ear, my hair cascades forward, and now on my back, my knees raised to wrap around you, my head twisted aside on the pillow—blah blah blah."

"Why don't you play like *I'm* Andy Garcia?"

"Being still was what popped it. Redford and what's-her-name in her barn. Horse leather everywhere, but you couldn't forget the Sundance catalog when you looked at it. He had a Sundance shirt on, I swear it, from that catalog. I saw the shirt in the catalog and I was thinking about ordering it, I had already thought of ordering it, and then a couple days later I'm watching TV and here he is humping what's-her-name and wearing the shirt."

"They weren't in the barn," Del said.

"That doesn't matter," she said.

"You want to pay some attention here?" he said. "Say we

pretend I'm this Garcia-Redford equivalent, you know, like for the turn of the century?"

"We could do that, but it would be stupid and depressing because you're about as much like Redford as I am like I-don't-know-who—I mean, you're *that* close, and besides, he's having serious skin problems that remind me of that other actor who got furry face syndrome, and he smiles like he's thinking Deep Thoughts most of the time, or looking at himself thinking and so on, and he's too precious, anyway, even when he's not smiling, or thinking, and the century's not turning for a few more years, and it won't make any difference to a couple of old farts like you and him when it does."

"Oh," Del said. "O.K. But Bob's a nice guy, really. Isn't he?"

She smiled again and brushed her ankle along Del's thigh. "Sure he is. I'm sorry. You're nice too. You're still sweet, both of you, worth the wait. I don't mind being your prisoner."

They sat there splayed apart, and Jen told him about her ex-boyfriend, a guy she'd last seen and last screwed a few weeks before on a rotting private wooden pier stuck out in Back Bay next to somebody's once-refined summer cottage. She wondered why all her boyfriends were fuck-ups.

"You're plenty old," she said, "but at least you've got the condo, a place to sleep, a decent car, stuff in the refrigerator. And you're not one of those shave-the-chest-in-a-semicircle-just-below-the-neck types that I always get stuck with when I get stuck with older men."

He pointed a scolding finger at her. "It's unkind to make fun of chest-hair victims. They have lives. They do not ask for the big hair. And besides, what do you mean, *stuck?*"

"Not you," Jen said. "I was talking about them and their chest hair. Yours appears nominal."

Her ex-boyfriend sold bikini swimsuits at the beach out of the back of his van. The van was black. The swimsuits were third-world products, shipped up from those hot Latin countries where the thong is king.

"His name is Itch," Jen said. "That's what everybody calls him. He ships the stuff to Itch Winston, after his cigarettes. We lived in his van most of the time. Living with him was hateful. When I finally told him he wasn't the man of my dreams, he said, 'Yeah, well. Sure.' Then he asked me if we could still do it, anyway, since we knew we were both clean."

"He sounds like a nifty guy," Del said.

"So I split, slept for a while hiding out with a girlfriend, Lisa, who runs a dump-grade motel stuck around the corner from the beach on Twenty-third Avenue. I met some guys and hung out."

"Then what?"

"Then I got the apartment," she said. "My dad sent some cash, and I got the place. It hasn't been that long. That's when I started putting out my handbills all over the place—coin-op laundries, groceries, telephone poles, newspaper boxes, restaurants—wherever. The first story I ever found was about a Long Island surgeon who sewed a man's right ear to his thigh after the ear was bitten off by another man in a fight. The doctor said the ear was too mangled to put back on the guy's head but that it could 'live' on his leg for five or six months and would have a better chance of survival there than if it were frozen. I loved the idea of this guy with his secret ear walking around."

"Uh-huh," Del said, lurching suddenly forward off the couch, knocking her feet aside, and landing on his knees on the floor. "I think we need to pray now," he said, beckoning her forward. He held out his hand so she could use it to pull herself off the couch. "Will you get down here? C'mon."

"What?" Jen said, taking the hand but not getting up. "I'm naked. You can't pray naked. Especially with a man, and especially after all this stuff we're doing."

"Please," Del said. "We have to."

He pulled her up, and she rolled off the couch and got on her knees alongside him, in front of the couch, both of them facing the windows that faced the highway that bordered the beach that bounded the Gulf. "What prayer are we doing?" she asked.

"It doesn't matter what prayer—just make it up," he said. "Just say what you have to say. But pray for other people first, not for yourself. It's bad luck to pray for yourself."

"It is?"

"It's very bad luck," he said.

So then they knelt together, naked and silent on the carpet in the dark living room of his fourth-floor condo at Tropic Breeze, and they put their hands together, and they bowed their heads. Out the window the stars were glinting fiercely.

4

AFTER JEN DECIDED she'd better clean up, she got to her feet and started collecting her clothes. She went into Del's bedroom, then came out of there and headed for the second bedroom. "I think I'll take my shower back here. Is that O.K.?"

"Sure," he said. "Either one."

"You can go ahead and finish up alone if you want to," she said, smiling prettily.

He looked at her over his shoulder, wondering how mean she meant that, but when he saw the smile he decided she had only the best intentions. He gave her a makeshift wave and said, "No. Thanks, though. I think I'll just hang on. You make me want to wait."

He sat on the floor, resting his back against the couch, the sweat drying on his skin, and watched the sliding-door glass, where, even with the room lights off, you could still catch reflections of cars on the highway, of searchlights circling the newest casino in town, of flickering hotel signs. Jen was more than he'd bargained for, more pleasing, more peculiar—he was ready to spend his life sitting on that floor, in that room, with her in the shower, soon to return.

But the shower didn't take long, and when Jen came back to the living room she was still naked. She sat down beside him on the floor and put on socks and her big shoes. She was lovely to look at as she moved—the small elegant breasts, the dish of her hips, the perfect soft skin, the complex curves of her shoulder blades, the thick nipple-brown lips, the dark shadow streaks where the bone rose over the flatness of her cheek. Looking at her was an uncommon pleasure, satisfying by itself.

"What about some TV?" she finally said, embarrassed by his gaze. She leaned across him, going for the remote.

The only furniture he had was the sofa, out in the middle of the room, and the TV, a thirteen-inch Sony, on the floor in front of the sliding door. "You want to watch something?" he said.

"I don't know," she said. "Maybe I should go. Maybe this isn't healthy, what we're doing."

He took the remote from her. "It's plenty healthy. It's lucky I'm not a drooler or anything, a flayer or any of that, so it's lucky about how we met, but it's healthy too. It was wonderful of you to let me in yesterday."

She flattened herself on her back. "It was fucking nuts. You broke into my house, you know what I mean? I don't know what I was thinking."

"I should have just knocked on the door," he said, remembering the light switches in her apartment, the ones that glowed when they were off, and the shelf in her bedroom, next to the bed, where there was an aquarium with two baby turtles in blue water. "Are those turtles O.K.?"

"What?" Jen said, twisting to see him. "Oh, my turtles. Yeah, they're O.K. You want them? They smell."

"I don't want them. I was just thinking that they weren't moving much, is all."

"They're fine," she said. She sat up and crossed her legs.

"You know, I sort of knew it at the restaurant. I knew you liked me. I knew you were coming, one way or the other."

"Uh-huh," Del said. "Me too."

"It always happens that way," Jen said. "But then we get to now, and I don't know you much."

"I'm a failed public relations person. Now I sell stereo equipment, but I probably won't do that forever. Born in Texas. Parents still alive, got a brother in town here. I'm six one and a shade, weigh two hundred pounds. I move well, considering my bulk and advanced age. My eyes are kind of green."

"You're a Christian," she said.

"No," he said. "In some bizarre way, maybe. Disorganized. That was about half a joke, that business. No, wait— that's not right. It was a truth joke. I was thinking I was lucky you were there. And it was my birthday."

"Forty-four," she said.

"I'm fond of girls in pictures," he said.

"Oops," she said, getting up and crossing the room. "That's far enough. Time for me to go, isn't it?" She leaned against the big windows, looking out at the Gulf. "I don't know why this is so filling, but it is, isn't it? It makes you feel like everything's all right." The room was dark. Lights blinked outside. Her skin drew colors from the glass, and when she turned, her body seemed to shine, catching red lights, reflections, blankets of shadow.

"Everything is all right," he said.

"So let's have some toast," she said, pulling her hefty torn-up T-shirt over her head.

Del struggled up and followed her into the kitchen, pointing to the refrigerator when she asked for bread. She got the loaf out and dropped two cold slices into the toaster.

He got the butter and the Bama grape jelly out of the refrigerator, slid them onto the small table, and then sat down.

She looked through the kitchen cabinets, standing there with the doors held open as she surveyed. Del started throwing the Bama jar up in the air as if it were a tennis ball, but on the second toss he missed it on the way down and it hit the floor like fireworks.

"Shit!" she said, jumping. She looked at the mess, then at him, then into the top of the toaster to see how the toast was coming along.

"Do you accept my apology?" Del said. He was tiptoeing around her, dragging hunks of glass out of the jam heap.

"You mean yesterday? Breaking in and that? I don't know."

"I really like you," Del said. "This is what happens when you really like somebody. You do demented stuff."

"Throw jelly," she said, pointing to the floor. "Is this my job?" She sighed, looking a bit forlorn, hoping it wasn't. The toast popped.

"I'm on it," Del said. "Just stay there. Don't move." He dumped glass into the garbage, then wiped at what was left with giant folds of paper towel.

"Do you want me to tell you my new story?" she said. "The one I'm doing for the next issue?"

"Sure," Del said. "Sit up on the counter, will you? I need to get this floor."

"This woman in London was having a fight with her husband," Jen said. "She locked him out of their bedroom one night and he was in his pajamas and tried to force the door, and when he busted the lock and got the door about half open she reached through and grabbed his crotch, and she had these really long sharp fingernails, fake nails, and when she grabbed him the nails just sliced him open, sliced his balls, and he looked down and she was holding one of his blood-covered testicles, and then she dropped it there on the bedroom floor."

"Jesus," Del said.

"The guy passed out on the landing," Jen said. "She said she had no idea her fingernails could do that."

"What did they do with it? The testicle? Did they put it back in? What happens when that happens?"

"I don't know," Jen said. "That's where the story stopped. You want some of this toast? Can I walk on the floor yet?"

"No. And yes," he said.

"I've got to get home," she said, pushing off the counter. "I've got to get these contacts out."

5

HE WAS NERVOUS about telling Margaret about Jen, concerned that Margaret might get upset about it or that
everything would suddenly have to be talked about, stuff
they'd done or almost done, and the whole situation would
get messy again, and they wouldn't be able to sneak by with
what he told himself was their small indiscretion. But Margaret wasn't even slightly upset when he called and told her
about Jen. She seemed happy for him. When the conversation
got around to her, she said Bud had moved out. "I told him
to go on," she said. "I told him he needed to get straightened
out and I wasn't going to be able to fix it for him."

"I'm sorry," Del said, managing to sound better than he
felt about the news. "I thought things were improving. This
stinks. You're not going to separate, are you?"

"Hey, hey," she said. "Take it easy. It's not you. Besides,
we've done it before. A couple of times. This time Bud got
himself an apartment at Valley Mondrian—have you seen that
place? The eighth wonder. Flesh-colored cedar siding and pine-
apple plants galore. We'll be fine; he just needs some private
moments."

"Are you sure?"

"It's an educated guess," Margaret said. "You ought to call over there and see. Besides, you guys need to talk."

Del couldn't tell if she was guessing or hoping. "What do we need to talk about? You mean *talk* talk?"

"No," Margaret said. "I just mean stick together. You know, like brothers. He misses you, too."

HE CAUGHT BUD teaching his cat, Walter, to walk on the tops of the doors in the new apartment. "This is a Flying Wallenda idea," Bud said on the phone. "I put the cat on top of the bathroom door one day at the house, and the cat did all right, walked back and forth like there was nothing to it."

"Great," Del said. "Very nice. Now, what's going on about getting an apartment and not telling me?"

"I have to tell you if I get an apartment?"

"It's not just that; it's you and Margaret," Del said. "What's going on?"

"We're just out to get a little moving-around room. It's not a big deal."

"I thought California was moving-around room," Del said.

"It was," Bud said. "But let me tell you about this cat idea. See, what's great is the way the cat looks up there, like a tightrope walker. You know that backing up and creeping ahead, the way those people inch around, hesitate, wag the pole, do that toe deal where they split the wire—it's really wonderful to see a cat do it."

Del tapped on the microphone part of the telephone receiver. "Oh, Bud," he said, calling it out as if he were trying to reach someone who'd slipped away. "Come in, Bud."

"She's the cat of the nineties," Bud said.

After that call he and Bud started talking regularly, hanging out, watching pro football on TV together—once they even went grocery shopping, although that was more awkward and embarrassing than Del had imagined it would be, and Bud must have felt the same, since he didn't suggest it again.

Del was spending most of his time with Jen, though he still found it hard to believe that Jen was with him in any sure way.

When she wasn't around, it was quiet at the Tropic Breeze condominium, and he liked that, liked staying there and reading, staring at the water, the pleasure boats going out and returning, the shrimpers crossing the Biloxi Channel on their way to work.

He didn't see Margaret at Bud's apartment, but Bud said they were getting back together. The week he was alone, Bud said, he'd gone a little crazy, rushing out every night to cheesy clubs dressed like people on TV, in laughable leather flight jackets and suit coats over tight white T-shirts. He'd spent his afternoons at the apartment pool, slicking up his tan.

"It was loony time," Bud told Del. "I walked around like women were checking me out day and night, like I was way down the coolest guy around. I'd cruise the middle of the street out here at twilight, flip-flops clapping and my hair slicked straight back, dark and shining. Wearing sunglasses and my little Speedo suit."

"Mr. Speedo," Del said. "Wears his sunglasses out way past their bedtime, right? Wears the cool duds. Walks the cool walk."

"That's it," Bud said.

"Don't worry; everybody does it," Del said. "When Karen and I split, I started unbuttoning my shirts a lot. I was the jerk who couldn't buy a clue."

"I don't know how these guys do it with a straight face. I see them all the time," Bud said. "It's like they're living from one long romantic shadow to the next."

"Maybe if you do it enough it doesn't feel so stupid?"

"I think it must feel stupid no matter how long you do it,"
Bud said.

A COUPLE OF WEEKS later they were in the oversize concrete
bleachers of the college's athletic field, staring down at the
pregame warm-ups before the season opener for a local wom-
en's football squad, the Biloxi Distilled Water Wildcats. The
Wildcats were sponsored by a bottled water distributor in
town. There were eight teams in the conference, the Women's
Southeastern Regional Amateur Football Conference, most of
which were sponsored by beer companies. Five were in the
northern part of the state, with an especially potent club called
the Hi-Time Girls being fielded out of Oxford. The two non-
Mississippi teams in the conference were from Alabama and
Arkansas.

"Margaret played one year," Bud said, pointing down at
the field. "First they played six-woman tag football, then eight,
finally eleven. It's real popular around."

The teams were at opposite ends of the field, distributed
like X's and O's, taking snaps, tossing balls back and forth,
doing calisthenics. They looked like men, except the hair.
From the bleachers it was any high school team in the country.
The field looked like a big green toy, mostly because the stands
were nearly empty.

"She played here?"

"Yeah. It was before the uniforms," Bud said. "A friend
of hers was the quarterback."

Bud held a hot dog, but he wasn't eating it. Del looked at
it and wondered if he ought to get one too. It looked good;
the mustard looked real good.

"This is my plan for my future," Bud finally said, waving
the dog. "I'm going to continue teaching Walter to walk on

the tops of doors. That's my whole plan. I know it's modest, but—"

"Can't the cat already walk on doortops if it wants to?" Del asked.

"He's a cat," Bud said.

"That's what I mean," Del said. "So what about this breakup? Is there something serious going on? Is it about anything?"

"You mean, is it about you and Margaret?"

That caught Del off guard, though he instantly knew he should have seen it coming. "I don't know. Well, sort of—I guess she told you we got a little more messed up than either of us felt right about." Saying it to Bud made his hair stand on end.

"She told me," Bud said, finally taking a monster bite, knocking off half the wiener at a single stroke. He was watching the field with too much intensity. "She told me. I don't think you ought to worry about it, though; it's just one of those things that goes on. And about us, well, Margaret and I always get over stuff. We've been through our share. I guess that's what's good about marriage: that it works; the bad part is that there's no escape." He finished the hot dog and crumpled the paper into a tight ball. "So what about this new girlfriend Margaret says you've got?"

"She's young," Del said. "She's strange. She wears a lot of Lycra and rayon. Good bones. She used to live in a van with her boyfriend."

"She's twenty? Is that what I heard?" he said.

"Twenty-four," Del said. "Graduated from somewhere."

Bud took a long drink out of his beer cup. "That's a blessing," he said.

The game had been Bud's idea. He wasn't a fan, but he thought Del ought to see the all-women's league in action. In fact, Bud didn't like sports much. He made fun of his co-workers at the college who were a little too eager to be fans —they read lots of sports magazines, repeated what they read, golfed gravely, and played in fantasy leagues in several sports. These were college professors who spent considerable leisure time in revealing study of some gigantic man's inflamed extensor, or of the historical averages for at bats by left-handed non-Spanish-speaking hitters more than three consecutive years in the majors, 1939 through 1964. Folks living in denial.

Bud's colleagues made him mad, anyway, even without the pathetic sports. They were always rustling up new grub for their vitae, or arranging presentations at local weekend conferences, or preparing insipid articles for publication in dim-bulbed academic journals with double-digit circulations, or letting on in whispers that they were at work on major books—perhaps even groundbreaking ones—that were soon to be under consideration at some prestigious publisher. It wasn't that Bud did a lot more—an essay or two every year —but he didn't kid himself about the worth of it.

In the stands, Bud and Del saw the first of the late-summer weather system they were having, something typical for the coast—dark skies before nightfall and a light drizzle that came and went. They'd brought umbrellas but hadn't opened them when the showers started in earnest. The huge rectangular racks of lights across the field cooked the rain as it came slanting down, making it a transparent sheet, something like a stadium negligee.

"So how is Margaret doing?" Del asked, thinking that if nothing else, he had to keep after this question, this answer. They were sitting high on one side of the stadium, staring out in front of them. The rain was delicate and cooling the way it hit his face. It looked as if it was raining hard on the other side of the stadium, but all they were getting on their side was the fine mist. From the other side, their side probably looked like nothing at all.

"Margaret's fine," Bud said. "She comes over, I go over. Nothing's changed, really. Why are you so worried about it?"

"I feel bad," Del said. "You've been together so long. I wasn't thinking about this separation stuff."

"She likes this kid next door," Bud said. "She's thinking we ought to check out adopting. I tell her first thing that happens is they find the parents living in a big tree out in Pascagoula—pinheads. Wearing a lot of Ralph Lauren discards picked off the Salvation Army. I don't really know anything about it, but I don't like it. We knew these people who took this little girl, and she was slow because her mother was some kind of freak, and these people, who were basically O.K., ended up treating this little girl like shit. Then they had their own kid, and things got ugly."

"You think you're too old?" Del said.

"That," he said. "And other stuff. I wouldn't be good. I'd worry. I'd have to change the way I think, and I can't, so I'd lie to the kid. It just seems like a bad idea."

"To you, you mean," Del said.

Bud gave him a look that meant he wasn't asking for Del's help on this, that he'd made up his mind and didn't want interference. "That's just one of the things between us, anyway. But you shouldn't worry," he said. "I'm a careful man. I'm going to cover all the bases before I'm through."

THE GAME WENT OFF without a hitch. One of the teams, their side, was wildly victorious, and in the end the little marching band that the announcer called "our own Phantom Regiment" marched right out of the stands and onto the stadium floor, the better to lead the victory tour in the light and sparkling rain. Bud insisted they stay and watch, and by the time the last happy prancer had followed the final trombone out of the stadium, the place was empty, just a cauldron of red and blue seats, concrete tiers, blue-glass-encased boxes. When the first set of lights across from them crashed off with that strange electrical release, Bud grabbed Del's shoulder and helped him to his feet.

"I guess that's it," he said. "You want to go to the Faculty Club for a drink?" He waited a minute before going on, his hand still on Del's shoulder, standing away at arm's length, regarding him. "You hate the Faculty Club," he said. "I know."

"Sure, I'll go," Del said.

"Tonight's the night," he said. "Women to dream of."

"Hair in buns," Del said. "Besides—"

Bud popped his shoulder. "I know," he said. "Spandex and Lycra. Chrome skin. Don't remind me. You're a cruel person. You're intolerant and sometimes wrong. Wait'll you see how wrong you are about the club. Beautiful women everywhere. A feast for the heart."

"I'm ready for correcting."

They filed along the row until they got to the stadium steps, then chucked down those to the exit. By the time they dipped back under the stands, all the field lights were dark and hissing. A few teenagers skidded by on Rollerblades and skateboards, shouting obscenities, as Bud and Del took the long slanted walk out of the stadium.

6

DEL GOT SOME KIDS Margaret knew, some students, to paint the inside of the condo on the weekend, so he and Jen took a room at the Royal d'Iberville, a ten-story hotel on the beach half a mile away. A little after midnight he was sitting out on the balcony, drinking a beer and feeling the warm wind that whistled through the tops of the oaks that jutted up from the parking lot below. They were on the sixth floor, directly above the driveway, fresh black asphalt that reminded him of a THINK ASPHALT bumper sticker he'd seen that morning. No picture, no logo. THINK ASPHALT. He'd pointed it out to Jen, and she'd said she was trying.

Jen was afraid of heights, so she refused to come out on the hotel balcony. She was afraid she'd lose her balance and fall six floors, or throw herself off and die a painful and contorted death. He promised her she wouldn't, but that didn't do much good. So he was outside and she was inside, in a chair, raising her voice a little to get it through the open balcony door.

"Here's my new idea," she said. "Until you buy me a dog you're nothing. You're dirt under my nails, like all the other chumps I've hung it up with."

"I want to buy you a dog," Del said. "Really."

"It's not a figure of speech," she said. "I want a real honest-to-God dog. Paws and all. The whole shoot-up."

"We can't have a dog in the condo, Jen. That's a problem."

"So we lose the condo," she said. "What do we need with a condo?"

"I thought you might like the condo after a year in a van with the swimsuit mogul," Del said. "Comforts of home and all that. Sitting equipment."

"You can go a long way in a van," she said. "And fast. You can go a mile a minute."

"You want to get a van?" Del said. "You want me to sell the condominium so we can get a van and become vagabonds and scavengers?"

"Vags and scavs," she said. "We already are, aren't we? We're bottom feeders. You just got that condo by luck. You married it."

"So what's wrong with that? You probably wish you'd married one too."

"I'm twenty-four, Del. I could have married ten condos by now if I'd wanted to."

"You probably did," Del said, watching the twirling Pecan-Waffle House sign down by the highway. "Oh, never mind. Forget I said that. That was wrong. I may have gotten the thing for free, but I've got money in it now."

"You need to get some money in *me*, Del," she said. "You buy me that dog, and I'm yours for life. In the biblical sense. In all the ways. No more fingernails. Details you can't even dream yet. Stuff that'll make your teeth wish they had teeth."

Dogs had been haunting Del all his days, is what it seemed like to him. Karen had wanted a dog, other girlfriends wanted dogs, now Jen. Everybody wanted one. It was part of their birthright, apparently. A happy woman is a dogful woman. Del's vantage was that getting a dog sooner meant you had to divvy it up later. He stared at the white moon sliding in and out of spoiled clouds, the light of it more limp than pale. The clouds were full of soot, like some cancer on the night sky, flowing, changing shape and texture, consistency, always moving on to kill more later, always spreading to the next clear patch of sky.

"These clouds don't look like tumors to you, do they?" he asked Jen.

She leaned out the door to look. "No, not really."

"I didn't think so," he said.

Salmon and green neon creased the horizon. Cars with trunks packed full of woofers thumped and walloped as riders whizzed by on Highway 90, the Biloxi version of a short seawall, with all the sand on the other side of it portable, tricked in by clever engineers. A lot of sand, he thought. He'd read in one of the Welcome to the Mississippi Gulf Coast pamphlets that Mississippi's was the world's largest man-made beach. It looked man-made. It was sort of pretty but seemed frail, as if it weren't really there at all, just some sand somebody'd thrown down and sooner or later it would be blown away or swallowed up by the Gulf. They hadn't done such a bad job of protecting the tern, though. He gave them that.

Sea & Sirloin, the restaurant across the beach highway from the hotel, was about ready to close up. He checked the clock over the Krispy Kreme doughnut shop; it was forty minutes after midnight. New doughnuts were scheduled for 12:47, the sign said.

"Why can't we just have a regular, adult relationship the way most people do?" he said. "Look out for each other, take the small pleasures, that kind of thing. What's wrong with that?"

"Nothing's wrong with it," she said. "As long as you have a dog to do it with. Without a dog what's the point? Then I know we're not made for each other and it doesn't matter what we do or don't do—I know we're headed for the end of the line."

There were sand fleas on the balcony. Del felt them popping around on him, scalp to forearm, forearm to calf, just a momentary wrinkle in some skin somewhere, a feeling that a tiny movement had taken place, always past tense when he noticed it, always just finished, just moved on, and on his body in improbable spots—in his trousers at the bend in his knee, the inner bottom of his left shoulder blade, to the right and a little above his navel.

"I'm getting bitten," he said.

"You want to come in?"

"Maybe it's my imagination," Del said.

A Chevy with what sounded like Steelpak mufflers hammered by, the note rising and falling with the shift. Then horns. He wanted to pull Jen out onto the balcony, force her to sit with him and watch the cruisers, smell the sand, and feel it too, the wind-carried bits she would catch on her cheek without ever having noticed their landing.

"I wonder where Itch is tonight," she said. "The poor fuck. You know what the big problem of sleeping in a van is? Getting it level. It's horrible sleeping at an angle, especially if it's like just a little angle, like it's *almost* level."

"Do you miss him?" Del said, looking at her over his shoulder.

"No," she said. Then she waved crosswise in front of her. "But we worked all these beaches. Mobile and Shatter Island all the way through here and on down to Waveland. We ate and slept in the van, like it was a tiny apartment. Seven o'clock in the morning Itch was up and stringing suits across the open back doors on these racks he got this guy to make for him. When the doors were done he propped up the plywood sheets we kept under the floor of the van. Put forty suits at a time on each sheet. He'd had that plywood forever. It was plywood his daddy'd given him, he told me. His lucky plywood."

"How can that be?" Del asked. "What's lucky about it?"

"Don't know. Maybe that he got it from his father. He told me it never let him down," she said. "He could always sell stuff off that plywood. It was always with him, solid and true."

"That's what I like in my plywood," Del said.

"I think we were in trouble for a long time," she said. "He grew fonder of inanimate things; they became his dearest companions. Once he told me the door on the van was the one thing left in the whole world he felt he could trust. That was an aggression, I guess. He knew something was about to happen."

DEL DIDN'T SLEEP well in the hotel. He woke early, tried to go back to sleep, then couldn't and got up to take a look outside. Early morning was, as always, delicate and constant, the light falling equally all around, foreshortening the visible world, flattening it by cutting the shadows but leaving the shine. It was seventy-one degrees on the d'Iberville sign.

From the hotel balcony the water of the Gulf started close and ran forever, as big as anything ever gets, and hugely glassy at six in the morning. It was the end of things, the point beyond which you couldn't go. Mottled and flat, and rising to meet the horizon, the surface went from silverish to a sentimental green and, at its uppermost edge, the point farthest from where he sat on the slotlike balcony of the hotel, a hazed and sky-matching blue.

A few people in beat-up cars bumped out to the edge of the water behind the Sea & Sirloin across the street and tried to fish, and others were doing the same down the way, behind

Rodeway Inn, Pecan-Waffle House, Open Palm Souvenirs, Winner's Casino. Small groups, two or three, stood together on the rock jetties lapped by tiny white froth. The Gulf at Biloxi wasn't actually the Gulf but a kind of giant brown-water sound protected by barrier islands a few miles out. The water was low and slow and without many of the watery virtues. There weren't any real waves to speak of, except when the weather kicked in, and the winds started going, and the rain started rocking things around. Then, like any other coastal water, it got heady.

Del went inside to get a new diet Coke. He'd made a special trip to a Jr. Foods drive-in grocery down the highway the night before at eleven because the Coke machines in the hotel were jammed up.

Jen was still in bed, with the covers up to her chin, her eyes shut, but she had her glasses on, so he knew she'd been awake.

"What's that?" he said. "With the glasses."

"If I put these on I can go back to sleep," she said. "It's a trick I learned."

7

A FEW HOURS LATER, after Jen really woke up and they'd both showered and changed, they went across the street to take a look at the jetty behind the Sea & Sirloin, a thirty-foot-wide spur of land running maybe two hundred yards out into the Gulf. It had a road going out partway, but after that dead-ended, the jetty was just chunks of concrete, old pieces of building, bits of streets, bits of flooring attached to the concrete beams, tiers of bricks, lots of riprap. Looking back toward Highway 90, there was a five-story motel on the water side of the souvenir place. The motel had been turned into some creepy apartments, and it looked as if it had burned recently. All the windows were gone, leaving just a black frame and a five-story tower of stairs around a concrete core. The water out at the jetty's end was army green. Two dozen telephone poles stuck up on the left in a perfect rectangle, eight feet out of the water. Something wasn't there anymore.

The Sunday fog was so heavy it turned everything off-white. The beach was a thin strip of cream. He saw a slab of concrete with a bit of Deco-green bathroom tile on it. The water was insistent the way it rolled up against the chunks of concrete. A hundred fifty yards out in the water, a buoy bounced in the water, and on top of it a tiny American flag was waving. Birds with bright-red stripes on their beaks sailed by in sets of four.

"I was thinking about this deal you were talking about," Del said.

"What deal I was talking about?"

"The pet deal. I was thinking about a hamster," Del said.

"Hamster?"

He nodded, then pointed out the algae that was water-shined on the pieces of concrete right at the jetty's edge.

"That's pretty," Jen said. "Like a forest seen from an airplane."

The slabs of concrete tipped as they walked from one to another of them. They were like tightrope walkers, their arms poking out for balance. He thought of Walter the cat.

To the west, the fog coming in from the Gulf was so thick that three hundred yards down the beach the whole world turned solid white—they couldn't even see the highway.

Jen found a purple cloth bag with *Crown Royal* sewn in yellow script on it. "I believe a hamster is a step in the right direction," she said. "Not a big step, but it shows you're getting your bearings."

"I want you around," Del said.

"That's arrangeable." She squatted on a California-shaped scrap of concrete at the lip of the water. "It looks like this water is playing here," she said. "Throwing up little white edges. And what are these water bugs? They look like bullets."

"Bullet mites," Del said.

A hundred yards east of them, another prong of land extended into the Gulf, only it was really land and it was bulkheaded. There were a couple of cars on it, a couple of trucks parked right next to each other, and another car farther out by itself. It looked like a place where people came to do car therapy, to work out their differences. Nobody over there was fishing.

They headed for the motel-apartments, the Cabana Beach. A dump lay behind it, a place where people expanded what jetties were made of, so there were chunks of wood, boards, shipping pallets, a couple of ten-foot bins filled with oyster shells, some kind of industrial oven mounted on little I-beams. There were corrugated metal sheets, metal boxes, refrigeration equipment, an eight-foot cement pipe, a huge metal column base bolted with two-inch-thick bolts into a slab of concrete the size of a car. Just in the water there were water heaters welded under channel iron—a flotation device now half submerged, rusted, slathered with algae.

"So what you're saying is no dog, not now, not ever? If we're having a relationship it's going to be dog-free?"

"What do you want a dog for?" he asked her. "Why don't you just have a baby?"

"A baby's got no fur," she said, eyeing him sideways.

"I'm sorry," Del said. "I shouldn't have said that. But can we just forget the dog? For a while, anyway? Wouldn't you rather have something else? A printing press?"

"And a hamster?"

"Anything that stays in a box," Del said.

"That's scary," Jen said. "Remember we don't know each other all that well yet. You've still got to watch what you say."

"I was talking about pets exclusively," Del said.

They got away from the water, and things quieted down. They could hear the tinny click of the big air conditioner behind the Sea & Sirloin. They were right along the beach, a prime tourist zone, so he was surprised what a wreck it was with all the junk out there—stacks of trashed jalousie windows, a pink stairway twisted off its mooring, galvanized-iron sheds on top of the third floor of the restaurant. Behind the

Cabana Beach there was a ten-foot rusted metal tank on its side, its weight drawing it down into the shape of a camshaft lobe. Both ends were gone, so it was a gigantic short tube. There was a kitchen chair inside, and some wads of carpet. It was a water tower, or a storage cylinder, on its side with the top popped off. Del could stand up easily inside. The walls were quarter-inch sheet steel.

"Get out of there, will you?" Jen said. "That thing will flatten you."

The corrugated-metal siding on the back of the Cabana Beach was waving in the wind. There were corrugated ceilings in some of the rooms that didn't have walls, and the penthouse was all broken glass. "Do you want to eat?" he called.

"Let's go to Back Bay," she said. "I like it over there. Maybe we can get a Blister Burger if that place is open on Sunday. Or we could go to the Gun and Knife Show at the coliseum. There's a guy there named Mr. Leather. I saw him on the TV ad."

The inlet behind the Cabana Beach was muddy. Out in this mud were more stairs and, along the side, what looked like a lot of kitchen equipment.

"People have died here," Jen said. "I can tell."

They started back across the street. The sun was barely coming through the fog, and the scene was stunningly white. On the side of the Cabana Beach, Del noticed a man sitting in front of one of the first-floor apartments, dressed in a tuxedo. He had on a red cummerbund and red socks, and he sat on a folding chair next to a stone doghouse that had cement pouring out between irregular pieces of stone. "Giraffe house," Del said, pointing the doghouse out to Jen.

She slapped his hand and hissed at him. "He'll shoot us, you goof. God. Don't you know anything about moving around?"

They got back to the d'Iberville and checked out, then took

a ride to the bay side of Biloxi, where hundreds of identical brick houses were oddly spaced along streets that ran in irregular concentric circles. Jen was driving.

"This must be air base stuff," she said.

The only difference from one bungalow to the next was that sometimes the carport was on the left and sometimes it was on the right. The buff-yellow houses were stupidly spaced and twisted slightly, so nothing was parallel to anything else. These houses looked like toys that had been put down there by some very large child.

They were driving through the streets of this playtown when they ran into a chain fence that surrounded an airstrip lined with stubs of red lights. Soldiers were driving camouflage jeeps up and down the runways, yellow lights blinking; fifty jets were lined up on one side of the strip, nose to tail, their fuselages all matching. At a little yellow-brick building at one end of the fence, a stub-nosed kid in full uniform, complete with gloves, stopped them, bent to look in the car, then waved them off. "Married cadet housing," he said. "Move along."

"How'd he know we weren't?" Jen said.

"No ring," Del said. "Let's get out of here."

They cut back along the water and drove onto the fishing pier that ran halfway out across Back Bay and then stopped dead. This was a two-lane concrete road from the fifties, sitting in the shadow of the new six-lane bridge that connected the beach with I-10, the superhighway running all the way from Florida to Los Angeles, through Mobile, Biloxi, New Orleans, Houston, Phoenix.

"This looks so cool," she said. "You can see what it was like in the old days." She stopped and they got out of the car near the end of the pier, which was the old access bridge, now broken in the middle, up on square concrete pilings. It was cut, as if hit with a bomb. A pair of two-foot-square concrete beams had been placed across the end of the road so cars couldn't drive off into the water. There was a barge out in the middle of the bay. Over to their right was the bay's mouth, a cluster of shrimp boats, some tin shacks, forty-foot trees competing with strings of telephone wires. Out in the water was a cage twenty-five feet high, made out of four tiers of creosote-soaked poles stacked up like Lincoln Logs, meant to keep barges and pleasure boats from smacking into the taller central telephone pole, carrying the lines.

You could hear the tires on the concrete up on the new bridge, tearing at it, knocking on the expansion joints. Some kind of little island lay in the mouth of Back Bay, low and brown, and a pelican floated by. Mist was still hanging back there.

Jen walked around reading the stuff scrawled in spray paint on the concrete. " 'Three BHS number six,' " she said. " 'Number two Untouchables.' 'Number eight, number four.' 'We Biloxi High School, kill the meat.' "

An inky-blue crane landed on one of the horizontal pieces of the nearest telephone-pole cage. There wasn't any white on this bird, and it almost disappeared into the background.

They walked out to where the roadbed just stopped in the middle of the bay, where there was a drop-off, no rail, no nothing, thirty feet or more down to the dark-green water. There were more of those phone-pole cages going across the bay. Some fishing boats were anchored on the opposite bank, near some places that looked like bait camps and shabby restaurants. A place called the Hygiene Crab Company was almost surrounded with two-story mounds of reef shells, clamshells, riprap, crushed limestone.

Standing on this fishing pier out in the bay, the stiff wind blowing across them, Del watched pelicans sailing by, dropping now and then like wind-driven kites into the water. It was getting dark. The sky was closing up fast.

"Check the train," Jen said, pointing to the girdered bridge that pivoted a center section so boats could get through.

The birds were amazing, the way they flew and then folded up like daggers and slammed into the water. Everything was turning a wonderful gunmetal gray. There were a few yellow lights shimmering on the water, reflected from car lights up on the big highway.

Fog was coming in from the Gulf, and it was thick. Out toward the mouth of the bay, toward the Gulf, it looked as though the water went maybe half a mile and then stopped dead. Everything past that was gray.

8

BUD WANTED to get Del a permanent job at the college. As a first step he'd gotten him a weekend deal as co-coordinator of the department's first annual faculty retreat, just to put Del into the picture. Del wasn't so sure he wanted to be in the picture, but since Bud was interested, he was going along. Bud had apparently already floated the idea about Del joining the faculty to the department chair.

"So we're doing a planning meeting," Bud said, when he called Del. "We're going to barbecue and talk about this retreat. The chairman thinks this is a big deal where we all get together for a weekend at a motel in Mission, Alabama, and feel better about each other. A happy faculty is a productive faculty, that kind of thing. He thinks it's a good way to 'lubricate' us. That's his word."

"This is Rudy?" Del said. He'd met Rudy a couple of times.

"Right," Bud said. "The other coordinator will be Rudy's friend Mimi, so you have to be nice. She's coming to the cookout."

In the background, Margaret yelled, "She's his executive assistant—nudge nudge."

Del heard them wrestling over the receiver, as if Bud was shoving Margaret out of the way. "He's poking her, O.K.?" Bud said finally. "He's been poking her for years. They're poking each other. Where he goes, she goes. They usually keep their distance when it's a college deal, but this time he's getting connecting suites on nineteen so they can poke till the cows come home."

Margaret said something in the background that Del couldn't quite hear. "What'd she say?" he asked.

"She said the cows have come and gone," Bud said. "She doesn't like Mimi that much."

"I think I know Mimi, don't I?" Del said. "Haven't I met her at your house?"

"I don't think anybody knows Mimi," Bud said. "Anyway, you'll be the troubleshooters—you know, check out the seminar rooms, be sure they've got the right chairs, the water glasses are full, ice for the panelists, that sort of stuff."

"I can handle it," Del said. "So why are we having this barbecue thing? What are we going to plan?"

"It's a get-together," Bud said. "Don't worry about it."

"Bring Jen," Margaret said into the phone. It sounded as if she was sitting in Bud's lap; she was right up on the handset. Then there was more wrestling noise.

In a minute Bud said, "She wants you to bring Jen to the cookout. O.K.?"

"Sure," Del said.

He punched the Off button on the portable phone Margaret had dropped by a few days earlier. It was an unfolding Toshiba bantamweight Bud had bought for himself, but when he found out it didn't work all that well, he gave it to Del.

"Maybe you'll like it," Bud had said to him on the test call. "Just try it. You can always put it back in its box."

Bud was always doing things like that, giving him cast-off equipment that was brand-new, in the original packaging. He had done it for years by mail, sending stuff to Houston. Recently Jen had returned a couple of things; she said it was a little much for Bud to be giving them all his junk.

THE STREET THAT ANGLED through the Mondrian was littered with kid stuff—three-wheelers, balls, bikes, little plastic men, stenciled skateboards. It was a family project, recently modernized in what somebody imagined were big new colors —dour raspberry, copper green, and plastic-flesh pink. It was as if the owners were looking to change the project's image, maybe attract a new crowd. Even made over it seemed beat-up and disreputable, about standard for a beach town. Salt air would destroy any improvements, so the owners just let it slide for as long as they could, and when nothing else would do, when the buildings were on the verge of collapse, they'd hire locals to nail up salvaged A-D plywood and revise and extend the colors.

Why Bud wanted Del to teach wasn't clear, especially since Bud wasn't thrilled with it himself. He always said teaching boiled down to "how much control you figure the cowgirls have over their Nissans," but he never explained what that meant, and Del never knew. He'd asked Margaret once, but she didn't know, either. Bud was terribly idealistic, she said, but he didn't want to show it much, so he always stashed it behind a huge cynicism about his co-workers, their pretenses, and the limited prospects of the students.

Since Del had moved to the Tropic Breeze he'd seen Margaret on and off, much less often than he would have liked. She had gotten a dizzyingly angular haircut and was skinnier, having started eating almost nothing. It was a crash make-over, going on during negotiations with Bud about their life in the aftermath of California. So when Bud and Margaret started slinking back together, it was the old Bud with the brand-new Margaret, completely redone, refurbished, reactivated. She seemed a different person—she might as well have been some being Bud had fetched out of the Arizona desert on the fly on his way back home, some new woman with supertanned skin and a long twisty flattop. According to Bud, Margaret had developed a "hair thing" and was always going after her body hair with scissors and tweezers. He told Del that except for her skull, she was utterly hairless.

He'd about given up trying to figure them out, what they were doing, living apart and living together. He knew Margaret didn't think much of divorce, because he'd talked to her about his while Bud was gone. "It's stupid," she'd said. "I don't mean you, but who gets divorced anymore? It's bad juju. Now we stick together, take what we can get, and arrange the rest."

"You spend a lot of time longing," Del said. "If you stay married, I mean."

"That's good for you," she said. "We used to say our growth and development was being impeded, that was a reason for divorce, but now we know we weren't growing or developing in the first place. Now we're just scared, so we're smart. It must have happened when Reagan was president."

"So whatever happens, it's going to be you and Bud forever?"

"Life and five years," she said. "Absolutely. I would die and go to heaven before I'd let Bud go. You get sick and tired of everything—every breath, gesture, every nasal note in the voice—but you get over it, and after a while it's like having a big pet around, a dog, a giant monkey lizard."

IN THE STREET OUTSIDE Bud's apartment at Valley Mondrian, Del said hello to a graying woman who was out on her nightly walk. He'd seen this woman walking her dog almost

every time he'd been to visit Bud. Sometimes Del said hello
and the dog would get up on its hind legs and start dancing
in circles. It was a toy poodle, old, going peach around the
eyes. The woman would nod at him, and they'd watch the dog
together.

"How you doing, guy?" he asked the dog, and the dog
started its hind-feet act. "Hey, look at that!"

"We haven't seen you in a while," the woman said, wiggling some slack into the leash, her face proud.

"You gotta watch the shadows to catch me," Del said.
"Somebody told me that once. That's what I do. You don't
want 'em to get a bead on you."

He figured she didn't get that at all. She gave him a blank
nod and yanked the poodle.

He crossed the street and let himself into Bud's apartment.
Margaret was on the sofa. He startled her, coming in with the
key. "What's the big rush?" she said, motioning her magazine
at him.

She looked striking and newfangled. The haircut made her
younger, and it looked right on her. She was wearing under-
pant-thin cotton pedal pushers, printed in zebra or alligator or
shimmering tarantulas—he couldn't quite make out what animals they were—and half of a black T-shirt over a full white
one.

"Bud's out back," she said, waving toward the kitchen of
the apartment. "He's getting ready for tonight. I don't know
why we have to have this woman Mimi, but we're having her.
It's going to be the treat of a lifetime for you, a man who just
stumbled into the halter-and-Spandex set. Mimi likes her little
shorts size one and light-emitting."

"That's not nice, Margaret."

"I know. I just hate her. She works for Rudy and I don't
like Rudy, and she's such a prick I don't like her, either. Bud
thinks it's savvy having her over. It's a cleverly disguised po-

litical maneuver. You know how clever Bud can be when he puts his mind to it."

"I thought Rudy was invited too," Del said.

"He was, but he has fallen away, leaving you with Jen and Mimi, an opportunity to double your pleasure—look but don't touch," she said, pulling him to her and grazing his ear with her lips. "Something we did just for you, Hoppy."

"Gee, thanks," Del said, pulling away. "What are we eating?"

"Halibut, probably," Margaret said, rolling her eyes to indicate that he was silly to ask. "Listen, I'm glad you're here —can you fix this TV?" She waved the magazine toward the TV.

"What's the matter with it?"

"It's on the wrong channel," she said. "HBO in ten minutes has a Billy Zane festival."

"Hot dog," Del said, mock-jumping toward the set. "Let me hurry up and get that fixed for you." The TV was old and small, one they'd had in their bedroom at the house. Suddenly he stopped and said, "Say . . ." He narrowed his eyes at her. "How come you don't get up and fix this TV yourself? And where's the switcher?" He made a remote motion with his hand, punching air buttons, aiming at the screen.

"I'm old and beautiful," she said. "Besides, the switcher's gone. C'mon, Del. Do it, please?"

He cycled the TV to HBO, then leaned away from the screen to check the picture. "That it? Is Bud in the kitchen?" Del pointed toward the kitchen.

"He's in the kitchen," Margaret said.

BUD WAS LEANING awkwardly over the sink, spooning soupy ice cream out of a peach-colored plastic glass with shatter lines of light cracked in its side. His door-walking cat, Walter, was sitting on the counter.

"It's diet Coke and diet ice cream," Bud said, a trace of the float still clinging to his lip. "I measured everything; I was careful. Really."

"You're going to eat your way out of Margaret's arms," Del said. "But it's nothing to me. Move the cat, will you?"

"And I wonder where she'll go?" Bud said, holding the spoon out with some float on it for Walter to lick. "Better than Vaseline?" he said to the cat. "Hmm?"

"What's for dinner?" Del said. He could hear the cat's tongue ring on the spoon.

"Girls," Bud said.

"Please, Bud. We're reaching a mighty reach for the normal."

"I forgot," Bud said. "We're having Budburgers and Bud-taters, fried by me in this pot over here, using a recipe known only to myself and Bob the Owner, owner of the Satanic Fish Town. I've got the lo-cal buns going at eighty calories each, got the good imported-from-Texas barbecue sauce, got the correct additives."

"What about fish?" Del said. "Margaret said fish." He opened the refrigerator, looking for a beer, but the only one in there was dark. "Didn't we give up dark beer right after high school?"

"You attacking my beer?" Bud said.

"Just warming up," Del said, grabbing the beer.

Bud twisted toward him. "We've got no fish for dinner—nobody promised you fish. All we've got are these two red-hot blast-me-off-to-Portugal women, one of whom is news to you."

"Margaret already discussed this," Del said. "Miss Mimi Everlasting. I'm to take visual pleasures only, right?"

"If there are any," Bud said. "Yes. She's a young person

with a life stretching out in front of her like so many unrented videos. *Exactly* like that."

"It could be worse," Del said. "It could be just us and basketball on TV."

Bud rinsed his glass under the hot tap, using three fingers like a bottle brush. "Hey, how would *you* like to be seven and a half feet tall? We got to pay 'em something for that. How would *you* like to screw twenty thousand women?"

"Squeak, squeak, squeak," Del said. "That's the feet on TV, not the screwing. Although maybe it's the screwing too —how would I know? On TV all I hear is the squeaks." He dodged Walter, who was interested in his shoes. "Why wouldn't Rudy come?" Del said.

"Because there is a God," Bud said. "And unlike everybody else, God don't like bike shorts. Margaret sees Mimi at the college health club. I can't speak for her brainpower."

Margaret showed up then in the kitchen door. "Yeah, and brainpower is everything to Mr. Bud. He hates them bike shorts, especially the lemon-colored ones." She crossed the kitchen, took a yogurt out of the refrigerator, and made some kind of forties glamour gesture, looping her free hand over Bud's shoulder. "But listen, don't you worry about Bud. He only *thinks* about these things." She smiled seductively. "We have limitations over here, Del."

"Del don't want to know," Del said, lifting his eyebrows.

She had the magazine with her, *Vanity Fair,* something Bud subscribed to in "his week," as he called that period between when he moved out and when he and Margaret started their renegotiation, and now was stuck with for the rest of the year. "Anyway," Margaret said, "what's this I hear you older guys still have for Julie Brown?" She flapped the magazine, and Del caught a headline that said WOMEN MEN LOVE III.

"She just *looks* smart, doesn't she?" he said, eyeing the page swivel-headed.

"She's cool," Bud said. "Lobot material."

"Lobot?" Del said. "What's Lobot?"

"She's not the stupid Julie Brown," Margaret said. "She's the other one. The sexy one with nasal tunnel syndrome. It says in here she's a favorite of older viewers, like men in their forties. And up. It says she has lots of energy."

"There you have it," Bud said, rubbing his mouth with a dishcloth. "You can't learn energy."

"I agree," Del said.

"I'll bet she's streetwise too," Bud said.

"She's a real stud muffin," Margaret said. "Last year's model."

DINNER WAS SCHEDULED for seven, so Del had time to get home for a rest and a clean-up. He took the long way back to the condo, enjoying the walk, the fresh weather, the sea birds. Around by the condominium pool, he noticed, the property manager had strung new barbed wire to keep out the neighborhood kids, and he wondered if he should complain about that. He stopped at his mailbox to see if he'd gotten any new magazines and found copies of *Spiff* and *Newsweek*.

There was also a letter from Karen, who had left her new husband and gone to Oregon and was working at a graphics studio there, doing desktop design. He read the letter, standing in the breezeway where the mailboxes were. Her script was tiny, black, angular, on gray laid paper. "So you ought to get out here sometime, Del. We could drive around. Every time I go by a gas station, one of those stucco places with stacks of tires off to one side and a couple of steel drums around, I think about you. I'm not sure it was such a good idea for me to come here. Maybe I should have tried somewhere else. These are the people who've been leading the Believers' Revolution all these years. All their cars are earth tones, Rovers and Cherokees, just like their clothes. They want to make a difference so bad. They want to start right now to build a better tomorrow for themselves and their children. I think there's something seriously wrong, Del. The Body Snatchers have made more progress than we know. These beings are too eager, too simple. What's most frightening is that they can make the world just what they want it to be simply by believing in it together."

Del felt air suddenly run streams around him, making him shiver. The letter tightened his stomach—it was lonely and small, hopeless-sounding, and so far away. Everything was Karen then, memories of how gentle she was, how sweet, of all the time they'd spent together, and how that was lost, of all the things they did, the ways they talked, the kinds of jokes they shared, the touches, the play. It was as though she were there with him in the breezeway; he felt her size, the scent of her skin, the color of it, the smell of her hair, the way she moved—all of the thousands of details came back instantly, flooded him, left him aware of how lonely she must be, how lonely he was too, in spite of everything. The loss was suddenly gigantic, impossible to corral, as if a whole life had been lived and was over, was dead, and yet here was this short letter, showing him that his life with Karen wasn't gone at all, it was still out there, circling in space but lost to the participants, some fragment of a planet momentarily in sunlight.

Then he was relieved, too, to be clear of her, clear of that time when they were together but it was obvious they shouldn't be. That was a hard feeling. Cruel. Not something he was proud of. He looked across the highway at a boat nosing into its slip in the rickety marina, then returned the letter to its envelope and went up in the elevator and inside to get ready for dinner.

He had gotten a few pieces of furniture from mail order

catalogs, but they were all stuffed over on one side of the living room, as if he'd just moved in. He liked it that way, liked the temporary feel of it, the sense that nobody had tried to make it charming, or correct, or even livable. Even with the new paint, the condo looked like a storage place for the furniture. There wasn't that much—a couple of chairs, a lamp, small cushions, a table still in its shipping box, and some posters. The posters leaned against the wall. There was a Braque—a huge framed thing from France—and a few smaller prints: a Giacometti he'd found in a used office furniture store, a framed postcard of a Giotto, all in stacks against the fresh white paint. The sofa was still in the center of the room, still facing the Gulf. The TV was by the glass door where he'd put it the night he moved in. There was a cardboard box he'd cut down so the cat would have a place to sleep if Bud and Margaret went out of town, though they hadn't yet.

When Jen wasn't around, Del spent most of his time at home in the bedroom, sitting in bed reading magazines, working up the new sales literature he brought home from the store, watching a new, second television out of the corner of his eye, over the tops of magazines, stopping every couple of minutes to punch up the sound on the news, a big scene in an "R" movie, a video that looked cleverer than usual, a bit of *Wings* on the Discovery Channel. Magazines piled up under the bedside table, and in the closets, and on the built-in bookshelves in the living room. He felt bad when he threw them out before he'd read them, so there was pressure; a magazine would sit there for ten days and then, when he started to toss it, he would realize he hadn't looked at it, so he'd rustle through it on the way to the garbage. Sometimes when he bought a new magazine he'd get home and find that he had it, that he'd bought it already, brought it home, never read it.

———

HE SLID Karen's letter into the kitchen cabinet next to the Lea & Perrins, which was where he kept the mail that he planned on doing something about, and headed for the bath. He sat naked on the floor of the bathroom, on the bath mat, reading through a copy of *Entrepreneur,* listening to the water run into the tub. Janitorial services were a big opportunity, the magazine said. The sound of running water was very restful; it was something he liked. Sometimes he thought he heard voices in the water and turned it off quickly to be sure there was no one at the door or in the house.

After his bath he dried himself, took two fresh towels, and stretched out on top of the bed, one towel under him and one carefully covering him, ankle to mid-chest. He rested that way for twenty minutes, then propped himself up against the wall behind the bed and called Jen.

"Are you going to Bud's?" he asked.

"Sure am," she said. "I'm looking forward to it."

"You want me to come get you?"

"Sure; that'd be great."

"Are you all right?"

"I'm fine. What, do I seem wrong?"

"No, you sound fine. Never mind," Del said. "I guess I figured you'd be nervous."

"I'll be perfect," Jen said. "Are you worried? Don't be worried. Can I stay at your place later?"

"Yes," Del said. "I'd like that."

His hair was screwy, but he slapped it into shape with a hairbrush, got dressed, packed some beer from the refrigerator, and then started for Bud's. As he was going out the door he made the sign of the cross and then began saying the Hail Mary, whispering it to himself as if it were some kind of assurance that the evening would go smoothly, that nothing would happen. He wasn't sure why he was nervous about it, what he expected might happen. Mimi was some kind of risk, maybe.

He knew the Hail Mary from childhood, but he'd heard it the night before on cable TV, on a channel run by Catholics. He was flicking through the fifty-one channels one last time, and there, on thirty-eight, in the no-fault zone on the television dial reserved for magic cleaners, muscle builders, big-hair guys forever weeping into the camera, and that weasel-faced preacher who knocked people over when he made the blind to see, the deaf to hear, the lame to walk—there Del found a priest in full High Mass regalia, the brilliant gold vestments over the crisp white linen, talking to the TV audience in a soft, careful way about the virtues of faith. Behind this priest was a tiny nun, a person the size of a nine-year-old, in traditional nun black and white, a half-circle cowl shrouding her forehead. The two of them were stuck in a charmingly pitiful rent-a-talk-show set complete with Sears office-at-home desk and chrome-legged chairs with nubbly off-white upholstery. But the guests were gone, the priest was talking to the camera, and this nun behind him was whispering the Hail Mary. When the priest finished talking about faith, he started talking about next week's guest, but Del wasn't listening to him, he was listening instead to the nun, and pretty soon he was saying the prayer along with her, first mouthing the words, then actually speaking them out loud, the words in her cadence, almost a song.

Since last night he'd said the Hail Mary hundreds of times, to himself at home, in the car, in the shower, watching other TV shows—anytime. He said it out loud sometimes, when he was alone, and sometimes he just imagined it, just kept it in his head.

He was surprised how short it was, how little it appeared to say, how lovely "blessed art thou amongst women" was, and he worried that the end should be "at the hours of our deaths" instead of "hour of our death," since it seemed to be plural. Then, when he couldn't remember which it was supposed to be, he quit worrying about it, because he figured that if the prayer had lasted this long it was beyond grammar. Now, on his way back to Bud's for dinner, he thought about all the prayers he'd recited as a kid, all the statues of the Virgin he'd knelt before, all the flickering candles in their red-glass cups, the perfumes of their flaring wicks an elaborate reflection of his prayers; he remembered the antique wooden pews, worn by hand after hand, the way they creaked when you settled into them, the pads on the kneelers, the withering flowers around the statuary—all the reassuring memories of Holy Mother Church.

JEN LOOKED gaunt and sweet with her big brown shoes, heavy socks, a thin black-lace leotard, white bike pants, a black denim skirt about eight inches long, and a copper-colored Sea World Maintenance shirt over a man's old-fashioned ribbed white undershirt. "It's grunge-revival," she said. "Is it O.K.?"

Her hair was pulled back, showing a widow's peak, perfect brows, the mystery in her eyes.

He opened the car door and let her in. "With this face you could wear socks on your hands," he said, eyeing her eyes.

"Hey, thanks," she said.

Mimi had already arrived by the time they got to the Mondrian. Bud was outside whacking the barbecue grill with a steel brush, and Margaret was in the kitchen. She did the introductions. Del felt awkward.

"Margaret told me about everything," Mimi said. She was older than Jen, maybe older than Margaret, but very small and sexy.

Del was caught a little short. "She told you about everything? What'd she say?"

"Oh, she was just telling about how you guys are together all the time," Mimi said. "About how you come over for dinner. That's nice."

"Oh," he said. "Yeah."

Mimi leaned against the counter with brown beer in a juice glass, the glass tilted at a big angle. "And," she finally said, "Margaret told me all about you, about how you two were all alone over there at the house while Bud did his turn out West."

"She said that?" Del said, looking at Margaret.

"Well," Margaret said. "Sort of."

"Oh, cut the guff," said Mimi. "I'm talking pre-Jen, of course. We know about these things, don't we, Jen?"

Jen made a face.

"We do business on the planet, if that's what you mean," Del said.

"Whoa," Mimi said. She looked at Margaret with an expression that meant the brother was a dork, then flipped Del off and said, "You too, Buster. I just want you to remember, when Jen gets tired of you, I'm about as available as space travel."

"I'm rushing for tickets," he said. He turned to Margaret. "Did I kill her Pomeranian? Have I missed a key part of this meeting?"

"Why don't you give Bud a hand?" Margaret said. "He probably *needs* a hand with those meat patties."

DINNER WAS EASIER than he'd expected. Mimi cooled off, though there wasn't any explanation for her first nastiness. She seemed more interested in leaning across the table so everybody could get a good view of her nipples, and in beating up on Bud, than in talking to Del. When they'd finished the hamburgers he helped Bud clear the table.

"So this morning," Jen said, watching Bud stack dinner dishes, "this morning at seven-thirty I get a call from this guy, wakes me up, and he wants to know if I want to buy some garbage bags made by the blind. He's selling garbage bags made by the blind. I tell him I'm asleep, and so he goes, 'Do you want me to call you back later?' I say, 'No, thanks.' So he goes, 'You want me to keep talking? I say, 'No—what's the matter with you? I'm asleep. I'm trying to sleep.' So he says, 'What about these garbage bags? They come in colors. Well, three colors, anyway. Black, brown, and green.' So I say, 'Listen, I bought light bulbs from the blind, six bucks apiece, isn't that enough?' "

"You didn't say that," Margaret said. "Did you?"

"That's what I said," Jen said.

"You're a tough study," Mimi said.

"Good for you," Bud said. "Those damn blind people are driving me nuts, always poking around trying to sell you something."

"Poking?" Margaret said.

"What?" Bud said.

Mimi turned and gave Bud a pained expression. "Duh. I don't think we say 'poking' when we're talking about the blind, Bud," she said.

"Poking, get it?" Margaret said. "Like with a stick?"

"Were those bulbs any good?" Mimi asked. "Somebody tried to sell me some, but I wouldn't buy 'em. I said, 'What kind of light does a blind person need?' That stumped the guy."

"Hail Mary, full of grace," Del said. It just came out, it was hollow-sounding.

They stared at him. He didn't know what to do next. He couldn't tell what they were thinking. They were startled, stopped dead, waiting. It was uncomfortable the way everybody shut up.

He said, "Hail Mary, full of grace, the Lord is with thee, blessed art thou amongst women, and blessed is the fruit of thy womb, Jesus." Right then Jen joined in with him, and they said the rest together.

"Holy Mary, mother of God," they said, "pray for us sinners, now and at the hour of our death. Amen."

Bud was a little way off from the table, between the table and the kitchen door, holding the burger platter. His hair was like brown wires springing off his head. He was grinning. Jen was grinning at her hand on the table. Mimi was looking at everybody else, everybody but Del. Margaret smiled.

Del started it again, and this time Jen joined in right from the beginning, and then Margaret was mouthing the words too. And Bud began to say it with them, carrying his platter out into the kitchen. When they finished the second time, nobody said or did anything, everyone just sat there—that's what Del saw, what it looked like to him. Sesame seeds from the buns dotted the tabletop. Finally Margaret patted her napkin across her lips and said, "It's pretty, isn't it?"

"Really," Jen said.

9

ON FRIDAY a week later Del met Bud in a classroom out at the college to talk about the retreat, since they hadn't actually gotten around to it at Bud's apartment. It'd been raining, and there were thunderstorms all around, and lightning, and the fluorescents were on in the building even though it was only four in the afternoon. It was already storm dark outside, the glass peppered with raindrops, the thick tree limbs weighed down with water they'd caught.

Bud had been to the Faculty Club for a few beers. "It's time we talked about this," he said, shutting the classroom door. "I don't get you. You're my brother, aren't you? So when I went to California you started fucking around with Margaret? No, excuse me—*messing around,* that's what she called it. What is that, messing around? Does that make it cleaner? Del, I want to be sensible here, I've been trying for weeks and weeks, but I don't get it."

Del felt dead, no remorse or anxiety—flat. He had imagined the conversation too often, too completely. "It was nerves," he said.

"Fuck your nerves," Bud said. "You're my fucking

brother. You screwed my fucking wife. What the fuck is wrong with you?"

"We didn't make love," Del said.

"Oh, *make love,* sorry," Bud said. He shut his eyes and shook his head. "That's good. That's sweet."

"We didn't do it," Del said. He was sitting in the front row, in one of the oak student chairs with initials scratched all over the writing arm. Two Oriental kids walked by in the hall outside, speaking loud Chinese.

"I feel a lot better now," Bud said. "You were short of actual, uh, penetration, right? There was no insertion. Have I got that? That's good, that's swell. I feel a lot better now. So, what, the two of you just rolled around a little bit, right? Jack you off, jack her off—that the idea?"

"Come on, Bud," Del said. "We can't do anything about this now. I'm sorry—everybody's sorry it happened."

"That's damned sensible," Bud said. "That's right. We should just forget it. Or I should shred your face and stick it in a dog pail."

"C'mon, Bud," he said.

"We don't have a dog, anyway," Margaret said. She'd come in and was standing in the classroom doorway with three diet Cokes.

"If we had a dog," Bud said.

She crossed the room, put two Cokes on the instructor's table, then went to the window and stood looking out at the weather, her reflection clear in the glass. "I thought I ought to be here," she said.

Bud was on the table, dangling his feet. "I guess you're right." He tossed a Coke to Del and snapped the tab on the other one.

"We didn't want to do anything," Del said. "We didn't know what the fuck was going on. It just started."

"Oh, Jesus fucking Christ," Bud hissed. He jumped off the

table and charged Del, knocking him out of the chair, knocking the chair over, then he locked his arm around Del's head, twisting it, and flipped Del over on his back. Del's feet were caught in the chair arm. Bud hit hard with his fist on the top of Del's head, two, three times.

Margaret turned around but didn't leave the window. "Easy, Bud," she said.

"You're a screwy little cocksucker," Bud said. "It's always simple for you, it's always fucking luck, first to last. You just wade on in and take your chances, and bang! everything works out. Jesus, you make me want to puke."

"Let him go, Bud," Margaret said.

"Yeah," Del said, his voice muffled because he was talking into the side of Bud's shirt, Bud's chest, his head still in the headlock. "Yeah, I'm one lucky motherfucker, all right."

"This is great," Margaret said. She turned and looked back out the classroom window. "This is really splendid and highly evolved."

"Are you going to let me go now?" Del said, managing to get his mouth uncovered.

"You smell kind of funny," Bud said.

"Oh, screw this," Margaret said.

"He does," Bud said, letting his brother go.

"Thanks, Bud," Del said.

"What do you wash with?" Bud said.

"Soap. The usual." Del got up and dusted himself off, picked up the chair and straightened it, then sat in it again. He snapped a cigarette butt off his pants leg.

Bud sat down on the instructor's table and took a long drag off his Coke.

"That was a flurry of activity," Margaret said.

"Sure was," Del said, rubbing his head.

"I'm sorry," Bud said. "I lost it a minute."

Del waved him off. "Yeah, well. I'm sorry too. You know,

we were there, you were gone, nobody knew what was happening. It wasn't like—"

"Oh, shut up, Del," Margaret said.

He waved a hand at her back and grimaced. "Right."

Thunder coiled outside and racked the windows. Margaret said, "I don't know how you can talk about this for so long, Bud. Especially now, after all this time. It's just stupid. It was a stupid mistake, and going on about it is stupid too. And look at this rain, anyway."

"She's a weather person," Bud said, holding his Coke can as if toasting Margaret. "She believes in the washing of the earth. She believes in God. She believes in grace. She believes in hope. She believes in the future. She believes in fucking the pants off her husband's brother—"

"No, Bud," she said. "I don't."

"O.K., sorry. *Almost* fucking the pants off him, right? Just about. Playing a little doctor on the couch with him, maybe, just a titty squeeze, and a dick rub, and an ear-tonguing, wet-between-the-legs, panty-fuck deal, is that right? That it?"

"You're disgusting, Bud," she said.

"Yeah, but I'm not fucking your sister," he said.

Bud showed a tight smile and then came off the table, throwing a wide right fist at his brother, catching him high on the temple, knocking Del and the chair over a second time. Instantly Bud grabbed his hand and doubled over in pain. Del hit his head on the linoleum going down. There was a cut where Bud's knuckle had caught the side of his forehead.

Swinging his legs wide, Del caught Bud and tripped him, knocking him to the floor. "Are you going to quit fucking around with me or what?" Del said. "Jesus." He wiped the blood off his forehead and stared at it.

"I think I'm probably going to kill you," Bud said, not moving.

"Yeah, well," Del said.

"I want her back," Bud said.

Margaret, who had turned around to look at them on the floor of the classroom, was yelling this time. "Who's her? Who the fuck is *her?*"

"You," Bud said. "Before this."

"You'd better talk that over with me," Margaret said, loud now but not screaming. "He can't do anything about who I was. All he did was mess with the packaging and worry. I did the rest."

Bud was making all kinds of faces. "I think I busted my hand," he said.

"Fuck you," Margaret said. "You're a weasel."

"Yeah, but I think I did," Bud said.

"There it goes again," she said. "Experience validates myth."

Bud sat up, leaning against the leg of the table. "I don't care what you people did, who did it, where you did it, how you did it, who started it or who stopped. Who would I believe, anyway? What if you say the same thing? Then I'm in trouble."

"You're in trouble, anyway," Margaret said, going toward him as if to help him up.

"Screw off," he said. "Get away. I'd trade your ass in a minute for any ten-cent rag in the country—anything young, hot, and sexy."

"What would you do with somebody sexy?" Margaret said.

"I'd try to remember," he said.

Del got up and righted the student chair. There was a pool of diet Coke on the floor, and a pie-size wet spot on his jeans. "That's enough," he said. He reached out to help Bud off the floor. "You guys can quit this now before it gets bad."

"Shut the fuck up," Bud said, taking his hand. "I'm talking to Margaret. When I'm talking to Margaret you just shut up. O.K.?"

"Got it," Del said. He pulled Bud to his feet, then started wiping at the blood on his head with the sleeve of his shirt.

10

DEL SPENT a few days nursing cuts and bruises from Bud's attack. The cuts and bruises were modest, but Del liked being hurt so much that he managed to turn these little injuries into wounds of some seriousness—lots of peroxide and Polysporin, lots of gauze bandages, lots of adhesive tape, lots of trips to the drugstore for supplies and equipment, right down to the Ace bandage for the elbow he'd banged up in one of the falls. He loved the Ace bandage.

Jen did the doctoring, playing along. While she circled him, changing the bandage on his head, he was thinking that there was something rare about her size, or maybe it was just the way she moved, so lightly, as if not required to have feet on the ground.

After she'd changed his bandages at two o'clock one morning in the middle of the week, he went out on the balcony while she did some computer stuff. He was thinking about Bud and Margaret, about how they were doing together, wondering how much heat went on when they were alone. He never reached any conclusions about them when he thought about them, in fact, told himself conclusions couldn't be reached, but he thought nevertheless, remembering Margaret after dinner while Bud was gone, with her elegantly long hands together, palms flat against each other, her perfect auburn hair swaying off to one side of her tilted head, telling him how surprised she was that she cared for him as much as she did. How had that happened?

He was out there wearing shorts and a T-shirt, his feet propped up on the rail, staring at the mostly empty highway and the Gulf, watching the docile waves roll up like crooked white lines to the shore, as if it was all they could do to arrive. Gnats bit his legs. He waved them off. A motorcycle accelerating in the distance sounded like some *Saturday Night Live* fart joke. Heard again, it sounded like a snore. The lights looked as though he was seeing them through star filters, gauzy centers with peaks streaming away from them. He rubbed his eyes and heard the sliding door open.

"You living out here?" Jen said, hanging on to the handle.

"You want to come out and sit?" he said.

"Will you keep me from falling?"

"Sure," he said.

"I don't trust you. What're you doing out here, anyway?"

"Wondering how I got into that business with Margaret. Maybe I worry too much, but it was a mess and I don't know why I didn't know that to start with."

"You did know," Jen said. "But you temporarily dispensated yourself. And you ought to forget it now."

"Yeah, I know. But I haven't. And if the circumstances were different, the timing, well, it wouldn't have been all that bad a thing necessarily, would it?" He turned to look at her, and she was firing her eyes back in her head.

"O.K.," he said. "I guess it was fucked."

"No duh," she said.

"I don't think Bud's going to get over it easy, no matter what he says. Even with this." He tapped the bandage on his head. "But he's got all this other crap happening to him; he's real pissed off generally. I shouldn't have fucked up."

"Why don't we leave it to them?" she said, creasing her hair with the faces of her fingernails. "Or is there more? Is this about something else, like you and her?"

"No," he said, reaching for Jen.

She draped a hand toward him, and he took it for a second, then let it fall. "You sure?" she said.

"Yes. Jesus," he said, sighing and rubbing his eyes. "Yes. I adore her, but—"

"I'm going to bed, then," Jen said. "Don't worry. Wake me up if you need me." She backed inside and slid the door shut.

On the highway below, the restaurants and the miniature golf courses and the souvenir shops were all screaming with lights and flags and flickering silver things that whipped around in the wind. There weren't very many people down there. Every once in a while he saw somebody walking on Highway 90. Sometimes people by themselves, sometimes couples would go by. They were an odd mix because some were tourists in full party performance and others were homeless, headed for a big meal over in the Dumpster behind the pancake house. These he liked better than the tourists, at least from the safe harbor of his high floor. He even envied them a little—they got to camp out in the woods behind Ritz-A-Dish Restaurant Supply, or to sleep out on the beach somewhere, and they never had to shave, and they could smell bad whenever they wanted, and they got to eat stuff other people had already eaten parts of—that held a fascination for him, eating after other people. He'd always wanted to do that, wanted to be hungry and need to do it, so he could get over the revulsion.

That afternoon, coming back from the mall, he'd seen a couple, a black woman and a white guy—the guy with tattoos all over, even up on one side of his face, and a saxophone case, and her with tight emerald toreador pants and an armless black-and-white spangle-style shirt—and they were walking along the highway talking vigorously, making lots of world-addressing gestures and big faces at each other; and then, two hours later, he'd driven over to the other side of Back Bay to pick up some unhappy customer's bad tuner, and he'd seen the same couple again, miles from where he'd seen them first, and they were still walking, still talking eagerly. Settling the planet's hash.

He got up, ready to go inside. The wind was sweeping by, buffeting treetops, rattling leaves, plastering his shirt against him. He liked that about Biloxi, the wind. It was always there, always blowing off the Gulf, so no place ever seemed completely still. There was always sticky air pushing against you, swirling your hair and tugging your clothes, reminding you that you were alive.

JEN GOT most of her magazine stuff off Compuserve Information Service, a computer network she called on the phone, linking her machine with giant ones in Virginia or someplace. Once on, she searched the wire services for stories she might be interested in. When she found one, she downloaded it to her computer, edited it, and then it was ready to be patched into her magazine.

The computer made finding the stories a lot easier than combing the papers, and it allowed her to get at stories she would never have been able to find in local papers.

"I thought it was too easy at first," she told Del. "I thought it was phony. Like, if they're this easy to get they can't be any good. But then I thought the stories were so beautiful it didn't matter where I got them."

He wasn't sure the stories were as beautiful as she said.

They were freaky and grotesque, but that wasn't new, particularly—the tabloids and MTV had been doing freaky for years. Still, there was something about the stories she chose that separated them from the run of the mill, something horribly charming, some little twist in each one that made it hers and not the *Star*'s. He couldn't put his finger on it—maybe it was just that they were stories about people, regular people doing monstrous things—they reminded him of paintings somehow, or even Weegee-style pictures, polished just a little for effect if necessary. The perfect economy was attractive.

She'd been brought up on computers in the schools, playing with Apples in grade school, Macintoshes in high school, PCs in college. She had an old Toshiba notebook, five and a half pounds, with a color LCD screen. Toshiba made the best portables, she told him.

Earlier that evening they'd been hooked up through his telephone to Compuserve, and he'd watched over her shoulder as she searched the wire services for key words she was interested in—brutality, dismemberment, sacrifice, ritual, severed, torture, violence, amputation.

She found a story about a teenage girl who gave birth to a child in her parents' bathroom and then stabbed it one hundred and seventy-five times with fingernail scissors and threw it out the window; the girl's father, who found the baby on the front lawn, thought it was a doll. Her second story was about a postal worker in New York who killed forty-eight cats. This guy was arrested because he brought a cat with two broken back legs to the ASPCA. Twenty-seven other cats, similarly brutalized, each with broken back legs, were found in the basement of the post office building where this guy worked. He said he had a preference for girl cats.

She also found a story about a Fellow of the Royal College of Physicians who said Jesus faked his death in a premeditated bid to survive crucifixion, that the whole deal was cooked up in the garden of Gethsemane the night before, that Jesus was up there only six hours and people watching the crucifixion weren't so sure he was dead, but he made this big show of crying out and then got taken down with what the Royal College guy said was probably a temporary deficiency of blood supply to the brain.

"Sure," Jen said. "And I suppose Jesus lived forty more years as a brain-damaged juggler in a traveling show. Where do they get these guys?"

The next story was about nineteenth-century academicians who wondered if the brain of a serial killer was shaped differently from the brain of an artist, so they developed a field of study they called cerebral morphology. It had a rundown on the brains that included in the Wilder Brain Collection at Cornell University, where large glass cookie jars hold them in yellow- or green-tinted formaldehyde. At its height, in the early 1920s, the collection featured thirteen brains of highly educated persons, along with 648 other human brains, of all ages; they were down to about seventy now. The largest brain in the collection, perhaps one of the largest brains ever known, was a "1770 gram behemoth" that belonged to a mid-nineteenth-century multiple murderer and genius named Edward Ruloff.

"I like this last one," Del said, as she downloaded the brain stories. "I'd like to see these brains in the cookie jars, you know?"

"I don't know why," she said. "They're probably just sitting there."

"Oh," he said. "Yeah."

It took only a minute or so to download each story. Sometimes she just turned on a capture file that transferred everything that went through the screen to her hard disk, but more often she scanned the titles of the stories, sometimes the lead paragraphs, then made her decisions.

She got a couple of cemetery stories too, one about Penman Memorial Park in Miami, where two guys were put in the same grave, and another about a guy in Alabama who watched a scary movie and then went to the cemetery, dug up a grave, opened the casket, and beheaded the corpse. He told the arresting officer that "he'd always wanted a skull and decided to go on out there and get him one."

The last story was about a war among hairless men in Seattle. Two or three hairless men had been found dead under a bridge, and later another hairless man was charged with the killings. There was factionalism in the hairless community there, the report said.

THE SUPPLY OF STORIES was endless; every week there were more, every time Jen hooked up with Compuserve. Del started getting interested and began reading more and more computer magazines. Whenever she went on the network he began looking forward to the next article, wondering if ghoulish things such as she was finding stories about were going on in Biloxi, right around the corner from where they were, maybe even in the building.

Slasher movies bored him because they weren't true, but the stories scared him. And immunized him. Bizarre stories were touching; they sent shivers down his spine. He could picture the people in the stories, in the news pieces, like characters in a novel. When he got out the old barbecued-dog story and read it, he could almost see the guy barbecuing his neighbor's dog, the neighbor watching over the fence. He could imagine what the dog's hind leg looked like on the grill, what the ribs looked like. He could imagine what the grill looked like—not a Weber, or an Old Smoky, but a gas grill, one of those with the propane tank underneath. The yard was well trimmed, maybe a few weeds out by the street. The house was brick, with white wooden shutters alongside the windows. The guy barbecued in his T-shirt. The arms were ripped out of the shirt, so that whenever he moved, whenever he turned anything with the big fork that he held in his right hand, you saw armpit hair. He had rings on his fingers. A stupid watch, a big gold thing. A beer in his left hand. He wore shorts and black shoes with black socks, but they weren't modern black shoes and black socks, they were office shoes. The socks were thin and ribbed. You could see the skin of his ankles through them. His hair stuck out from the sides of his head in spikes, glistening in the sunlight, jiggling when he threw his head back to drink the last bit of beer out of the can. The guy had a wife, but she'd left him a year or two before. His house was a mess. Somebody from his office had started to come by to watch sports on television. They drank beer and scratched themselves together. Mr. Barbecue didn't like his neighbor because his neighbor was too young and happy, too clean, too earth-toned, too well maintained, and he had too nice a car, too nice a wife, too easy a life. And in that easy life the neighbor had an annoying dog, and that was how it all started. The dog barked too much. The dog ran back and forth too much and banged into the fence between their properties too much. The dog shit too close to the fence. The neighbor was too fond of the dog, spent too much time playing with it in the backyard, threw the stick too many times, threw the ball too many times, combed and washed and walked the dog far too often for Mr. Barbecue's taste. So then one Saturday he had asked this neighbor if he could borrow a VCR just for the afternoon, just to tape a ball game while he was watching another one. His VCR was on the fritz, he had told this neighbor. They weren't friends, these neighbors, they didn't talk to each other ordinarily, so the neighbor was taken aback by the request, and he was hesitant. His uncertainty was an insult. It was an insult that Mr. Barbecue could have gotten over but didn't. Eventually he got the VCR, but then after he had taped his game, he wanted to watch his game, which meant he had to keep the neighbor's VCR, which he'd promised to return immediately after the game was over. The neighbor called and asked about the VCR, and Mr. Barbecue explained he couldn't return it because he wanted to watch the game that he had recorded. The neighbor said *he* had to record something and that he needed the VCR back right then. He didn't, of course, and Mr. Barbecue knew that, knew the kid was just scared about having his precious VCR too long in Mr. Barbecue's shabby home. So he took the VCR outside and tossed it over the fence, where it landed in a bush, and then the dog started up, and that was it. He got the dog, smacked it with a shovel, butchered it behind the garage, cooked it on his grill with the neighbor looking on.

JEN KEPT CHANGING the name of her magazine. First it was *Blood & Slime Weekly,* then *Jen's Total Puke,* then *Organ Meats.* She changed the subtitle to "The Hi-Speed Terror Vendor." She printed it out on the small laser printer she'd brought from her apartment, printed it on Day-Glo paper that she bought at the K & B drugstore. Searing orange or lemon, bright green, shattering red. Big headlines, big type, short stories. She'd print twenty or thirty at a shot, then they'd drive around posting them at grocery stores, restaurants, laundromats, sometimes on telephone poles at busy street corners, places by the beach where people were walking.

Sometimes, when she and Del were driving around in Biloxi or Gulfport or Pass Christian, or any of the little towns along the Mississippi coast, they'd wait and try to catch somebody reading the issue they'd just put up. She liked to watch people's reactions, if they had any. Mostly they didn't. Mostly they just read for a while and then walked away. Sometimes they shook their heads or scratched their heads or wiped their foreheads or smoothed back their hair.

Occasionally, someone would yank a copy off the bulletin board or telephone pole, fold it up, and put it in his pocket.

11

THE COLLEGE RETREAT was in late October, and when they finally got there and Del met Rudy Glass again, he didn't like him. Rudy was working too hard to be just one of the guys. He was a big man who wore a beaded buckskin jacket that didn't fit right, and jeans, and motorcycle boots. He invited Bud and Del for an early dinner Friday in the hotel restaurant, the Schipperke.

After they'd ordered drinks, Rudy said, "What is that?" He was tapping the name on the restaurant menu.

Mimi said, "Who cares what it is? Aren't you excited about the retreat? Personal Makeover Institute says get people out of the office and you see what they're made of."

"I don't know about that," Rudy said. "But there's kind of a spiritual overtone I think may work for us."

"It's a dog," Bud said.

"People need a chance to open up," Mimi said. "Show themselves. The PMI manual says they'll strip down for you, uncover their scars."

Bud pretended to wave for a taxi. "Cab!" he said.

"They send you all this stuff," Rudy said to Bud. "They have great graphs, really killer graphs, in their brochures."

"Beautiful," Mimi said.

The waiter brought their drinks, and after they'd been delivered around the table, Rudy said, "I'm glad Margaret could come." He reached for Margaret's hand. "Bud said you were thinking of not coming—why was that?"

"Mammogram," she said.

"You going to eat these crab claws, Bud?" Del said, snapping four or five of the fried claws off Bud's plate.

"PMI reps gross sixty to eighty thousand the first year," Mimi said. "I may moonlight for them."

"No kidding?" Del said.

"Even if it doesn't work, there are worse ways to spend a weekend," Rudy said. "You see George Willis brought that graduate student of his?"

"The one he's always doing crossword puzzles with in the lounge?" Bud said.

"See, that's exactly what I'm talking about," Mimi said, her face brightening as she pointed a crab claw at Rudy. "People need a chance to go public with their stuff."

"We're damn modern," Rudy said. "I like that about us."

THE MOTEL WAS a six-story building, as clean as beach places ever get, given the traffic. The staff was used to dealing with the small-bore conference trade, so Del's job turned out to be easy—he did the setup, then stood around outside the meeting rooms, taking care of people who couldn't find the public rest rooms or the bar.

After dinner Friday he made sure the correct conference rooms were going to be available when they were supposed to be available, unpacked some handouts Rudy and Mimi had prepared, and went over the luau plan with the motel's director of conferences and workshops. Then he set up the projection video system in the Matrix Room for the nine o'clock showing of a program Rudy had taped off C-SPAN, a panel on the film *JFK*, which was back in the news for some reason. That was followed by a discussion period moderated by a regional assassination buff who had slides and reexamined the evidence, including new material released the previous year from Dallas police files, details about the detention of the "three tramps," and some CIA materials leaked recently to the press. He had a lot of slides of car crashes too. Snapshots taken right after the crashes, with body parts strewn around, splashes of blood dripping down windshields, ripped-up faces.

It was hard to know, since Del was in and out of the conference room, whether these deaths were related to the assassination or a separate interest of the speaker.

Finally there was the two A.M. Late Sky Seminar. An astronomy guy took everybody to the beach. They stood in a circle holding hands and staring up, while this guy told them what they were looking at. Jen stayed in the room, but Del was out there, squeezed between Mimi and a hefty woman with wolflike hair.

Most of Saturday was free—the faculty people went into town, or sat on the beach, or slept. There was a late-afternoon round table discussion of departmental priorities. Del made sure there was coffee and the correct number of Style Three snack trays, but that was it. Saturday night was the luau.

ALL AFTERNOON a pig had been roasting in one of the two fish ponds in the courtyard. The pond, which was twice the size of a Jacuzzi, had been filled in with dirt, then dug out again to make a pit to cook the pig. Mimi had made Xeroxes of "Pig Hawaiian" handouts, which explained the long Hawaiian tradition of cooking a pig this particular way, buried in dirt, covered in palm leaves and pineapples. She had encountered this style years before in her travels for the Geiger

Foundation, the handout said. In Hawaii this method of pig cooking was a native ritual.

The luau was scheduled for the courtyard, but as soon as people got their first drinks it started storming, and everybody had to trail inside. At first they all stood there staring out the huge glass. Mimi had gone overboard on the decorations—dime-size glitter disks, Christmas lights, tiny white paper flowers, sagging used-car-lot boas of twisted mirror-finish plastic. It was third-worldish when the rain hit.

The pig was hustled out of the courtyard strung between two six-foot Pier One bamboo poles carried on the shoulders of Ken and David Whitcomb—twin homosexuals who team-taught a class in rock video, baseball, and Madonna—and taken to the hotel kitchen, where it was cut up into oven-friendly portions and rushed to completion.

Jen had dodged most of the weekend, so she'd agreed to attend the luau, but when the rain hit she caught Del in the lobby and said, "I'm retiring to the room. I believe I'm bringing the bad luck."

"You're forgiven," he said. "Just as soon as I get all these pig-eaters squared up."

"I'll wait for you," she said.

Del moved everybody to ballroom two, the Blue Conquistador Room, which he had arranged to have available against just such a contingency. When he got it set up, he went and sat out in the courtyard for a minute. The rain was spotty by then, unnaturally large spurts of water that looked as though there was somebody on the roof shooting a hose.

He sat on the lip of the working pond and stared at fat goldfish circling in the alarming blue water. There were hidden lights in the pond, and when fish swam through them it was as if the fish themselves were strangely shaped bulbs. One fish was almost as big as one of his new cross-training shoes. The shoes seemed much bigger and brighter than they had in the store; he'd been thinking about it all afternoon, wondering if he'd made another shoe mistake. He stared from fish to shoes, then back to fish. The fish was much smaller, he decided, about the size of a personal loaf of French bread.

WHEN DEL GOT BACK to the room, Jen said, "Thank God they roped it off." Jen was on the bed in her ribbed underpants and a kid's T-shirt. "I thought for a minute we'd be staring into the burning eyes of that thing as it was yanked out of the dirt. I thought we'd have to watch them burst."

"They take the eyes out," Del said.

"In Hawaii they probably suck them out," she said. "Like they do out of chickens in France."

"They're too big," Del said. He stood at the mirror, pushing the tip of his nose to make it a pig nose.

"Mimi told me it was the most beautiful pig she ever saw," Jen said.

"Let's go home," Del said. "Or leave here, anyway. I'm ready."

"What, tonight?"

"Let's tell them we're going home and then move to another hotel—what about that? Just you and me on a high floor. Romance. Wind. Pounding rain."

"Sounds good to me," Jen said.

They were sprawled together on the satiny comforter that spread over the bed like simulated icing on a microwave cake. "I hoped it would," he said.

"But we're probably not going anywhere," she said. "Are we?"

She'd spent Saturday rooting through a few stories from the local newspaper, then she linked up with the network for a quick scan. She told Del she'd found a piece about a woman who was out of work and who beheaded her three children while they slept, then told her neighbors she was offering them as a sacrifice for the Darlington 500, a stock car race. The woman's name was Lolita Portugesa. She had gotten up at midnight in her trailer in a quiet fishing village north of Tampa, grabbed a Chicago Cutlery carving knife that had been a Christmas present from her ex-husband, Fernand, and slashed off the heads of her children: Miniboy, eight, Squat, six, and Junior, three. All this was from the police report, Jen said. The woman then hacked at her own wrists in an unsuccessful suicide attempt. The Florida authorities said she would be given a psychiatric evaluation to determine if she was sane. A note Portugesa left in the kitchen for Fernand read: "I am leaving to you the heads of our children. This is what you have deserved."

There was a knock at the door as Jen finished telling him this story. "Jesus," she said, getting out of the bed and pulling on jeans. "What, now they catch us?"

Del put his hand over his eyes as if to hide.

Margaret was at the door. "Rudy wonders if you will join him in the garden," she said. She was wearing a swimsuit, one-piece, way low in the front, with a long but open wraparound skirt and backless heels.

"What's the Big Rudy want?" Jen said.

"He wants to thank you," she said. "Both. He's proud of the way things are turning out."

Del said, "I guess he's deaf, dumb, and blind."

Jen frowned at him and said, "It hasn't been so bad."

"You haven't been out of the room—how would you know?" Del said.

"I didn't like the pig," Jen said.

"You didn't like the pig?" Margaret said. "Everybody downstairs loved the pig."

"Well, I guess they're in the preponderance," Jen said.

"So do you want to come down with me?" Margaret said.

"Or later? Like in a minute or two, when you have time to get straightened away?"

"Take Del," Jen said. "There's one other story I want to download. It's a guy who caught a fish with a human thumb in it. Six people disappeared in this lake recently, so they don't know whose thumb it is. It's a detective thing."

"Yeeech," Margaret said. "We have to talk, Jen."

"What other kind of thumb is there?" Del said.

Jen tapped Del's shoulder. "Go on. I'll find this, and then I'll change, get my makeup all straightened away, and then I'll be right down. Show Margaret your elevator moves."

"She likes me in elevators," Del said.

"I do not," Jen said, ushering them out the door. "I just said it was possible."

THE ELEVATOR WAS LINED in seat-cover vinyl, dusty rose colored, with a thick padded handrail all around the interior, something to prevent kids from hurting themselves when they bashed their heads against it while rampaging up and down in the building, as the designers apparently knew they would. Margaret leaned against the rail on the far side of the car, her head turned to stare at the clicking numbers over the door. Del studied her calf.

"I need to get away for a while," she said, not taking her eyes off the numbers. "Maybe I should go back early. Maybe tonight."

"Ah," Del said. He smiled and nodded, but felt even as he was doing it that it was too vigorous. "We were talking about leaving too. Everything's done, really."

"Yeah. Maybe we'll go together," she said. "Why not?" She hit the Emergency Stop button.

"What's this?" Del said, pointing to the control panel. "What're you doing?"

"Let's rest a minute," she said. "O.K.? Let me just rest a minute here, Del. I don't ever get to just rest, you know? Since Bud's back. I'm all over the place and I don't say a thing. I argue and smile and nod and wave and make my eyes twinkle and draw my lips back and do my nostrils—but I never rest. I'm not like most women."

"Margaret," he said.

"Have we ever talked, just you and me?"

"Yes," Del said. "We talk all the time. We talked the hell out of those weeks Bud was gone."

"I like you, Del. I always did. I love Bud, but that's not the same thing. I suppose you know what I'm talking about, don't you? One of those suddenly-out-of-whack things?"

"We did that, didn't we?"

"Yeah, that was fun. I kind of miss it."

Del caught himself nodding again in a silly way. He stopped.

"I used to want children," Margaret said. "I always figured I'd be good at that. I always think of the kinds of things I'd say to them. I'd tell them not to let anybody kid them, that people will say anything, they'll say they love you, but they really don't. They try, but no matter what they're after, they're not after what you're after. Not usually."

"That's kind of depressing, Margaret. I don't think we're supposed to tell kids that kind of thing," Del said. "It's O.K. to get depressed, and maybe it seems like it's that bad sometimes, maybe it even is, but we're supposed to keep it to ourselves, I think." Del had his arm around her. They were slumped against the back wall of the elevator. The call bell was ringing.

"That's why I don't have any. I keep pointing to Bobo, talking to Bud about Bobo," she said. "But he isn't buying."

"Well, with Bobo you're beyond projectile vomiting."

She gave him a look and the only laughing in it was in her

eyes, and that was only barely there. "I'm pretty dreary to-night," she said. "Sorry."

"Never mind. It was stupid," he said, gently finger-combing her hair.

"Once I was at the store and this guy who looked like Bud came in and held a stun gun on this checker. I'm standing right there. I couldn't get over it—Bud's double. After all the TV shows, the cop shows, the movies, the mystery books, here was this guy in Pass Christian. Anyway, so I talked him down. Just like TV. We had a talk about stun guns. I told him the way he was holding his, he was going to take big electricity."

"When was this?"

"Couple years ago, I guess. Before you."

"He was holding it wrong?"

"How do I know?" she said. "I saw a guy say it on *America's Most Wanted* or *Cops*—one of those—so I tried it. Said he was going to burn if he zapped her. He was thin, sick thin like AIDS or cancer, so I asked him if he'd been checked up recently. I pointed at this spot on his neck with my fingernail and asked him if anybody had looked at that. There wasn't anything there, a smudge, but I made it sound like there was something, trying to get him a little doubt. He said he thought he was holding the gun right, he'd read the instructions, he'd shot it off on a dog that way. I asked what happened to the dog. He said it spit up and then bit him, and I just shook my head. 'There you go,' I told him."

She was threading her fingers in and out between the buttons on Del's shirt, pressing him against the back of the elevator.

"Bud likes gun magazines. You don't, do you? He gets dozens of them, but he never reads them. *Soldier of Fortune,* stuff like that. He's always decoding the mercenary ads in the backs of those magazines. Like, when it says 'rotunda work O.K.,' that means the guy is willing to kidnap or do something else. 'Wet work' used to be one. Stuff like that. And *Paint Ball*—have you seen that one? Bud's dying to play paint ball. The magazine's full of Desert Storm masks and paint ball guns that are crossbreeds between forties futurism and nineties street weaponry. Full head dressings, choice of ball colors. I look too, but I'm afraid of guns. Aren't you?"

Del caught her hand, slowed it down, then held it for a minute. "Let's see. I shot a squirrel once, a long time ago. I felt bad afterward—it was worse than that guilt you get sometimes after really ugly sex. Once I shot a bird out of a tree, one off a wire, and I killed a groundhog at my uncle's farm when I was ten. I think that's the complete catalog."

"I guess killing's not about manhood after all," Margaret said. "I'd be afraid to have a gun, though. How would you avoid using it? How would you stop yourself from playing with it all the time, pointing it out the window at passersby and stuff? Going over the line?"

"That'd be a problem." Del eyed the panel with the floor numbers on it. "Bell's ringing," he said.

"At least there'd be the risk," she said. "Don't we all go a little nuts and slam the hammer through the bathroom wall sometimes? Crack up one of those hollow-core apartment doors? Wouldn't we use a gun then, if we had it? Or like when Bud started to jump up and down on the mini satellite dish because it wouldn't find G2-A? That's his favorite. The things we do in private are scary sometimes, aren't they? Maybe that's a good reason not to have a gun."

Del started to slide out from behind her but didn't make it. She had him pinned. She had a bittersweet aroma, a new scent, dark and slightly overdone in a nasty way.

"I figure we can do anything we want, Del," she said. "Whenever we want to do it. Anytime. Anywhere. Just get right down and do what we want, and nobody ever knows the difference, nobody ever knows what goes on."

"Rudy's waiting, isn't he?" Del said.

"I guess, but he's way down there and we're way up here."

"And what about Bud?" he said, sliding sideways on the rail, pressing out from behind her.

She backed away, holding up her hands the way TV wrestlers do when they want to persuade the ref they're making a clean break. "Hey, if that's what you want," Margaret said. "I was thinking you might want to open up some, like Mimi says—you know, show yourself—but if that's not the way you feel, O.K. It's up to you—I'm just following the keys here. That's what these things are for, right? These retreats? To let you guys catch up?"

"You are completely lovely, Margaret," he said. "Really."

Then she stalked him playfully around the edge of the little elevator, and when she caught him they held each other for a few long seconds, then separated. Margaret smiled at him, traced his cheek with the backs of her nails. "I'm fine," she said. "I'm a lot better than I appear." She fingered the red Emergency Stop button for a minute, eyeing him, then shoved that button in and hit the one that said Lobby.

"You know," she said, as the car lurched down, "I used to be out there at night, clubs and parties, I used to see people, I used to do stuff. I remember what it's like, what night smells like when you're out there on your own. Sometimes, when I watch MTV, or the dance shows with the kids jerking at each other every way they can, it just carries me away, you know? I feel every single thing they're doing."

RUDY WAS ON the edge of the goldfish pond, staring into the lighted water at the big things circling in the thickened sea grass. "I love these," he said to Del, pointing into the water. "If I had it to do over again I'd be a fish, I swear to God. See how they move? Look at that, look at the white one there."

"Margaret said you wanted to see me?"

"Yessir." Rudy leaned to one side to look around him. "Where's your partner?"

"She's resting. Too much Hawaii, I think."

"Ah." Rudy shook his head and stared at the fish some more. "I tell you, that Jen. She looks a little like Margaret, you know? She's a hell of a piece of business."

"Pardon me?" Del was surprised at how easily Rudy said this, as if Rudy thought it was all right to say.

Rudy looked up, then shimmied a hand by his face. "Nothing. Sorry. I was thinking out loud, I guess."

"That can get messy sometimes," Del said.

"Take it easy. I apologized. I didn't mean anything. She's just real nice and young. And so on."

"Thank you," Del said. "I'll pass that along to her, with your compliments."

Rudy handed Del a sealed envelope. "Your stipend," he said. "How'd you like this weekend? No problems? Go O.K.?"

"It was fine," Del said. "Couldn't have been easier."

"Good," Rudy said. "You and Mimi get along O.K.? She's peculiar sometimes, you know? Like, she seems one way at school, and then she seems like a different person when she's not there."

Del took a minute, then shook his head. "I don't know what you mean. I've never seen her at school."

"Well." He reached out to shake Del's hand. "She's over on the beach now, waiting for me."

"O.K.," Del said.

"I think your brother left," Rudy said.

"Probably not," Del said. "We came together, so I expect he's around." Del caught sight of Margaret in the lobby, watching them.

"He hates me," Rudy said. "He thinks I'm some kind of

jerk. I don't like him that much, either. The California deal was a screw-up. What was he trying to prove, anyway?"

"He was taking a vacation, I think," Del said.

"Uh-huh." Rudy noticed Del looking into the lobby at Margaret. "I like *her*, though," he said, waving at Margaret. "I wish I liked him as much. She's so calm all the time."

"I guess," Del said.

"You stayed at the house while he was gone, right? Just you and Margaret? How'd that work out?"

Del gave Rudy an edgy look. "I don't know what this is about, Rudy, but it's not working for me."

"Hey, that's cool," Rudy said, rocking his head back. "Whatever." He dropped a fingertip into the water, and a potato-size goldfish swam up for a look. "Margaret come down with you? You guys heading out?"

"As soon as Jen gets here," Del said.

12

BUD WAS IN THE ROOM with Jen when Margaret and Del went back upstairs. "He thinks you took off," Del said. "I told him you couldn't leave without me."

"I'm right here," Bud said. He was in one of the easy chairs, reading the Hotel Activities Schedule for the next day off the television screen. "Dentists are meeting in the morning. Oral Surgery Seminar is at nine A.M. in the Ticonderoga Room. Anybody want to go over to the beach?"

"No," Del said. "Rudy's there."

"With Rudyette," Margaret said. "They're probably over there opening up to each other."

"I saw some of Jen's stories," Bud said, raising an eyebrow. "A child-head-slashing story and a gallery-of-brains story." He turned to Jen.

She said, "That's all you remember?"

"A gallery of brains where all the brains of serial killers and other heinous types are kept, weighed, measured, and so on. Cut up into little sausage parts for testing. The heaviest brain is the brain of a small-appliance salesman—is that right?" Bud turned to Jen, who nodded. "There is no relationship between the size of brain and serial killing. This is in Ithaca or someplace."

"Is that it, I hope?" Margaret said. She put her forehead down on Del's shoulder as if expecting the worst.

"Gallbladders," Jen said.

"Yeah. Somebody was trying to smuggle one hundred and seventy-three bear gallbladders from Alaska to Asia," Bud said. "Gallbladders are really small, apparently. Between a gearshift knob and a tennis ball. Bear gallbladders, anyway. Each one has a small tail-like protrusion."

"The sergeant said it was the biggest bladder seizure he'd ever had," Jen said.

"O.K. Thank you. That's enough," Margaret said, waving her arms. "I guess we should be happy nobody was hacked to death. Why are all these stories so messy, anyway?"

"They're not *that* messy," Jen said. "Not as bad as what's on TV every week. There are lots worse ones."

"These are bad enough for me," Margaret said.

"Some of them are messier than these," Del said. "There's nothing hideous and repulsive about gallbladders and brain collections."

"I guess those aren't so bad," Margaret said. "But the others, the head-hacking ones—those are grotesque."

"Yeah, but they're clear," Jen said. "There's no mistaking them. They're grotesque enough so there's no disguising what goes on in them. It's like all the cartoony plot stuff in books and movies—it makes them easy to follow, easy to understand. You don't get lost, and you don't have to worry about what things mean all the time."

"Like in life, is what you're saying," Bud said.

"Yeah, exactly," she said.

———

THEY LEFT THE HOTEL at three the next afternoon. Jen was driving. Bud and Margaret were in the back. They took a turn by the beach long enough for a last look, then slipped back up to I-10 and headed west toward Mobile. They were riding alongside an eighteen-wheel truck that had big lemons and limes painted on its side. The traffic was surprisingly heavy. Jen pulled in behind the truck and hit the cruise control. "I'm just following this guy," she said. "Wherever he goes."

"We probably should have left last night," Margaret said. "Rudy expected it, anyway."

"He says Bud hates him," Del said. "That's what he said to me when I went down."

"I do hate him," Bud said.

"Not really," Margaret said. She was rustling her hair.

"I hate everybody," Bud said.

"You're just trying to make yourself attractive to the rest of us," she said.

"Rudy *is* kind of loathsome, though," Bud said. "He's the worst kind of loathsome, as a matter of fact. He tricks everybody into thinking he's swell, evenhanded, enlightened, when he's really sneaking around doing all this cheap stuff to get the best twigs in his tiny nest. He's sort of like middle management in that way."

"He is middle management, isn't he?" Del said.

"He's a wuss," Jen said, as they moved through the highway traffic in a four-car snake—the lemon-sided truck, a minivan, then Jen, and behind them a woman in a Jetta. Way out front, a thick line of military-colored clouds clustered low along the horizon, spreading toward them, looking like rain. The cars swept through a cloverleaf of overpasses under construction, arteries jutting in at all angles, a Stonehenge-like preview of the remains of the future.

"I love that shit," Jen said, eyeing the rearview. "It's instaruins, just add water. I wish I lived there. I wish that's what my yard looked like."

"You don't have a yard," Bud said.

"Sure she does," Del said, tapping Jen and pointing her toward two jets cutting across the dark-gray sky in tight formation, circling out of the Mobile air base.

"I saw them already," Jen said.

"What about this?" Del motioned to a flea market sign, a life-size elephant up on one back leg, impaled on a huge pole, its trunk raised high, screaming. "You see that already too?"

Jen just made a sound, a grunt.

"I guess I don't hate him that much," Bud said. "He's O.K. He leaves us alone most of the time."

"Make up your mind," Del said.

"You don't care enough to hate him," Margaret said.

"I wish that were true," Bud said.

"Don't people always loathe the people they work for?" Jen said. "Isn't that a rule?"

The rain came more like wet dust than rain. The windshield was speckled with tiny gray bits of mud, as if they'd had it tinted a powdery white. They passed a place called Bag Town, where three eighteen-wheel flatbeds with John Deere tractor housings on them—green bodies, big yellow wheels— sat parked by the edge of the highway.

"I'd stay out here if I could," Bud said from the back seat. "If I had the guts. Imagine what it's like out here when all these people like us are gone."

"It's like being an explorer," Margaret said. "That's what I think."

"They're never gone," Del said.

They shot under a crossing four-lane. Construction cranes were everywhere, sticking up at sixty- and seventy-degree angles, splattered with white paint. North of the highway there was a small bay intercut with roads, berms, more tilted cranes.

The bay must have been drilled once, or used for loading sand or shell. There were a half-dozen rusted flat-topped barges in the water, a couple of tugs—a dead harbor.

"These people are all on the phone," Jen said, signaling toward the cars going by them on the left.

"Leave 'em alone," Margaret said. "They're lonely."

"It's fun," Bud said. "I've done it. You call people, jack around, look good in the bargain. Everybody wants to look a little bit arrogant nowadays. Pretty soon the kids in the malls will take over."

"They already have," Del said. "Saw them at Edgewater."

"Oh," Margaret said. "You guys are so cynical."

"Yeah, Bud," Del said. "Grab a clue."

A dark-skinned guy walking along the side of the road waved as they passed. He had on white socks and a white undershirt, and he was carrying his boots. Both his arms sported big spidery tattoos.

"Hey," Jen said, returning the guy's wave. "It's Bobby De Niro. What's he doing out here?"

"I need to say this," Bud said, sliding forward, hugging the back of the front seat. "Don't worry, everything's O.K. I'm not going to do anything now, but I want to say I think sleeping with Margaret, or whatever you did, was real crummy. That's for the two of you. I thought I was getting over it, but I don't know. I've been trying to figure out how I can say, like, it's a normal thing a brother would do, like it's natural for you to be attracted to each other, and so if you go out of whack once or twice, well, it makes sense, but I can't think that. I come up short of that."

Margaret sighed. "This is not a good time, Bud, O.K.? Let's just watch the scenery and get home."

"I'm fine," he said to her. "I'm openly fine." He slid back, away from the front seat.

Jen gave Del a tilted look. "You said that you just—" She looked in the rearview mirror at Margaret.

"True," Margaret said.

Del checked the speedometer. She was streaming along at eighty. They passed a country Olds dealership, acres of brand-new cars with soap-writing all over the windows, cheaper than town. Next to the dealership was a wired-off gravel yard stocked with gray cement statuary, mostly horses and angels.

"We never did," he said.

"We're not discussing it," Margaret said. "O.K.?"

"Who?" Jen said, eyeing her in the rearview.

"I keep thinking about it," Bud said. "I should forget it, but I don't." He sounded listless. He was staring out the side window of the car. They went by Silverado, a metal-shack cowboy club. The traffic was throttling down, as if somebody ahead spotted cops. Jen kicked off the cruise control with the brake, then let the car decelerate. The right lane was closed. Just beyond a rest area, behind a row of pines, there was a refinery, a forest of silver towers a hundred feet tall wrapped in pipes and wires and ladders and stubs, small platforms, burn-offs. Some of the towers were smoking, and all of them were glinting.

Margaret leaned over and whispered something to Bud, something long and complicated, complete with hand gestures and occasional little kisses.

"Oh, Jesus Christ," Bud finally said, shoving her off him. "You can't get around it like that. It's not just some guy you're drooling over."

"Nobody's drooling," Margaret said, her tone suddenly flat and acrid.

"I think we should handle this individually," Jen said, cocking her head to get Bud in her mirror.

"It's easier for them to lie that way," Bud said, returning her glance.

"I don't want to hear this," Margaret said. "There's no fucking lying going on, Bud."

"Let's shelve it, O.K.?" Del said, staring out the window to where workers had cut a ten-foot-square hole in the road. Men were standing looking at this hole. "That's typical," he said. "These guys standing here. I've seen that a hundred times."

"I'm really interested," Bud said.

"Shut up, will you?" Margaret said, before he could say anything else.

An unmarked cop car was sitting off the road. Del touched Jen's arm, but she'd already seen. "They love this part," she said. "They go for the big angles. You see that? The way he's parked?" She sawed with her hand to show how the cop was parked at an angle to the road. "They always do that. It makes them feel powerful."

This one was a state trooper with a big hat that had a strict horizontal brim. Under it his eyes looked like Marks-A-Lot scribbles.

Jen liked driving. She seemed younger, as if she was from another world, not the one Del knew, but one where the rules, the ways, were all new. He traced three fingers along her arm, and when she turned to see what he was doing, he said, "Are you O.K.?"

"Sure. I'm Speedy," she said. "I'm fine. Really."

They were over water, a long, low concrete bridge over the tan edge of a bay. A truck full of cans marked Flammable Waste slipped by on the right. Whatever it was, it burned if you got close. Jen went into the right lane in tandem with the lemon truck, the van, the Jetta. They went around a slow-going Tommy Lift that had a couple of white boys in it, country boys, one with a big straw dripping out of his mouth.

At the top of an overpass Del looked out at the level world

in the distance, and then looked closer, just over a rim of trees, at a pea-green flat of water dotted with white gulls and white cranes. "What are these, exactly?" Del said.

"Big birds in water," Bud said.

"Herons," Jen said.

They got by a pickup pulling a four-wheel trailer with a midget racer on it, number 84, bright red, yellow letters. A roll cage and a polished metal fin above. On the side it said Eddie Stores was the owner and driver. A burly guy with a beard was driving the rig, chewing and driving.

"How come you always see race cars on the highway?" Jen wanted to know as she cut by a second one, on a slick black trailer.

"How else are they supposed to get to the races?" Bud said.

Four clapboard buildings stood incongruously on the roadside, looking weather-beaten and classic. They were a hundred years old easy, obviously trucked to the site. It was like the start of a used-car lot for old wood buildings. Next to the buildings there was a ten-by-ten lime-green shack with a single small sliding glass window in front and a hand-painted sign that read FINE MEXICAN FOOD nailed over the window. A dark woman standing by the window was talking to an extremely short person whose head was just barely visible inside the shack. "Must be a *Dances with Wolves* thing," Del said, clicking the passenger glass with his nail.

"What must be?" Jen said.

"This Mexican dump back here." He waved off to the right and behind him. "There was this real swarthy customer, and something reminded me of what's-his-name, the actor. You know how earnest he is, and these were real people there, living real lives. I could just see him feeling real stuff for them, you know? Something wrong like that."

"Earnest is O.K.," Jen said, turning to check on Bud and

Margaret. "We have more than we really need these days, I guess, but it's something."

"It's a weapon," Del said.

AN ELEGANT WHITE BIRD standing just off the edge of the asphalt in the tall grass fluttered its wings, then refolded them, as Jen went by. "Brancusi," Margaret said. The bird had a thin gold diamond of feathers slipping down its back.

After that two Peterbilts from Waytown, Montana, struggled into the Turtle Bay RV Park, and a ratty Chevy with Louisiana plates cut in front of them. Two businessmen were in the front seat; bags were hung up in back. These guys were talking it up big, wiggling hands at one another. "They need Hawaiian shirts," Jen said as she pulled out and passed.

"Put one on the car," Del said.

The left lane was closed. There were station wagons ahead, and log trucks with double puffs of smoke shooting from their stacks as they slowed. The road was littered with toppled red rubber pylons, only they weren't red, they were sherbet orange. Workmen were out in force, repaving the center section of the highway with a huge machine the size of a small building that straddled what they were paving, maybe forty feet wide, a trough spreading the concrete evenly across the span. The stretch they'd just poured was a foot and a half taller than the old highway. Hundreds of reinforcing rods stuck out of this slab, threatening to rip tires if a car got too close.

Jen glanced in the rearview at Bud and Margaret, then tried to whisper to Del. "Is this going to get better?"

"I heard that," Bud and Margaret said together.

Del looked over his shoulder. The mood in the back seat seemed to have changed. Bud and Margaret were laughing together. "I took half a blue," Bud said, meeting Del's look. "I'm doing well, thank you."

An Oscar Mayer truck driven by a fat guy with goggle shades pulled up alongside. He had a giant jacket hanging up in the seat beside him. The guy gave Jen a glance, then pulled ahead. "PUS256" was stenciled in blue in a box on his rear bumper, next to a sticker that said PECAN QUEEN FESTIVAL.

"We ought to stop at a fruit stand," Del said.

"Yeah," Bud said. "Boiled peanuts."

Just then the lemon truck put on its blinker and pulled off the highway to the right, churning up bleached dust. Traffic was merging into one lane, slowing. Pretty soon everybody was almost motionless on the highway. A road sign propped up in the median had a vertical line with a crooked line alongside it. The tall weeds in the median leaned over, looking tired from just standing there all day in the heat. Jen checked her hair in the mirror, dug at it a couple of times, stuffing it back from her forehead. She stretched, no hands on the wheel. They were barely moving. Two miles an hour, five miles an hour, through the road work.

Del wanted to kiss her. "Why don't we talk about this whole situation a little later? Will that be O.K.?"

"We can do that," she said.

He settled into his seat, slipped down so his head would hit the headrest when he leaned back. He watched a trailer full of longhorns inch by. In a minute they picked up speed. Jen kept a steady twenty-five miles an hour through the end of the construction. The landscape was flat, verdant. The sky was thundered with dirty clouds. There was a skid sign on the left, surrounded by a crowd of Mexican-Americans with hard hats that had lamps attached, and as Jen drove past, Del caught a ruddy foreman type in a blue shirt holding a cellular phone he was staring at and shaking. There were three or four Caterpillar tractors in a row, then a very old white pickup being filled with dirt from a lift. They were picking up speed. Jen went by a shiny waste hauler, eighteen wheels and a big silver canister. Straight ahead there was more road work, but this time it didn't slow her down. She went through the dust at seventy. Off to the right, a dump truck was doing idiot circles. They went around a pickup pulling some railroad ties on a little flat trailer, and then Jen had them back up to eighty. An American flag floated high over the Ice Pick Restaurant. As they cleared out into the open, the highway got hot and drab. The rush of slinging through traffic died. Everything thinned out. There was a mosquito-control truck from Alcove County. On one edge of the highway, an abandoned gas station was overgrown with cars covered by orange tarpaulins. They went by a Younger Brothers Waste Savers truck, a Goodyear chemical plant, and then, in the shallow dirt ravine between the highway and the feeder, a ditched '58 Chevrolet station wagon with all four doors wide open and a guy alongside it washing his arms out of a water jug that was perched on the roof.

"Does this seem like Pluto out here?" Del said. He pointed at a billboard for Chuck Was Famous Tattoos. There was a huge shoulder painted on the billboard, with a tattoo of Jesus with extremely long blue fingernails, in a shiny pulpit. All of this drawn as if shot up close through a fish-eye lens. "I guess Jesus is a Howard Hughes thing for Chuck, huh?"

"For all of us, maybe," Margaret said.

"Vice versa," Bud said.

"He likes me, and vice versa," Margaret said, her voice singsongy. "He likes me, and vice versa."

"Me and this Jetta woman make up the shortest cavalcade in history," Jen said, pointing out the window at the Jetta, which was now in front. "We're a team. We're the littlest wagon train. We've lost everybody else."

She cut into the lane that veered off east, and Del's heart jumped. The road was full of bumps. She went right and hugged the concrete barrier as they cut through another highway construction site, where a big guy who looked like Hulk Hogan in a safety vest strode along reading a magazine. They went under an incomplete overpass, where a single concrete beam about ten feet tall bridged columns on either side of the road. The beam already had a sign: CLEARANCE 16 FT. 2 IN.

"I'm ready for my bath," Margaret said.

They crossed the seven-mile bridge over Mobile Bay, past the USS *Alabama,* Pinto Island, Polecat Bay off to the north, and went underground, where the high arch of the tunnel was lined in cream-color glazed tile that reflected headlights and taillights, blinking instruction lights, truck running lights—a Hollywood movie car tunnel.

Coming out, they passed another field of rusted erection cranes. "These look like steel people with stick arms," Bud said.

"Remember when industrial stuff was pretty?" Del said. "Is that gone, or what?"

"You just have to deal with the fanatics," Jen said. "The environmental twerps, dumping twerps, poison-waste twerps, half-life twerps, spill-off twerps, fecal twerps—you can't just *look* anymore."

"Take me now, Lord. Take me now," Bud said.

"I'm not saying that's me," Jen said, trying to catch him in the rearview. "Don't get me wrong. I'm part of the gum-it-up crowd."

"Good," he said. "Me, I want to stop over here at We Treat You Better Baptist Hospital, or back there at Cimabue's Low-Price Meats. Either one."

"You're going to Mauriceville, Bud," Jen said, jerking a thumb at a sign to her left.

The sky was thickening again, more rain to come. They slipped around a blue Buick, a red Riviera, and Wayne Ducat's company truck. Jen hit a McDonald's cup at eighty miles per hour. They crossed Calamine Bayou, then went by National

Trampoline & Barbecue, where big round trampolines were tilted up on their edges and a herd of black thirty-gallon barbecue pits gathered in front of a tin shack. A Cadillac went by, a sailboat behind, standing up on its trailer as if it were shot full of meringue.

Jen said, "Check this," pointing forward to a bumper sticker on a new car in line, which read: BE YOUR OWN BEST FRIEND, SAY NO TO DOGS. "I ought to give him a little bump, huh?"

On a small old steel-girdered bridge they went through a snow of eight-and-a-half-by-eleven sheets of paper somebody had dumped. Hundreds of sheets flashed across the bridge at the exact moment of their passage. A guy with SUPPORT OUR TROOPS signs all over his car was beside them, chewing vigorously. The bay off to the right looked stark and artificial, as if it had been painted in.

The sun lowered ahead of them. Jen seemed to get more radiant every minute. She saw Del looking and ruffled the fingers on both hands as they went over a tiny bayou and then under some tall concrete overpasses that were heading out south toward Dauphin Island. There was a cop under one of the underpasses, so she slowed it to sixty-five and let it go for a while. He wedged his fingers, palm down, under her thigh in her seat.

"Hello," she said, grinning at him.

"Thank you," he said.

"Here's what I'm thinking," she said. "It's the thirties and we're hitting City Ballroom at midnight, rain shimmering the sidewalks, headlights raking across the scratches in the blacked-out glass. It's an upstairs joint with a Latin band. The players are a little older than the building, and they don't move much, they just cook. Everybody in the room is touched with lamé."

"We swoop in there, up the painted stairs," Del said. "We move like wild animals."

"Lots of strut happening," she said. "Black-shoe shuffle."

Alongside the highway near Bigpoint, Mississippi, five more police cars were all lined up, ready to work. There weren't any cops in four of the cars; they were all in the first car, drinking coffee out of white Styrofoam cups.

They passed signs for Little Capital Motor Inn, Prudomme's Cajun Café, Hotel Acadianna, Davis Mechanical Inn, Starlight Motor Inn, and Tiger Night Motel.

"Lots of highway patrol," Jen said, fingering two more cop cars.

They were creeping up onto the concrete like big white cockroaches, crawling slow, looking mean. Above one there was a giant purple dog on a sign advertising a nightclub called Rodrique. High new lamps lined the interchange where I-10 crossed above I-17, and the road was washed with pale supplemental daylight. Kids were juking around in the rest areas tucked into this cloverleaf. After Jen went through some RV traffic, she hung the speedometer at seventy and hit the cruise control again.

At the turnoff for Commerce, four black-headed sheep were grazing in a small pen to the right of a highway Exxon station. A billboard overhead touted the refurbished Courtlight Inn. "Bold new design startles industry!" it said.

Crossing the Singing River Bridge at Pascagoula reminded him of the swamp between Baton Rouge and Lafayette, where there was twenty miles of concrete road over tree-stumped swamp water. Two highways, dead straight, a hundred feet apart, on huge round pilings that lifted them forty feet over the water when the swamp was down, twenty feet when it was up. Each side was two lanes, with a little extra in case somebody needed it. Driving that stretch was like going into one of those fifties movies where all the roads are suspended, way up, and they just stay up there, floating across the cities. Only this went over luminous greenish swamp, through the tops of cypresses; and where limbs opened for views, there was this otherworldly swamp that swallowed trees right up to their tops. There were always guys with bright hats out in the swamp in small brown boats.

When he'd come through this last time, making the move to Biloxi, the swamp was high and dazzling. The water was a sharp dirty-green reflection of the trees. He'd cranked up the tape deck, listening to Phil Glass as he watched the two roads in the rearview like huge white slices through the dark water, clutched on either side by treetops. In the middle of the bridge he crossed the Achafalaya River, where the water turned coffee brown and the highway came briefly together, then separated again into two strands. Twenty miles without an exit, without a change, twenty miles with only one way to go. He crossed this bridge listening to *Koyaanisqatsi* at deafening levels, like thunder in the operatic late afternoon, with the sky dark and low, and soft as the feathers of a dove.

JEN SLIPPED ACROSS the Whiskey Bay overpass, roaring by a handful of slower cars, some United trucks, a guy with a fishing boat upside down on top of his Corsica. There was still more precast-concrete raised highway over pretty green water to go. On the left, in the distance, was Pascagoula, hidden in the trees. Terror by night there—nobody ever went to Pascagoula.

Jen backed out of the gas. In the next lane a couple of black kids, teenagers, were cooling along in a trashed pickup with a fatigues-green rowboat stuffed in its bed. They kept tossing beer cans out the window. They were going through beer cans faster than seemed prudent. A can kicked up in front of Jen and smacked into the right front fender. It made a big noise and then spun up, aloft, into the air. Jen shot these kids the bird as she went by.

Bud, who'd been quiet enough to be asleep, jerked up and said, "What's this shit?"

"Nothing," Del said. "Drinkers."

"A lot of people are wearing those sunglasses with the Day-Glo arms," Margaret said. "Are they cool now? I guess they are."

"Painter's goggles are cool," Jen said.

They went by an appliance-white Chevrolet Lumina pulling a brown plastic football fifteen feet long on a trailer. The driver was a laughing big man who was about seventy-five percent forehead. He was trying to drive and play guitar and talk on the phone all at the same time, and when he caught Del's eye, he gave him a strange wink. Then, almost suddenly, the traffic stopped dead. There were four lanes across, bumper to bumper, inching forward a couple of miles short of Biloxi. Everybody in the car yawned at the same time, then they all tried to stop. Just ahead, a double-wide trailer had flipped, crunching a Celica and a couple of motorcycles. People in the cars up front were craning and bobbing their necks like chickens.

13

"**I**'M GOING HERE," Jen said, cutting two lanes across crawling traffic and pulling off the highway into the pumpkin-colored dust of the parking lot in front of Polly's Interstate Peanut & Fruit Hutch. "The wreck is going to take time."

"I don't want to see it," Bud said.

"We can get some fruit," Jen said.

The sign was hand done on an eight-foot-tall inflated peanut that was roped to the door handle of a dusty Continental parked on the far side of the lot, facing the highway. The building was chicken wire and tar paper on two-by-four framing, open on three sides. Someone had attached a prefab eight-by-ten storage shed out back. The late sunlight, just about gold, was washing into the car. Jen looked as if she was beginning to fade as she steered in next to a blue panel van with a center-console fishing boat attached.

Del nodded at the thick-chested guy with the rub-on tan who was sitting up behind the console in the boat.

"Howdy," the guy said. "Bad crash, huh?"

Jen looked over at the highway and wiped her hair back. "Nobody moving," she said.

"You see it?" Del asked the guy in the boat.

"Yeah. Well, no. We heard it," the guy said. He was wearing flip-up sunglasses, flipped up, sitting there with a black portable computer in his lap.

"Anybody hurt?" Del said.

"I don't know," the guy said. "Probably."

His companion was a woman with dark skin and chestnut-color hair. While he typed, she transferred fish from the boat to some ice chests she had open on the ground. She'd gaff a fish, lift it out of the boat, drop it into the chest. Then she'd climb down, split the top of a bag of ice from the row of bags she had lined up, tilt ice into the chest, go back up into the boat and do it again. It was like Super Mario Brothers.

Bud rolled down the back window and said, "What's that you're writing, a list of all the fish you caught?"

The guy grinned. "No, not really."

"He's writing a book," his friend said. "Mystery."

"Oh, yeah?" Bud said.

The guy said something to the woman, and they both laughed. "She reads them for me," he said, poking his thumb over his shoulder.

The woman lifted another twenty-inch fish over the side of the boat. "I'm just looking for myself in there. It's a *Where's Waldo* deal."

"You coming in?" Del asked Bud.

"Go on," Bud said. "We'll be there in a minute."

Del waved and followed Jen into the fruit shed. There wasn't much inside—handmade two-by-four bins with half-inch plywood bottoms, but not much fruit, not many vegetables. The woman who was running the place was in her mid-thirties, tall, with long, straight blond hair parted in the middle, a lovely face with freckles, and a quick, teeth-flaunting smile.

"I just don't even know why you people bother to stop,"

she said, covering Del and Jen, as well as the people outside, with a single swipe of her hand. "Polly ain't got no vegetables. Polly ain't got no fruits. All this stuff you see here, why, this is runt stock. This here's Runt World, fruitwise and vegetablewise."

"We're just looking," Del said.

"Look away," she said. "Enjoy yourself. Truth is, I should make me up a sign, Runt World. One of those bumper jobs."

The woman was right. She didn't have anything anybody would ever buy. Red dust floated in from outside.

Jen pointed at a watermelon that was holding one of the flimsy doors open. "How about this?" she said.

"You take a close look at that fella, honey," the blonde said. "I'm not sure that's the genuine article, you know? It's a big something, but I don't know what. Only watermelons I been getting are those yellow kind. You seen those? Those'll turn your stomach. You don't want yellow watermelon—that's my persuasion."

Jen said, "That one's yellow inside?"

"I'd be surprised if that one *had* an inside. You go in there and what you've got is a gift certificate for four square inches of watermelon at some time in the future. My name is Polly, by the way. Like the parrot."

Jen introduced herself, pointed to Del, and said, "My friend Del."

Polly shook her head, flipping blond hair back over her shoulders, then stuck her hand in her jacket pocket and pulled out a tiny plastic model of a house, a forties-style bungalow, that had some kind of red and yellow peaks around it that looked like whipped cream pulled up by a knife.

"Take a look at this," she said. "I got this down in Vero Beach." She put the little house on top of the cash register and snapped a switch on its side. The whipped cream peaks turned into flames, and there were tiny shrieks from the house, mouselike shrieks.

Polly slapped her thigh and watched this house burn. "Why, that's a good one, isn't it?" She laughed. Then she said, "Eeek! Eeek!"

The guy from the boat came in, and on the ground he was very short and about twice as red as he'd looked outside. His clothes were uneventful. He came over to see what all the nearly inaudible shrieking was about.

"Howdy," he said to Polly.

She gave him a little popped-off-the-eyebrow salute, like something Cagney might have done in a movie sometime.

The guy nodded, then leaned close to the little house, as if he was trying to look in the window. Then he stood up and patted his stomach, then pointed at the house. "I think I used to live there," he said.

"Well, I'm certainly glad you got out before all this started," Polly said. She did an odd giggle, her eyes big like a frog's, and awkwardly draped an arm over the bookman's shoulder.

He backed off a little. "Me too," he said, picking up a jar of preserves from the counter.

"Whoa! You don't want to be messing with that." She came out from behind the register and took the jar, tapped it on its top, holding it up to the light. "See there?" she said. "We got air-lock problems. This stuff'll shoehorn into the walls of your arteries, bury itself. You ever see that movie *Alien?* Same thing."

"Dangerous," the guy said, making a squinty face, eyes balled up, nose wrinkled.

Polly dodged down, pretending to be short. "You got it. I don't really do business here; I just come out for the fun of it. I own apartments over in Simington for a living."

Jen nudged Del, steering him toward the back of the shed, where there were three Polaroid snapshots pinned to one of the two-by-fours. One photo showed Polly in a denim jacket, with long strings of firecrackers crossed over her chest in the style of machine gun belts. The second was a picture of a crucifix on a heavily spackled wall. The third was a picture of Lincoln. Del looked over Jen's shoulder at these pictures.

She picked up a perfectly ordinary-looking apple that was hiding in the squash bin along with four squashes and a pulp television-guide magazine called *TV Blueprint*. "I wonder what's wrong with this apple?" she said.

"Looks good to me," Del said. "It's an apple, isn't it?"

Jen looked over her shoulder toward Polly, then turned back to him and whispered, "Are you O.K.?"

"Sure," Del said. "I'm fine. I've got my overthruster turned way up. You want to go?"

Jen grabbed his shoulder and yanked him back, pointing into the bin in front of them. "What's this curly black stuff?"

"I think it's part banana," Del said. "Are you ready?"

"Getting close," Jen said, moving toward the far end of the shed, where there were a few white-dotted jelly jars on a sagging pine shelf.

Polly yelled, "Careful of that jelly, O.K.?"

Del waved at her. "I love this woman here," he whispered to Jen.

The short red guy was leaving. Polly amused herself flipping an ice pick into the countertop in front of her.

"Maybe Margaret would like a nice zucchini," Jen said, holding up a miniature chili pepper with a bad case of bump leprosy. She froze like that for a second, then shrugged and tossed the pepper back into the bin. "No, that's a bad idea. I'm a bad person with a mean streak. I should have my head examined."

"I don't get it," Del said. Then he said, "Oh. O.K., I get it now. The zucchini jokes."

Jen hung her head in mock contrition and waddled down the aisle toward the parking lot.

"I guess we're going," Del said to Polly.

"Hell, I would be, if I were you." She was cleaning her nails with the ice pick. "I'd give you something for the road, but it'd probably devivify before you cleared the lot."

She finished with her nails and scraped the point of the ice pick between her front teeth, which were large and pretty. "You all take care of yourself now, hear? You stay low and outside." She made an overhand pitching gesture with her right arm and then did a fishlike movement with her hand, as if mimicking the route of the ball.

"Thanks," Del said, trailing Jen out the open chicken-wire door.

The guy with the boat and his friend were gone, and the traffic was moving right along out on the interstate. Theirs was the only customer car in the lot. Then he noticed Bud and Margaret kind of wrapped up together in the back seat. They had slipped down about halfway, inclined against the far door, and they were mouth to mouth. Jen caught it too. She grabbed Del's hand and steered him off toward the big inflated peanut sign, and they walked in that direction hand in hand, kicking up carrot-colored dust that seemed to linger in the air.

14

JEN BOUGHT a carving knife at Kmart, one of those ser-
rated, cut-anything knives that guys were always demonstrating on TV by slicing cans and sawing through finger-size
bolts. She was playing with this knife the week after the retreat, cutting some things for fun—a book, a shoe polish
bottle—and waving the thing at Del to make a point, which
was that he should never have gotten involved with Margaret
and that he wouldn't have if he had any sense at all.

"And you never really told me about it, either," she said,
pointing the knife tip at him. "Not the whole deal, anyway.
After hearing Bud's side, you guys look pretty slimy, doing
that stuff. Especially you, with Margaret upset about Bud leaving and everything, going to California."

Del said, "Maybe it was stupid, but it wasn't about Margaret being upset. We were just there together. At least we had
enough sense not to screw each other."

"How do I know that? What if you guys just agreed to say
that and stick to it? Like Bud says. How close did you get,
you want to tell me?"

"I don't want to do this," Del said.

"I want to know," Jen said.

"We like each other," Del said. "It was affection, that's it."

"Sex," Jen said.

They were in the tiny condo kitchen, and there wasn't a lot of room; things were tight. Cabinets were chock-full of cookery, spices, electronic aids. Stuff she'd brought was all over, packed in, crammed on the countertops.

"Not really," he said.

"Oh, yeah? You just kind of hugged and kissed? I suppose you never got your clothes off or anything?" she said, swerving the knife at his shirt, then down at his pants. He was moving across the kitchen, and she was moving too. When she drew the knife back in front of her it accidentally caught his cheek and gave him a four-inch slice from the front of his ear down to his chin line and forward.

"Jesus Christ," he said, surprised more than hurt, stunned by the blood scattering down his neck. He grabbed a paper towel roll and used it whole to mop the side of his face.

Jen screeched for a second, holding the knife, then suddenly stopped, as if she realized that she was in some kind of fright-movie pose. Then she said, "Are you all right?"

"I don't know," he said.

"It's not that deep, I don't think," she said.

"Motherfuck," Del said.

"I mean, it's messy but, like, I don't think it's that bad, really," she said. "It wasn't that hard a hit, was it?" She got another roll of paper towels out of the cabinet and reeled off big swaths, that she used to wipe down his shoulder and his bloody shirt.

Del bent over the sink, dropping blood onto the metal.

Then the phone rang. Del said, "Fucking answer it, will you?"

"What'll I do? What if it's for you?"

He pushed by her and reached for the receiver mounted on the wall by the kitchen door. "Who is it?" he said into the handset.

He listened for a second, then shut his eyes and handed the phone to Jen. "Your mother. She always calls at midnight. Tell her you sliced me up and you've got to call the hospital."

He leaned over the kitchen sink again, watching the blood, which was slowing some, thread its way into the running water circling the drain. There were white specks in the drain, and he couldn't figure out what they were. He was soaking towels in faucet water, holding them on his cheek to stop the blood. It wasn't working.

Jen seemed very calm on the phone, though she kept wiping at the blood on Del's neck. She said, "I just cut him accidentally with this knife and it's bleeding real bad but I don't think it's really *that* bad, at least I hope it's not."

Her mother must have missed it, and Jen repeated it right away, louder. "I just accidentally cut Del's face with a knife I bought. We were playing around, and I cut him a little bit. He's bleeding, and we have to go."

Jen listened for another half minute, then hung up the telephone without saying anything else.

"She'll call back," Del said.

"Shouldn't we go to the hospital? The emergency ward?"

"Or the Urgent Care Center," he said. He had his head turned sideways, cut side up, trying to stem the bleeding.

She was leaning on the counter next to him. "They're going to have to stitch the hell out of that," she said.

"Thanks. That's great to hear."

She said, "I didn't mean to do this, you know. I was just playing around."

"You play hard," Del said. "You were mad, and you didn't mind hitting me."

"Oh, sure. Like I really want to cut your face open. I want to suck your brain out of a tiny hole. Just like TV. It's my obsession."

"O.K.," Del said. "Sorry."

"After you're patched up we can go rip skins off rabbits, huh? Maybe carjack some cars. Throw shit at people, break some glass, get modern."

"Can you just hand me a towel?" Del said.

He was still bleeding, but it was slowing. He pressed the paper towels to the cut, and when he took them off, blood just bulged out, forming a line down his face to a point where it dripped off his chin.

He pointed at his face. "Would you get with it? Are we going to the doctor, or what?"

"Fine," she said. "If you think that's necessary."

He was mopping his face with the towel she'd handed him, then he went into the next room, looking for his shoes.

"I'm sorry," she said, following him out. "I'm nervous, I think. Are we going? What're we doing?"

"Have you got the keys?" he said.

She shook the keys.

"O.K., let's go," Del said. He was at the door.

Jen was driving, fast but not too fast, whipping her head back and forth checking cross streets. "I didn't really cut you," she said. "If we were Mexican, I'd have cut you. White trash, cut you. Middle class, no. Too many jobs, too many cars—I can't cut anybody. Unless I go crazy, and then I can cut the shit out of whoever I want to, because there'll be an explanation that fits. But I'm not crazy, so I can only fuck around in the kitchen and accidentally slash your face a little." She stopped and tilted her head, looking at him. "You know, this cut might look pretty good after a while. Before it heals."

"It's going to look like a cat scratch," he said.

"It's way too big for that. You're going to get a lot of compliments on this down at the shop. They'll regard you with a new fear. It's just what you always wanted."

AT THE EMERGENCY ROOM a tiny doctor, an Asian, took a look at Del's face, then looked at Jen, then back at Del, and just shook his head. His black hair looked as if it was shivering. He pointed to some chairs. "Sit down," he said. "I'll be right back. Keep that towel on it."

Then he left. Del and Jen sat at opposite ends of the examination room. It was cool there, lots of spun aluminum and shiny steel.

"How's it feel?" Jen said.

"It doesn't feel like anything," he said. He took the towel off his face, tossed it to her, then unspooled some paper towels from the roll she was carrying, folded them, dampened them under the faucet.

"If you think this is all about Margaret you're crazy," Jen said. "I just wanted you to know that. I don't like the elevator business with her, though."

"I don't think it's about her. I was joking," he said. "I think you slipped."

"That's right," she said. "So what about the elevator?"

"It was all right," Del said. "She was just checking. Now we're back where we started."

"Where's that?"

"We like each other a lot," he said.

"Oh, great," she said. "How do I know that's where it stops? Wouldn't you rather we have this really open relationship, tell each other everything, every little notion, every feeling—that way it'd be easy for the other guy, you know?"

"We have that already," Del said.

"Yeah, but it'll get more open. It'll be great. We'll tell the truth. We'll tell more truth than anybody ever told before."

"Good," Del said, pulling the towels across his face.

"And nobody'll have to pay too much attention, because everything's right up on the surface. And we won't have any peculiar or difficult thoughts, either, you've got to promise that, so it'll be even easier. It'll be like *I Married CNN*."

"C'mon, Jen. Who buzzed you in here? Settle down, will you?"

"Let's go on Arsenio, anyway," she said.

"What?" The bleeding was slower. Del smeared it with his finger, then blotted it with the towels.

"He's black, he's modern, he's happening, he's huh-huh-huh." She made the grunting noise and did that business circling her arm. Then she slumped on the stool she was sitting on. "Oh, crap. He's bad meat. He's over—I know that. It's fast out there. What do I think, they're going to wait for me?"

"Jesus," Del said. "Put a rag in it, O.K.?"

"What a romance this is," she said. "Here we are in the middle of the night at the hospital, and you're telling me that. What is that?"

"You're babbling," he said. "I'm trying to get my face fixed and you're raving about Margaret and sex."

"Hey," she said. "It's not sex, I got plenty of that." She got up and leaned against the wall of the exam room, popping her shirt snaps, loosening her pants, and slipping her hand down under the zipper. "All you have to do is watch. Every man I ever met wanted to watch. 'Get over there, stand this way, stand that way—' "

Del got up and shut the door, stood in front of the little glass porthole so nobody could see in. "Put that shit back on, Jen. Christ. What's wrong with you?"

She was still at it. " 'Do this, do that, move this way, rub it, finger it, squat, bend over, twist that, squeeze it, hold 'em up, pull it this way, lick it, bite it, hold 'em apart, rotate, ride it way up, kiss it'—every man I ever met. That's the kind of babbling I get. You're no different."

"Crap," Del said. "Fine. Just get dressed, O.K.? Snap the little snaps."

"I don't know what happened to the old days when people felt things for each other, touched each other, cared for each other—I had better sex in high school than I've had since."

"Good," he said. "If that's what you think. Just button up."

"What, am I scaring you like this? Hey, we can tape it and sell it to Cinemax. We'll be real modern," she said. She closed her pants and started on the shirt.

"What's with modern?" Del said. "Have we been sticking a little too close to *The Week in Rock,* or what?"

"Well," she said. "Modern is making a difference, it's having our voices heard."

"That's great. You have one of the nine recognized attitudes," Del said. "You get heard. But if you have a complicated attitude, outside the nine, forget it."

"What nine?" she said.

"Check your local listings," he said.

"You sound like Bud," she said, sitting again. "It's depressing. I have my own ideas, sort of. I pick and choose, anyway. I don't buy it whole."

Del opened the door and stuck his head out, then redampened the paper towels. "Thank God for that," he said.

They had been in the exam room about ten minutes when a nurse came in, took the towel pack off, dabbed some Mercurochrome on Del's face, pushed the towels back into place, and told him to go home.

"I thought he was coming back," Del said.

"Who?" the nurse said.

"The doctor," Del said.

"We saw a Japanese doctor," Jen said to the nurse. "Short guy? Black hair?"

Right then the Japanese doctor came in. "What's going on?" he said.

Del said, "I don't know. The nurse was thinking I was ready to go on home."

He said, "No dice. We've got to do a few small stitches. We're very well trained in stitches, but we've still got to practice sometime."

Sending the nurse out to get some things he needed, he washed his hands in the metal sink. He had Del sit on a low white stool and cleaned the cut with cotton and alcohol, then shot Del's face in three places with tiny bursts of anesthetic from a yellow plastic syringe. When the nurse returned he took twelve mean-looking black stitches at the front end of the cut, along the curve of Del's chin.

15

A T FOUR IN THE MORNING Del cleaned up the kitchen, wiped the counters and the floor, and rinsed out the sink with soap, then alcohol. He packed up all the garbage he could find in the house and took it out to the Dumpster at the back of the property, across the parking area from the building.

The street that ran alongside the condo dead-ended into Highway 90. It was a quiet, tree-shaded, narrow street lined with a few old houses and a group of rental town houses. There was a flash of high lightning as he carried the garbage bags across the parking lot, and then the sky looked a calm midnight blue. He flipped the two bags one after another into the Dumpster, and he was standing there looking distractedly across the street when all the street lights, and the porch lights on the buildings across the street, suddenly flashed off. There wasn't a noise, just the sudden withdrawal of the light—he could still see, of course, but the buildings were faced in shadow, were almost silhouettes. It put him on edge, gave him a pleasant but slightly nervous feeling, as if something might be happening. It was like one of those movie scenes in which an intruder cuts the lights in the house where the woman is hiding, before he goes in after her. It was silly to think any-

thing at all about it, but the pleasure of the anxiety was genuine, so he stood for a few minutes there on the blacktop,
arms crossed, scanning the town houses across the street for
a clue, a movement, anything out of the ordinary. There was
nothing. He waited another couple of minutes, then started
toward the highway and the beach. The air was peculiar, the
way it was just hanging there, almost motionless, drifting off
the water, and the only sound was the faint hiss of little breakers running over rock jetties. There weren't any cars on Highway 90, and only one street lamp burned, about a hundred
and fifty yards down the road. He stood on the corner in front
of the Tropic Breeze, then walked out into the middle of the
empty highway and crossed to the beach side, where the sand
was gritty under his shoes, then he came back, looking all
around. Everything seemed to have lost its power.

16

AT BREAKFAST THE NEXT DAY Jen said, "I can't stand to go out with your brother tonight. Can you call it off? I can be sick, have a headache, PMS, something. I'll be throwing up. I really don't think I can go tonight."

"What's wrong with my brother?" Del said. "Is there something wrong with *him* now? You always liked him, I thought."

"I like him fine," she said. "I just don't want to mess with him tonight. I don't want to mess with all this stuff that's hanging out there with you, and Margaret, and whatever else is bothering him, which seems like almost everything in the world. I just want to do my magazine, hook up and get some new stories. I want to play, and I don't want to have to worry."

Del had bought three new rolls of two-inch gauze and was making himself a new bandage, a strip four inches long, folded and run over the stitches and the rest of his scar. He put small tabs of adhesive tape across the gauze so it looked like a big white version of one of those scars kids always draw on pirate faces.

Jen was ready to leave. She was going to her house to pick

up some paper and a disk she'd forgotten. "You're not going to work like that, are you?" she said.

"What do you mean? What am I supposed to go like? There's a big cut in my face, and I can either go like this or not go."

She rolled her eyes. "C'mon, you're making a big joke of the thing. Get a more discreet look there."

"I don't think it's so bad," he said.

"It's stupid-looking," she said.

"I'll stay home," Del said. He called Audio Instincts and told the store manager that he couldn't come in, that he had a fever, maybe a twenty-four-hour flu.

"That's it," he said, getting off the phone. "I ought to just quit this selling business. I'm tired of working. I did all that PR crap, and now this—"

"I thought you liked it. I thought you were one of those rich guys who goes off and gets a job working in a garden because he likes flowers so much."

"That's not me," Del said. "And it's not the stuff, either; I like the stuff. It's the wads who buy it that kill me. One more stupid, sweet-smelling, close-shaving, car-phoning, Saab-driving, Kenny G–loving know-nothing comes in to chat knowledgeably about a wow and flutter meter for his DCC setup, and I'm going to go off."

"I'm sorry I asked," she said. "Even if I didn't. Anyway, I'm going to my house, so why don't you take a rest here, and then we can figure out how to get me out of the Bud thing later. O.K.?"

"Fine," Del said.

"Del?" she said. "I'm sorry I cut you, really. Maybe I'll bring you a surprise. Is that a good idea?"

"I don't know," he said. "I don't feel all that good."

HALF AN HOUR LATER he was still on the sofa in the empty living room, staring at the Gulf, when Jen called. She said she'd been on her way to her house and she'd seen three police cars, a hearse, and an ambulance at this other house, so she stopped and parked across the street and watched.

"I'm ashamed of myself," she said.

"What happened?" Del said.

"I don't know. They were there, there were a lot of people talking, they were in the yard and then they were back inside the house, then they were back in the yard again," she said. "I don't know. I thought it might be a murder or maybe an old dead guy."

"Yeah," Del said. "Great."

"So then after a while a guy comes out of the ambulance with a gurney, one of those folding jobs, and he snaps it up to full size and rolls it in the house, and two minutes later he comes back out with something on the gurney covered in black plastic, and he and this other guy put that in the ambulance and then off they go."

"You're in the car?" Del said.

"Yeah. I'm taking a few snaps of all this. The cops are still standing there in the front yard, talking, smoking, spitting," she said. "One cop holds two fingers to his face, to his mouth, so he can spit farther. I don't get that. How does that help you spit? That must be a man deal."

"I've seen it," Del said.

"How does it work?" she said.

"I don't know," Del said. "I've seen it for spitting and for whistling, either one. Spitting contests they do it."

"I wish he'd been whistling," she said.

"I've decided to quit," Del said. "Really quit. Stay home all the time. I've got fourteen thousand dollars in the bank."

"Big deal," she said. "Who doesn't?"

"Lots of people," Del said.

"So a couple months from now you can be just like them, right? That's thinking things all the way through, Del," she said.

"Well," he said. "I don't want to work."

"Why don't you become a shrimper?" she said. "You could go out and catch the shrimp and then come back and sell them. You could become a shrimper or a crabber. Or maybe you could become a flounderer."

"That's funny," he said.

"No, no," she said. "I mean it. A flounderer, a person who catches flounder, who fishes for flounder, kind of an exclusive deal. Kind of a flounder deal."

"You weren't making a floundering joke?"

"I wasn't making any joke at all," she said.

"That makes me feel better," Del said.

THE SURPRISE WAS a sexy pale-gray-and-cream outfit from Victoria's Secret, all lace and filigree and straps and silver snaps, and Jen looked good in it, as if she'd just walked off the pages of the catalog. So they played Sluts on a Boat and Knife Me, Baby, and then told each other what they wanted to hear, and meant it, and ended up making a kind of dirty love that took a while. When they were finished with that they were winded, so they rested in each other's arms.

"That wasn't bad," Jen finally said, relaxed across his shoulder. She rolled over and kissed his cheek, then sat up and turned her back to him so he could undo the hooks and eyes that ran up the back of the bustier.

Then they were up and into the bathroom together with Cokes he brought from the kitchen and bath oil she found in her overnight bag. He sat on the floor next to the tub, leaning against the wall, and talked to her as she bathed, and when she was finished and out and wrapped in a big white towel she returned the favor, sitting with him as he bathed and telling him about a woman she'd run into at Dance City, where she'd gone to buy leg warmers.

"This woman said, 'Are you buying those for your little angel?' " Jen told him. "I told her I wasn't, and she said, 'Oh, I'm so relieved. Those are terrible things; they trick the little legs into thinking they're more ready than they are. They seduce the little muscles.' She said that. Really."

When things were straightened away, they went out on the balcony. She didn't balk. He said, "I probably should get some of those leg warmers for my mother. She could use some tricked legs. She has that circulation thing."

"You told me that already," she said. "You're repeating yourself. It's real early to start repeating yourself. Maybe you need a smart drug or two?"

"I need some Bob's Fish Town chicken," Del said. "But I'm too tired to go get it."

"Maybe I'll go later," she said. "What are you going to do now that you aren't going to be working anymore? Do you think I ought to keep working?"

Del said, "You're not working."

"Somebody ought to be working," she said. "We need the money, don't we?"

"I guess we do," Del said.

"What about working half time?" she said. "It would give us more time to mess around. I could help you get started in a new business."

"What kind of business? I'm just quitting," Del said. "I want to rest, think big thoughts, range free."

"Great idea," she said. "But you need a business. You could be a desktop publishing entrepreneur, how about? That's a good idea. Design letterheads, business cards. You can use my machine."

"I've always wanted to do that," he said, rolling his eyes.

"It'd be O.K.," she said. "People need that stuff."

Del gave her a look.

"They want it, anyway," she said. "You should see some of the bozos who have their own personal stationery. Back in college people did that. I even did that. Or you could do brochures. They could use some mailing pieces, advertisements of various kinds, yellow page advertisements. There's a whole universe of DTP."

"If I quit I don't want to turn around and do dime handouts for Twisty Kominsky."

"Who's Twisty Kominsky?" she said.

"Twisty Kominsky's this person I made up," Del said. "I don't want to design her advertising pieces. She's a small-business person, say."

"O.K.," she said. "Well, what about throwing in with me on my magazine? We could make it bigger, maybe try and get some subscriptions."

"Why, exactly, are people going to subscribe?"

"Gore," she said. "Mysterious blood-soaked stories. They make you feel alive, glad it didn't happen to you, but you still get some of the buzz just knowing it happened to somebody. Like what a strange world it is."

"Oh, yeah. But, Jen? It's well chronicled. How many times do we need to be told?"

"We don't need it, we *want* it," she said. "We want constant reminders, ghoulish stuff just to keep our hearts pumping. Maybe it's that these things aren't really ghoulish, like gerbil sex is ghoulish."

"Gerbil sex?"

"Sex with gerbils—it's a story I got off AP, but it was too horrible. A gay thing. The stiletto-in-your-penis set. Maybe if you have the freaky stories you don't have to have the freaky life. Think of it that way. Therapy."

"There are different kinds of freaky, yes?" he said.

She smiled. "Yeah, that's the point. See, under certain circumstances, slicing heads off people makes some kind of sense."

He screwed up his face. "What kind?"

"Well, you know—dramatic sense." She covered her eyes. "It's, like, that's what you do when things get to that point. Oh, I don't know," she said. "There's just something wonderful in these things, something beautiful. I feel it when I find them."

Del reached for her hand. "How come you can sit out here in daytime and you can't at night?"

"I don't know," she said. "I don't have the same impulse to throw myself headfirst off the balcony in the daytime." Then she backed her chair against the glass, as if having the subject come up made her suddenly aware of her fear. "O.K., never mind desktop publishing, forget the magazine, let's go back to crabbing and shrimping."

"I'm scared of water," Del said. "Scared of shrimp and crabs. I don't like to kill stuff. Killing's a bad idea except for bugs."

"Wait a minute," she said. "Is this that whole routine about eating what you kill, or killing what you eat, or whatever, and just killing what's needed for survival, and being at one with nature, and feeling like a real man, beating your chest with your foot up on the kill? And, like, wiping the blood on your kid's face so he's, like, initiated and everything? And so you pass along to the next generation the moronic values of the last? Performed with all the tokens of genuine feeling: the bitten lip, the rubbed eye, the wiped jaw, the boot in the dust, the sinewy muscle flexed, the shaken head—is that what you're about to say?"

"No," he said. He leaned back in his chair and shook his head. "No."

"Oh," she said. "What then?"

"I kill bugs because I'm afraid they'll get on me. I don't bother if they're not going to get on me. I'll eat the other stuff, but I don't want to kill it."

"Let the professionals do the killing, right? In the slaughterhouses and that? Chop the hooves, throw the rest up on the hooks, upside down, still bleating, and cut their throats? That's it?"

"I saw that show too. It was ugly. But at least they're not doing it for fun."

"So you're not Naturalman," she said, doing a superhero flying move. "I hate that shit."

"I can tell," he said. "And fishing's out for the same reasons. Also because I don't want to take something out of somewhere and take it somewhere else and sell it to somebody. So there goes shrimping, manufacturing, farming—there goes a lot of stuff."

"Got it," she said. "Nothing in death or sales. I just thought shrimping or crabbing—you know, out on the water, the sun, the wind in your face, kind of a day-to-day out-in-the-elements deal with a good tan, those weathered looks—I just thought you might like that for a change."

"I want to eat something," Del said.

"How about blood?" she said. "No, what I'm saying is, how often can you give blood?"

"I have the AIDS virus," Del said. "I got it from sleeping with athletes, male and female. I slept with two thousand male and female athletes last week alone. Besides, I don't want to give blood because if I don't already have AIDS, I'll get it there and bring it back here and give it to you and we'll both become heterosexual stats."

"Maybe we could go into pornography," she said. "People make a lot of money in pornography. I seem to be gifted and talented in this area."

"Amen," he said. "We could call you Ashley O. They'd

pay the long bucks for Ashley O., is what I'm thinking. Plus we'd be working together."

"It's a bad idea," she said. "After I get older I'd be tossed aside like a used-up TV dinner, while my breasts lived on in 3-D."

Del squinted, as if sizing her up. "Maybe we ought to go in and take some trial snaps, you know? Just to get the feel, get the flavor. A couple of test rolls, know what I'm saying?"

"I know what you're saying," she said.

THAT AFTERNOON they drove down the beach to distribute Jen's latest issue, which was called *Really Nice Stories,* out of deference to Bud and Margaret. They had to stop at Kinko's to run off a hundred copies of the issue, which featured three stories about women: "Our Lady of the Trunk," about a woman who survived nine days in a car trunk by eating a bag of peanuts and drinking the "sweat" of the trunk lid; "Household Chemistry," about a thirteen-year-old girl who broke into houses, turned on stereo systems, and then killed all the fish and rabbits she could find but left other pets untouched; and "Pen Pal," about a woman who was discovered in a secluded pen at a local veterinary clinic run by a female vet named Chastity, who said the captive woman "deserves to be treated like a dog for what she did to my husband."

"Where do you want to start with these?" Del said as they were coming out of Kinko's.

"Let's go down to Waveland and work back," Jen said.

So they crossed the bridge at Henderson Point and headed down South Beach Boulevard through Bay St. Louis. It was a windy day, the usual rain in the forecast for the late-fall afternoon, and the water was high and choppy. The coast along there was rattier than most of the Mississippi coast, but it had something of the forties or fifties about it, almost as if there wasn't enough interest in a section of coast this far from the usual amenities. Junked-up beach houses on stilts stood right next to each other, across the two-lane from the narrow beach and the water. Unlike much of the Mississippi sound, the water there got deep pretty quickly, so you couldn't walk out a half mile and still be only up to your knees. Jen snapped the car radio off and rolled down all the windows.

"I just love this," she said. "I don't know how people live without it."

"It's pretty good," he said. "It has a way of making you feel everything's O.K." He watched the water smack against the private piers running out into the sound.

"That's it," she said. "I think I'm happy to be around."

"That's because you're a young person," he said. "You've got stuff to look forward to."

"You, for example," she said.

They drove through Waveland and Clermont Harbor, past a trailer park that sat right on the edge of Buccaneer State Park, and Jen pulled off into the sand shoulder of the road. She pointed out ahead. "Nothing up here but the shrimp station, the Cone Island Fishery. After that it's all marsh, all the way over to Slidell. You have to go inland to drive over that way."

"So you want to start back?"

"Not really," she said. "I want to sit here."

"Do you want to get out and go over to the beach? Walk over there?"

"Not really." She cut the engine and slipped down in the seat, leaning her head back against the headrest and closing her eyes. "You smell that?" she said.

"The Gulf?"

"Yeah. Salt water, fish, whatever." She took a deep breath, her nostrils flexing. "Remember when you used to live somewhere else and you drove to the coast and before you got there you could smell it?" She sat there breathing through her nose for a minute, then opened her right eye and turned over to Del, who was watching her the whole time. "I guess you think I'm silly."

"I think you're as perfect as this air here," he said. "That's what I think."

Her eyes lit and she smiled, letting out a closed-mouth chuckle. "Very nice of you," she said.

"You're welcome," he said.

In a few minutes she restarted the car, made the U-turn, and headed back up the coast. Del rode on the water side, his head resting on the window's vertical track, letting the wind whip his skin. They stopped at a tiny food store in Closed Corner, and another in Waveland, and Del stapled issues of *Really Nice Stories* to likely-looking telephone poles along the way and to a town bulletin board on the little stretch of East Beach that ran through the eight curved blocks of seawall that was downtown Bay St. Louis.

When they got back on the bridge to cross the bay to Henderson Point, Del said, "There's a gas station up here I want to stop at, O.K.?" Then he reached down and untied his new cross-training shoes, yanking the tongue up so they'd slide easily off his feet when he got to the gas station.

17

BUD AND MARGARET came over and brought an air con-ditioner with them. It was a 6,500 BTU unit, still in its box, which Bud rolled in on a dark-green hand truck. He said it was good for a small bedroom. "It really churns the air," Bud said. "It's much more powerful than sixty-five hundred BTU suggests."

They wheeled the box into the living room, got it off the dolly, then flipped it over so the This Side Up arrow was point-ing up. "I don't know what to say, Bud," Del said. "That's a great present."

"I just wanted you to have it," Bud said. "We were going to put it out on the sun porch, but I decided I didn't like the way it looked out there."

"It's brown on the front," Margaret said. "Simulated wood grain."

"That's all right," Jen said. "They simulate everything else. I don't know where we're going to use it over here, though."

"Del can figure that out," Bud said.

"Sure," Del said. "Might put it in the back there, though I don't believe they allow that, now that I think about it. We could use it at Jen's apartment. You've got window units like this, don't you?" he asked Jen.

"Yes, we do," she said.

Bud seemed a little uneasy at that idea, but he nodded thoughtfully.

"Let them worry about it, Bud," Margaret said. "You gave them the air conditioner, let's let them use it where it'll do the most good."

"I know that," Bud said.

"You'd rather we didn't take it to Jen's?" Del said.

"No, it's only that I was thinking of it as a housewarming present, kind of. It's fine."

"Bud, it's theirs now. Just as soon as they opened that door this air conditioner became theirs," Margaret said.

"I just got it last week," Bud said.

"It's very nice," Del said. "What kind is it?"

"Arvaratum," Bud said. "A new brand."

"It's an Arvaratum?" Jen said.

"Yeah. It's a new brand. I've heard of it," Del said.

"It's good," Bud said. "It's made by Fedders. Or maybe by Frigidaire."

The box was in front of the couch, sort of like a coffee table. Jen put her Coke can down on the box and asked if Bud and Margaret wanted something to drink. They wanted beer. Bud went to the window to look out.

"Del quit his job today," Jen said, heading into the kitchen. "He's not going to work for a while."

"Oh, yeah?" Bud said. "It'd be hard to work with you stabbing him all the time."

"I'm thinking about quitting," Del said.

"That's great," Margaret said. "What're you going to do?"

"I don't know," Del said. "I guess I'll take it easy, look at the water. I've got a little cash saved. I think I need to take it easy."

"Yeah, I think you do," Margaret said.

"Why does he need to take it easy?" Bud said.

"Just because," Margaret said. "People need to take it easy every now and again."

"They need to do something first, don't they?" Bud said. "Besides, if he sits around he'll just start feeling sorry for himself, getting mad at the stuff people say on television."

"No, Bud," Margaret said. "You're confusing him with you. You'd do that. He won't do that."

"I might," Del said. "I worry about things I see on television. People think you should feel a certain way, believe a certain thing. People think you should have certain values. Right, Bud?"

"Used to be Republicans, now it's liberals," Bud said. "The liberals disguise it better."

"We're all liberals, aren't we?" Jen said, coming back with new beers.

"We're not that kind of liberals," Bud said.

"Bud's an anarchist," Margaret said. "We're seriously non-aligned. When we're paying attention we're against any rule, at least any rule we didn't make up."

"So what's that mean?" Bud said. "It doesn't say anywhere you have to do it twenty-four hours a day, does it? That's just another prissy rule."

Everybody was using the new air conditioner box as a coffee table. Del, who was on the couch with Margaret and Jen, had his feet on it.

"He's got a point," Jen said.

"You kind of promote disorder, don't you, Bud? In small ways," Del said. "Isn't that the idea?"

"I guess," he said, waving at the question.

"It's sort of Anarchy Lite," Margaret said.

"There really isn't so much range available anymore," Jen said.

"This is real handsome out here," Bud said, ticking his bottle against the sliding glass door. "What do these places go for now?"

"Karen's father got it for sixty-five, or that's what he told me. But that was twenty years ago. And there was some kind of trick deal on it—bankruptcy, or like that."

"Hmm," Bud said. "I moved back to the house and dumped that apartment, the Mondrian, so I was wondering if we ought to look at one of these. It's nice."

"We've been thinking about a child," Margaret said. "One of our own."

"You are?" Del said. "Is this, like, timely?"

"It's borderline," Margaret said.

"So if you had a real family, what would you want, boy or girl?" Jen said.

"Boy," Bud said.

"Girl," Margaret said.

"I see," Jen said. "Well, I'm sure you can work it out."

"They're not going to have all that much to do with it," Del said.

"That's what I meant, genius," Jen said. "So are you guys trying now—I mean are you *trying?*" Jen said.

"Sort of half trying," Bud said.

"We're trying pretty seriously," Margaret said.

"We kind of tried this afternoon," Del said.

"Jesus, Del," Jen said.

"We did," Del said, laughing.

"You didn't try that hard," Jen said.

"Now, Jen," Margaret said.

"We haven't decided," Bud said. "There are problems, especially at our age. We're a little old to be having children. We're thinking, really, is all."

Margaret raised her eyebrows and made a blubbery face, then pointed at Bud. "He thinks slow."

"Did you know a guy was killed in this building last week?" Jen said. "One floor down, at the end of the building. I couldn't believe it."

"Jen is obsessed with death," Del said. "This morning she stopped to watch them take some old geezer out of his house where he'd died. She took pictures."

"You didn't have to tell them that, Del," Jen said.

"It's true, isn't it?" Del said.

"I was curious," Jen said. "But I don't know if he was so old. It could have been anyone—a rape victim, a child, a gay pioneer. Did I say it was a geezer?"

"So then tonight we have to watch to see if it makes the news," Del said.

"I want to know," Jen said.

"That's really corrupt," Bud said.

"I don't think so," Margaret said. "I think it's very understandable."

"How?" Del said. "Sometimes I don't understand you, Margaret."

"It just is. It's one of those things. You see something and naturally you want to know what the story is, and you don't want to go right up and ask somebody. So you try to figure it out and then maybe catch it on the news, if it's the kind of thing that might be on the news, in case you got it wrong."

"Like some old geezer dying in bed," Bud said.

"Right," Margaret said. "That's the kind of thing. A car crash where somebody got hurt, where you saw somebody mangled—you'd want to see that on TV, wouldn't you?"

"You're darn right I would," Jen said. "I'd want to see that even if I hadn't seen it in the street."

"She's having a little fun with the oldsters now, Margaret," Bud said.

"No I'm not," Jen said. "I think it's interesting. It's like there's nothing phony about it when people are dying. They're just dying. They just go away."

"Why are you so worried about phony?" Bud asked. "There's nothing wrong with phony stuff; it's just more stuff."

"SO THESE ARE the famous stitches," Bud said. He had Del on the couch, with a lamp bent over his face, and he was looking at the stitches the Japanese doctor had put in Del's jaw. "They look pretty good. I like this thread."

"I think you should leave it uncovered," Margaret said. "It's got a kind of look."

"That's what Jen said," Del said. "She said it made me look dangerous, said it was a babe-magnet."

"You don't need any more babes," Margaret said.

"It doesn't look all *that* good," Bud said, tracing his first finger along the upper part of the cut, where it wasn't deep enough to have needed stitches. "This stuff up here helps, but you're no Mickey Rourke."

"Yeah, plus you don't have the right hair," Jen said.

"That's not a great loss," Bud said.

"I'd take Mickey's hair," Del said.

"Ditto," Jen said.

Del went into the kitchen and fixed himself a peanut butter sandwich and a dish of ice cream. When he brought it back into the living room he offered sandwiches to the others. "I'm sorry to be so rude," he said. "I couldn't stop myself."

"Yeah, the jar unscrewed all by itself," Jen said. "The peanut butter came out like a tornado, spreading itself on the big white slices."

"There was a lot of wind. The jam lurched at the bread," Del said between bites.

They watched him for a second, then everybody headed for the kitchen. Jen made more peanut butter sandwiches, and

Bud banged around until he found a few bags of chips, and Margaret dished up more dishes of ice cream, and pretty soon the air conditioner box was covered with plates and glasses and bowls and corn chip bags.

"I can't believe you live like this," Bud said, finishing his second sandwich. "How old are you, anyway? You're almost my age."

"I'm not even close. I'm years younger," Del said.

"You're not young enough to be having people over for peanut butter sandwiches," Bud said.

"For a fellow who's complaining, you're knocking them back pretty quick," Margaret said.

"You can cook yourself something," Del said. "Get some burgers going, though I don't see the difference. Anyway, there's plenty of stuff out there. Jen's probably got some venison out there. Or crabs. Or shrimp or flounder."

"You have flounder?" Bud said.

"He's making that up," Jen said. "That's about an argument we were having before you came."

Bud gave him a look and said, "Gee, thanks, Del. What a great brother you are."

"It was a joke. She was talking about me being a flounder man earlier."

"A flounder man?" Bud said.

"Yes," Del said.

"A flounderer," Jen said. "I was saying that since he's quitting his job he could become a fisherman specializing in flounder, or crabs or shrimp, maybe."

"I haven't actually quit the job yet, you know," Del said. "I'm still in the thinking stage."

Cuts of lightning shot through the sky, brightening the whole scene so they could see the light reflecting off the water and the low white clouds against the darker sky. Del got up and opened the sliding doors to the balcony, leaving the screen doors shut. "This is why I wanted to move to Biloxi, these storms."

"They *are* pretty," Jen said.

"They're more than that. They're dazzling," Del said. "They transform everything instantly. It's like suddenly you're in a different world and the junk of your life slides away and you're left with this rapture, this swoon of well-being and rightness. You get the world in its amazing balance."

"Del's having a romantic moment," Bud said.

Margaret gave him a withering look. "Well, then, for this moment, in this time and place, he's a lot better off than the rest of us, isn't he?" she said.

BUD AND MARGARET went home after the first of the storms had cooled down. Del and Jen went out for a drive, figuring to stop at a grocery store somewhere along the way. They rode through Gulfport, listening to the air whip around the car windows, to the intermittent wipers wipe, to the spatter of the tires on the wet highway, and to the constant low rush and recession of the Gulf water. And there was that hiss that water makes as it stumbles over rocks. It was nearing midnight, and there was a surprising crowd on Highway 90. People seemed to be having trouble with their cars, and where they weren't having trouble they were having loud conversations, with lots of bass-heavy rap music backing them up. Three or four cars would be grouped at the side of the road, and those people would be out of their cars, drinking canned beer and yelling at each other, and at other groups up and down the highway, and at people out on the beach. It was big fun. The wind was blowing; there were American flags on the fast-food restaurants. There were cars full of guys, riding low, and lots of motorcycles, though at this time of night they weren't the family Harleys with all the chrome but jagged, cut-down bikes whose riders looked as if they were kicked way back in La-Z-Boys. Kids were coming out of souvenir shops and video game parlors, straggling in groups three and four strong along the highway with their low jeans and their flappy shoes. Some guy in a phone booth looked as if he was getting into it with a cop just out of his car. Farther down, this one guy was shadowboxing, doing wicked karate moves with a pool cue. There were more American flags.

Del started to count them, and Jen said, "I hate all these flags. What's a flag doing on a McDonald's? A Burger King?"

"Marketing bonanza," he said.

"It's cheating," Jen said.

They turned around at the Sea World Water Park and headed in the other direction, going past the condo, through Biloxi, across the bridge, and straight out past Pascagoula to the Singing River Mall in Gautier. The rain was periodic and delicate, just barely wetting the asphalt, so that it glistened kind of gold from the sodium vapor lights. The mall was closed, and the huge parking lot was nearly empty. There was an atrium at the entrance, with red and blue strips of neon in a circular pattern, and those lights, too, were reflected in the asphalt. A few cars were around, not many. Del thought it was beautiful. "Nobody really gets this," he said. "Nobody sees how gorgeous this is or knows why."

"Sure they do," Jen said. "Kids. They love parking lots. It's the space, the color—blacks out here are especially good. And it's always fresh here, cleaned by the wind."

"Well," Del said. "That's a start."

They sat for twenty minutes listening to the rain, the car windows rolled down, the light drops like bites on their arms. Del got his pushed-up shirt sleeve soaked. Interesting kids in crappy cars with bad mufflers drove by slow, then doubled back to check them out.

A guard walked through the atrium, checking the doors.

"Look at that," Del said, nodding toward the guard, who was two hundred yards away, rattling the locked doors from the inside. "I swear he's staring at us." Del leaned toward the windshield and ran his hand back and forth on the glass to wipe away the condensation.

The atrium was thirty feet tall, a two-story space with a peaked roof and skylights, and that snappy neon. There was something about it that reminded him of the forts he built when he was a kid. Forts made out of wood blocks, some a couple of inches square, some with semicircles cut out of them, some like dowels or columns, about three inches high. That's what the mall looked like. There was light streaking across the parking lot, streaking the buildings, and the outside names of the stores were done in Franklin Gothic or some trademark script, lit against the white brick. "I guess people don't see it like this, do they? They come here looking for Odor-Eaters."

"Most people are asleep about now," Jen said.

They stopped at an all-night grocery and got some Mrs. Smith's cinnamon rolls with raisins for breakfast, then they headed for the condo. They had the windows down on the way, and the car was filled with the fragrances of mimosa and gardenia, and the smoky aroma of charcoal as they went through a subdivision where someone had cooked earlier.

Del noticed the dark, slightly sour odor of his sleeve and rode part of the way home with that wet sleeve pressed against his face, just so he could take its scent.

18

THE MORE JEN BROUGHT her portable computer around, the more Del got interested in computers, and software, and networks, and buying lots of computer magazines—*PC Magazine, Windows User, Computer Shopper,* and others— and shopping for new hardware and software. Eventually he mail-ordered a Gateway 486 with a lot of fancy add-ons. He was particularly interested in drawing and painting programs, word processors, and utility programs. He was using Windows, spending hours creating new icons, making drawings that he thought Jen might use in the magazine, doctoring photos to take guys' heads off or to remove the lingerie in the lingerie ads he scanned in from catalogs with Jen's old hand-held scanner. He was also getting new shareware programs off bulletin board systems that Jen set him up with, and going on Compuserve, using Jen's account to look up information on diseases he thought he might have, or might get, and to download consumer reports, reviews, news. He wondered what the point of a weather map was, inasmuch as the ones on TV were always more detailed and up to date, but he got them, anyway. He was linking into what journalists and excitable futurists were pleased to call the neural net, which was fundamentally mundane but fast and a little magical.

One night, just after he got off Compuserve, the phone rang and the guy on the other end introduced himself. "Hi," the guy said. "This is Marco D'Lo."

"Uh-huh?" Del said.

"You don't remember me, do you?"

"When you say that, pal, I know it's time for me to hang up and pull the shades, to bolt the big sheet metal over the windows."

"I'm sorry," the guy said. "It's Father Marco D'Lo. From St. Anthony's."

It came back at once. Father Marco D'Lo had been the assistant at St. Anthony's Catholic School. Father Marco D'Lo was a diminutive, delicate, and winsome fellow in an immaculate matte-black cassock, flowing across the campus of St. Anthony's like a small saint.

"Father D'Lo," Del said, sitting up, pulling the tail of his shirt down. "How are you?"

"To begin with, I'm not Father D'Lo anymore. I'm just plain Marco D'Lo. I'm out of the priesthood, and now I'm married."

"Hey, everyone is these days," Del said.

There was a pause, then D'Lo laughed. "Oh, I get it," he said.

"So what're you doing now that you're not Father D'Lo anymore?"

"The usual stuff," he said. "I'm thinking about Biloxi as a place to settle down, uh, maybe get in on this dockside gambling thing some way or other. Try to, maybe. See the other side of things." He laughed at this last remark. Father D'Lo's laugh was a dinky little trill.

"Great," Del said. "Uh-huh. What, you're going to be a

dealer? Probably going to invest in one of these places? Get in on the ground floor?"

"You never know, Del. I've got some things in the fire; I'm working with some people."

"I hope it works out for you." Jen was sitting on the floor across the room, staring at him. Del made freaky facial expressions at her and at the phone, indicating he didn't know what to do.

She sliced her forefinger across her throat two quick times. "Dump it," she whispered.

"So listen, Del," Marco D'Lo said. "I think it might be a good thing if we had a meeting, a get-together to refresh our memories, so that we can get back in touch and all that. If you're interested. I think it would be good."

"I don't mean to be rude," Del said.

"We've got a lot of old times to go over," Marco said.

The only old times Del could think of were he and Father D'Lo in the confessional. The prospect of meeting him now, for any reason, was not appealing.

"So, Del, are you there?" Marco said.

"I'm here," Del said. "I don't know, Father D'Lo. I'm real busy, lots of work, you know how it is. Things pile up, you get behind—I don't know."

"Your mother said you were in public relations?"

"You talked to my mother?" Del put his head in his hand.

"Yes. We had a nice talk," D'Lo said. "She gave me your number. And Bud's number."

"Ah," Del said. "I'm into this desktop publishing deal, a small company, and I'm in audio sales—and I'm traveling some too, so I'm kind of hard to catch."

"Audio?" he said. "Wholesale audio? Now that's a good business."

"Retail," Del said.

"Who'd have thought it when we were back there at Saint Anthony's?" D'Lo said. "You in that little brown uniform, playing on the playground and singing in the choir, straining that little voice of yours—who'd have guessed that we'd end up here in Biloxi together all these years later? It's an astounding world, isn't it?"

"We're not really *together,* are we?" Del said. "Excuse the expression."

"Those were good days," Father Marco D'Lo said, his voice drifting a little. "Everything seemed easier then." He stopped talking a second, then cleared his throat and went on. "But I guess it's better now in spite of that. That's my opinion. You can take that to the bank."

"Maybe you can give me a number and let me call you," Del said. "In a week or so, when I get straightened away."

"That'd be good," Father Marco said. "I really would like to get together while I'm here."

"I look forward to it," Del said. "How long will you be here, by the way?"

"Hard to say," D'Lo said. "All depends how things play out. Things are kind of loose right now. I'm just testing the waters."

"I see," Del said.

Father D'Lo gave Del a number, and Del scratched it on the pad next to the telephone. When he hung up the phone, he went into the bathroom and washed his hands, then rinsed his hands and forearms with isopropyl alcohol.

"O.K.," Jen said, standing in the bathroom door. "What's the story?"

"It's this guy who was a young priest when I was a kid. He taught at the school, or he was the assistant pastor, and now he's quit the priesthood, and he's here to get in on the gambling."

"That's horrible," Jen said.

"The only other priest I ever knew who left was that guy Bradshaw, the inner-child freak or whatever he is. Get you in touch with your little weenie."

"You knew Bradshaw?" she said.

"I had him for algebra, maybe," Del said. "Everybody thought he was real smart. This guy was just a regular parish priest, a go-along guy. The pastor was a twit, so this guy was a big improvement by comparison."

"What's he want?"

"Wants a meeting, he says," Del said. "Wants us to get to know each other. How do I know? Maybe he's lonely."

"Are you going to call him back? Isn't this kind of queer?" She took a towel off the rack and handed it to Del.

"Maybe," he said. "It's creepy. I wish the damn priests would just stay in there and be quiet. Jesus."

DEL WOKE UP suddenly at three A.M. Jen was out of bed, back in the living room, messing with her computer. The pale-blue backlit LCD and the night-light plugged into the wall socket were the only lights in the room apart from what was coming in from the street outside.

He stood in the doorway. "You have to listen to this now, O.K.?" Del said.

"What?" she said, still punching keys. Text was scrolling up her screen. "Are you all right?"

He shuffled to the couch and sat down crosswise, his back against the arm. "I had this dream that we lived in a power station."

"You're mumbling," she said.

"There's a group of us in this concrete place," he said. "The scale is amazing, like the Grand Coulee Dam, mesmerizing it's so big. So we walk down this long steel stairway, rattling and clanking, you and me and these other people, into this concrete place that's like a train station with oversize tracks, and they're vacant, and we're on top of these immense concrete beams, maybe sixty feet in the air, twenty feet wide, and up on huge round columns, and there are lines of these beams, jagged, not continuous, shooting off at little angles to each other—it's like a swollen underground world. It's open on top. People are climbing down and crossing the track space, but there's some trade going on down there, sixty feet below, in the dirt and muck. As far as you can see, there are these post-and-lintel ranges, some stable and some half collapsed, beams balanced on a single column precariously standing, columns fallen, and the channels between these rows of beams are muck and slime and sewage and rubble, deep ditches a hundred feet wide with people moving around in them, carrying stuff, camping around fires."

"So what happens?" Jen said. She'd turned around to face him, but there was still stuff going by on her screen.

"We've come to see this place, but we don't know who runs it or why we're there. And then something goes wrong. Huge earth equipment and trucks as big as houses start ramming out of one end, going down these long channels, scattering the people. There's no way to escape. People are being crushed all over the place, screaming, blood splashing everywhere, torn limbs skittering through the air, huge chunks of the beams are collapsing, and we can't get out.

"The scale of the place is terrifying. The channels between beam lines are a hundred feet wide, filled with rubble and water. The sky is dark gray. All these things are like the structures under highway overpasses, only they're much bigger than that, and people are living in groups on top. There's constant noise—loud and strident and industrial, and large sections of beams are moving, easing back and forth, ratcheting left and right, twisting, shifting slowly.

"We go back up to the surface, and it's like we're rebuilding the borough up there; then we're at a stadium, but we're not watching the field, we're watching a giant screen on the side of a blimp across the street, but all it's doing is glowing different colors and showing bits of packaging, like the flaps off a toothpaste box at a giant size, and then in the night we're back down on our concrete beam. We're rebuilding the world, recivilizing it, that's what we're doing, and we've got to do it using the rubble and stuff down there below. Our beam is like our own island in the middle of this huge rubble world. At night my job is working in a restaurant on our beam, and I'm telling them in the back of the restaurant not to throw away the leftover food people leave on their plates. I go into the kitchen through some flapping doors, like the rubber-edged steel doors leading to a butcher department in a grocery store, and there are beds lined up there, hundreds of beds out in the open on top of our concrete beam, cots lined up on one edge with a walkway in front of them, and after that just nothing, just a long fall down to the sewage river below. Rubble is piled up off into the distance.

"This one guy on a bed is making a speech. He says he's a doctor and that he's gone mad, and he starts out making a speech about something, and I don't know what he's talking about. It seems garbled but still intelligible, but I don't get it. Gradually he speeds up, so he's talking so fast I can't hear a single word he's saying. It's like line hash. Then these four guys in oily rags and silver rings and junk come along, step onto our beam, and they're outlaws, and they stop and sit with us, and the doctor calms down when he spies them. We're in a precarious position because it'd be easy to slip off the side of the concrete and fall sixty feet into the sewage and rubble. There are big concrete towers between us and the next beam line. Ragged pieces of steel have fallen at angles all around us, car-size pointed shards of rusty steel. There are people moving about down around the sewage river, and they're doing something wonderful, the way they're living out there in the middle of it all. It's dusk, the sun's sinking below us, boiling red. I stare at the outlaws for a long time, and nobody speaks until finally this one guy, the fat one, his charred face flat and expressionless, says to me, 'You'd like to be out there, wouldn't you?' He waves a huge hand at the river of sewage, and it hits me hard because he's right, I want to be out there living that outlaw life, but I'm not, and I know when he says it I'm not going to be, so I start crying."

Jen looked at him across the room. "In the dream you were crying?"

"That's when I woke up. I was crying in my sleep."

"Jesus. That's crazy," she said. "So what's all this stuff mean, the towers and the sewage and all that? What's the story, exactly?"

"There isn't any story. It's not the story," Del said. "It's just this breathtaking world, that's the point. It's like the story's not important—what's important is the way the world looks. That's what makes you feel the stuff. That's what puts you there."

MARCO D'LO looked like a lounge singer. Like a Days Inn version of a lounge singer. He had stringy black hair that was too greasy and sideburns that came down and went forward in points like little boots in front of his ears. He had oily skin and wore black plastic glasses of a kind that could probably be made popular only by a strangeness-seeking rock star. But Marco was proud of them. He had on a shirt of thick string woven loosely, a see-through shirt. This was what Del noticed first when he answered the doorbell Saturday morning.

"I called Bud," Marco D'Lo said. "I called Bud and got your address, and then I came over. You look great, Del. You look like a great big version of you."

"Bud gave you my address?" Del said. "Why don't you come in? I'm kind of surprised to see you. What time is it?" He knew what time it was, but he wanted to suggest maybe it was too early to be visiting.

"It's right at high noon," Marco said. "Time to be about my Father's business, as we used to say."

Del led him into the hall going to the living room. Jen was in the kitchen in her Hanes underpants and a half-length sleeveless undershirt that would have fit a thirteen-year-old.

"Hi," she said to Father Marco as he went by.

"Hi," he said, stopping to duck into the kitchen. "How are you?" He stretched out a hand and she took it, shook it once, then let it go. He didn't seem to want to take his eyes off her.

Del said. "Jen, this is Father Marco D'Lo, only he's not *Father* Marco D'Lo anymore, he's just plain Marco D'Lo now."

"That's it," Marco D'Lo said. "I dropped the Father."

"You want something to drink?" Del said, steering Marco into the living room.

"No, thanks," Marco said. "But you do look great. And isn't this place something? Damn. Look at that view there—what is that out there? That island I'm seeing."

"That's Dog Island," Del said.

"Boy, it's fine-looking," Marco said. He sat down on the couch. "Del, the reason I came over is, I may need your help." He waited while this had a chance to sink in. "Del, I'm starting something new here, and I'm wondering if maybe we could get together and work something out, you and me. Maybe we could get Bud in on it."

"Bud goes for the long shots," Del said, smiling and shaking his head. "I don't mean that you're a long shot, of course. I just mean new things, Bud goes for new things. Me, I'm an old-thing person, know what I'm saying? I'm just getting ready to take some time off and retool."

"Hey," Marco D'Lo said. "You're late, kid. I dumped that priesthood; that was my retool. I guess when you gotta go, you gotta go."

Jen was leaning into the pass-through between the living room and the kitchen. "I saw on TV that they've got a big pedophilia deal in the priesthood. Is that right?"

"Yes, it is," Marco D'Lo said. "But I wasn't part of that problem."

"If you're not part of the problem, then I guess you're part of the solution," she said, and smiled at him prettily.

He smiled back. "Thanks. I guess I am at that."

"I wouldn't want Del sitting around with no pedophiliac," she said, drawing out the last word as if it had a Pronounce Me sign on it.

"I wouldn't be much good at that, because I always get kids and feet confused," Father Marco said. "I can tell the difference between kids and feet, but—oh, you know. You'd think I'd know the difference by now, wouldn't you? Having done my time in the confessional?"

He gave Del a look that seemed riddled with suggestion, and Del wished he'd never seen it. It meant: *I remember you, I remember everything about you, I know all your secrets, you'd better be careful how you treat me now.* Then Del realized he was being silly; it was probably just the guy's idea of a friendly look. How could he remember everything? Besides, what had Del confessed that a hundred others, a thousand others, hadn't?

"You don't mind if I call you Father Marco, do you?" Del said. "I can't get used to that other. To me you're still Father Marco, big as life."

"I'd rather you call me Marco," he said, making moon eyes.

"Me too," Jen said from the kitchen. "I want to call him Father Marco too."

"O.K., just the two of us," Del said. "O.K.?"

Father Marco wiggled a finger at Del to get him in close for a private question. "How old is she?" Father Marco whispered, pointing toward the kitchen. "Is she, like, twenty-one?"

"More," Jen said from the kitchen. "And I've got good hearing. I've got good eyes. All of my physical equipment is pretty good."

He laughed and shook his head, turning to see her bare midsection through the pass-through. "She's a little sharpie, isn't she?" He slapped Del's knee a couple of times and made another clownish face.

"She sure is," Del said. "So what did Bud have to say?"

"About the same thing you said," Marco said. "Hi, how are you, like that. He said there were some problems going on between you two, the usual kinds of things, and maybe some a little less usual."

"He told you that?"

"Yes, just that you and he had some trouble last summer. He didn't say much in particular, but you know, I'm piecing these things together—I've been doing that all my life. I got the sense that he didn't want to see me so much, really."

"You were a priest," Del said. "It's kind of an out-of-the-past thing, like meeting up with the warden when you're out on parole. It makes you nervous. Sleeping dogs, you know?"

"You believe you were a prisoner of Holy Mother Church?" he said.

"Not me," Del said, showing both palms. "I love all that stuff—the incense and genuflecting, that big monstrance. I remember that monstrance best of all. Altar boys eating hosts before they were consecrated, serving Mass—I liked that so much I used to practice at home, holding my hands that way, up and open like you do when you're reading the prayers, keeping those special fingers together, the thumb and second, right? Or first? I even liked going to confession. You and Father Pooch. You could murder somebody and he'd give you seven Our Fathers and seven Hail Marys."

"Harold Pooch," Marco said, smiling. "Father Pooch. He was the pastor of pastors."

"I didn't care for him," Del said.

"Maybe today isn't such a great time," Marco said. "Maybe we just want to get reacquainted today, but down the road we'll want to sit down together. Talk things out."

"What are we going to talk out?" Del said. "I don't mean to be impolite; I'm just puzzled about it."

"Business," Marco said. "How we can make out with it, what we could do if we put our minds to it. That sort of thing. Maybe I can help you with this other business, with Bud—that's a possibility. We don't have to talk it out if you don't want to, but it seems to me that the opportunity is there, and it's ripe, and it might be a good idea for us to stick together, all three of us. You, me, Bud. Old Texas boys."

"I thought you were from Chicago," Del said.

"I *was* from Chicago," Marco said. "But then I moved to Texas when I was a priest, and after I was a priest, when I got married."

"Who did you marry, again?"

"That's one of the things I thought I'd tell you today," he said. "You remember Sandra Romano? You remember her?"

"Uh, maybe. Yes. She was in my eighth-grade class, and we used to have parties at her house," Del said. "That's what I remember. You married Sandra Romano?"

"It was years later, when she was grown up. She wasn't in the eighth grade when I married her."

"Thank the Lord for that," Jen said from the kitchen.

"What grade was she in?" Del said.

"She was almost out of high school when we started seeing each other," he said.

"When did you marry her?" Del said.

"A few years after that," he said.

"Wait," Del said. "You were seeing her in high school? When she and I were in high school?"

"Yes. Sort of privately," he said.

"Jesus Christ," Del said.

"Yeah, I know. It was bad," Marco said.

"So when did you leave the priesthood?" Del said.

"After that," he said. "We quit seeing each other, and I tried it again as a priest while she went off to college. But of course it didn't work at all. We tried to do better, but we couldn't, so then Sandra and I got back together."

"So she moved here with you?" Del said.

"We haven't actually moved yet," he said. "We're just thinking about moving. We're planning on moving. We came over to check it out. We're in Beaumont now. I'm at the library there."

"Good town," Del said, rattling the Coke left in Marco's can. "You want another one of these?"

Marco shook his head. "Sandra told me all about the two of you, so you shouldn't worry about that. In fact, what attracted me to her in the first place was her—you know, her inclinations."

"Uh-huh," Del said. "Right. Sure. I just remember she was real nice. And a smart girl, wasn't she? Good scores and the rest of that?"

"Excellent scores," Marco said, nodding.

Del nodded too, and the conversation seemed to stop right there. Jen came out of the kitchen and dodged into the bedroom so she could get dressed, and after Del and Marco had been quiet for a minute, Marco said, "I guess I'd better be going. I just wanted to drop by. Let me give you my card here."

"You don't want to stay for lunch?" Jen said from the bedroom. "We're having peanut butter. Del's on a peanut butter sandwich diet. It really works, but it limits what we can have in the house."

"We've got a few other things," Del said. "Not much, maybe, but—"

"I'd like to, but I can't," Marco said. "I've got to pick up Sandra. I left her over at the mall."

"She's about my age now?" Del said.

"She's early forties," he said.

"And you're what, fifty? Fifty-five?"

"A shade over that, actually," Marco said.

Del got up and followed Marco to the door. "I'm not holding that against you, Marco," he said, patting the ex-priest on the back.

The business card had his name printed on it. That was all. Under that he'd hand-written a local number.

DEL CALLED BUD. "You gave this guy my address? Are you crazy? Jesus, I'm sending him to your house."

"I thought maybe you needed to go to confession," Bud said. "Get some absolution, get some penance. He came over there?"

"Yes. He told me he married Sandra Romano. We're lucky, though. They haven't moved here yet."

"Don't give him my address. I can't see him. There's nothing I hate worse than a fallen priest. He's probably got a lot of opinions about things now—about the church, about religion, about God, about the way things are. He's the last thing I want to see. Is he gay?"

"I don't know. He married Sandra Romano," Del said.

"Oh, right," Bud said. "I guess that's a strong signal. Who's she?"

"She went to St. Anthony's. She was in my class. She was one of the little girls in the little plaid uniforms," Del said. "She was one of my girlfriends."

"No shit? He married her?" Bud said.

"He married her later," Del said.

"What's he doing here?" Bud said.

"He says he's going to get in on the gambling. He wants you to get involved," Del said. "I told him you were hot to trot."

"I don't want to see him," Bud said.

"Oh, and he's going to help out with our troubles too. The ones you told him about. I opened the door and there he was, wearing this see-through shirt."

"I didn't tell him that much," Bud said. "Whatever I said just slipped out. I wasn't thinking clearly."

"That puts you and him on the same wavelength, pretty much," Del said.

19

JEN AND DEL went to the fishing rodeo because Jen wanted to get some close-up pictures of dead fish and scan them with the new Logitech gray-scale hand scanner she'd just ordered to replace the one Del was using. She was planning to incorporate the pictures into her magazine. Since Del had started working on pictures, she decided that she'd neglected the graphic aspect of her magazine, which was renamed *Warm Digits*. The fishing rodeo was east of Biloxi, across the bridge in Ocean Springs. There was some rain, not much, when they parked in the sand.

A six-foot-six bald policeman with a full brown beard that stopped just short of his cap, a reverse-sideburns effect, told Del to move the car. "We're not parking on the beach, son," the guy said. "We have manners in Ocean Springs."

Del and Jen got back in the car. "I wish I could get a picture of *him*," Jen whispered. "Why don't you go talk to him." She was craning to look out the back window at the policeman, extending the electronic zoom at the same time. "Wait. Don't move. Maybe I can get him from here."

She clicked off a couple of shots.

"Let's just ask him," Del said. "Just walk up and say how freaky he is and could we take a close-up."

"Great idea, wonk," she said. "I'll bet he's a wrestler. We could ask him that: is he a wrestler? That might work."

"Ask him if he's a land mammal."

"He's probably highly educated," Jen said. "It took some education to get that beard on there. Probably an Oxford guy, Mississippi version."

There were a lot of women in halter tops at the fishing rodeo, a lot with their shirts off and wrapped around their butts, knotted in front right about dead center on their zippers. It was a style thing. A lot of fat men were sitting out there drinking beer in dirty jeans and black T-shirts that pried up to show slabs of skin, or tattoo parts, or scars. Most of the scars were a lot better than Del's, which was disappearing since he'd had the stitches taken out.

The fish were terrific-looking, packed on big four-foot trays of ice, some fish six feet long, some oddly shaped, some delicately colored. There was an alligator gar that stretched across two trays, it was so big. There were some big drum, some redfish, snapper, trout, lemon fish, jackfish, squid, yellowtail, flounder, mackerel—Jen got pictures of all of them. Close-ups. Lots of eyes, bloodshot, mostly. Jen said she liked the gar because it had a face like an alligator and a tail like a fish.

Some girl in blue-jean shorts that were ripped up to her panties was dancing on a redwood table, a beer in one hand and a joint in the other. A couple of the big bruiser guys with stomachs the size of cash registers were standing around the table, cheering her on. She had a silly little boom box, and it was screeching out sixties R&B. The panties were pink, lace-edged.

"I wonder what these fish are worth?" Jen said, tugging him away from the girl on the table. "Let's look at these fish again and try to figure out whether they're in your future—want to? Or do you want me to get up there and dance with her? I can do that stuff, you know."

"I know," he said. "You're the best. Especially at hospitals. But for now just tend to the fish."

"I'll do that stuff for you later, if you want me to," she said.

"Deal," Del said.

"I could do some now and some later," she said, unbuttoning the top of her blouse.

"Jen," Del said.

"O.K. I'm sorry. I was just joking, anyway."

They took two folding chairs that were under the corner of the barbecued-shrimp tent and moved them over to where the incoming fish were being laid out. There was a chalkboard at the back of the tent, with a form drawn on it, fish names on the sides, days across the top—this was the last day of the three-day rodeo. In the blanks were the weights of the biggest fish of each type caught so far in the rodeo. These were the fish that were in the ice right there in front of the chalkboard.

"Where's the drum?" he said to Jen. "That giant one must be it, right? That look like forty-three pounds?"

"I think I saw that one on TV last night," she said. "It says the gar is ninety-three." She was snapping pictures of the dancing girl. "You know, if things keep going this well, we're just going to have to start a new life together. Under one roof."

"We just started one this summer," Del said.

"Let's start another one," she said. "Let's reintroduce ourselves to the American people. We could sell bikinis, if you want to. I can teach you how to do that."

"I know that you can," Del said.

"You see the guy over here with the LIVE FAST OR DIE T-shirt? The guy with the other T-shirt tied on top of his head?"

"That's not your boyfriend Itch, is it?"

"No. But I know this guy. They call him Fifty-nine."

"That's his name?" Del said.

"No, that's what they call him. He gets fifty-nine cents on the dollar for this game he runs. He runs it all over the coast. Every fair you ever see, every deal you see in the mall, every parking lot and flea market, Fifty-nine is there running Pop the Boobs."

Fifty-nine was in a booth three tents away. He looked as if he weighed three hundred pounds, although he was only about five feet tall; he was dressed all in black, with a black T-shirt tied on his head. His game was a T-shirt on the wall with two balloons inside where breasts might be. You got two darts to try to pop the balloons. If you got them both, you got a prize. It cost a dollar a dart.

"Where's the forty-one cents go?" he asked Jen.

"He's got a partner," she said. "The guy who put up the money to start with. Plus he's got overhead—T-shirts, prizes, darts, balloons. He's got that little booth thing he's got to cart around. I never slept with him, I promise you that."

He looked at Jen as if she were crazy. "I didn't think you had. Why would you?"

"That carny thing, you know? When you're out here, you do strange things," she said. "Things come up. You don't know why you do them, you just do. They seem like good ideas at the time."

"This guy never seemed like a good idea," Del said.

"Right. Right," she said. "Charlie Manson seemed like a better idea than this guy. I knew this chick once, a runaway from Florida. She was fucking gorgeous. She slept with him. She was his girlfriend for a while, a month. He broke her wrist, then her jaw. After that she got out of town. I don't know where she went. People just float away, you know? She was a real good friend of mine for two months. Her name was Linda

Linda. That's what she called herself, Linda Linda. She was out of time somehow; she thought it was Haight-Ashbury in the sixties, or maybe she just bought the revival bullshit."

Del took the camera from her and looked through the view-finder, sweeping left to right across the rodeo. He had the zoom out at 135 millimeters. "Do you know anybody else here?" Del said. He took a few pictures of the crowd—fat guys, guys manhandling fish, guys running booths, guys selling foot-long sausages on sticks. "Do you know the rest of these people?"

That made her mad. "No, I don't know the rest of them," she said. "I know this one guy. Isn't that enough?"

"I thought you were saying that these were the people you used to hang out with," Del said. "Did you look around? Maybe you know some of them."

"I looked," she said. "That was the first thing I did. I was scared of coming here, and then I looked around and I only saw this one guy I recognized and I told you about him and now let's forget it, O.K.? That was another life. I've forgotten that. I don't want to look anymore. I want to get married and have your baby." She drew a baby in the sand with her toe. It was amazing how good a baby she could draw with her toe, just whip it out with a couple of quick curves, and bang! there was a baby there in the sand. "No, never mind," she said. "That was just a joke."

The water in the Gulf seemed kind of smoky, especially out toward Dog Island. It was always dark green, army green, mostly opaque. But when the weather was right, when the wind was blowing southwest, the water cleared up but stayed this dark-green color. There was mist coming up off the water out by the island. A pair of shrimpers went by in the deep-water channel, and then some guy was trying to water-ski in the middle of everything. Sailboats puttered by, with their sails carefully wrapped in sailboat blue.

"I like this dirty water," he said. "It's better than all that crystal-clean water they've got over in Florida."

"Yeah. All those sugar-sand beaches," she said.

"Father Marco D'Lo could do the ceremony," Del said. "If we get married."

"He's not going to be a fixture in our new life, is he? Why was he dressed like that?"

"It happens when you're a priest. You kind of lose touch with reality. Then, when you try to get back in touch with reality, the closest you can come is what's on TV. Or what *was* on TV when you last watched it. It's a hard job leaving the priesthood. It's kind of like beaming yourself up."

"How do you know that?" she said.

"I'm guessing," Del said, fiddling with the camera lens.

"You people never quite get away, do you? Look at you, still praying all the time, getting on your knees when you think nobody's looking, sneaking around saying Hail Marys and Our Fathers."

"I love that stuff," Del said. "It reminds me of what things were like. Besides, you never know. It was better then."

"That's the saddest thing I've ever heard," she said.

"Well, then, it's a good deal we're starting a whole new life, isn't it? There won't be any sad men in our new life." He zoomed in on the dancing girl's panties, but the girl kept jumping out of the frame.

"You know," Jen said, "this whole thing with you and Margaret?"

"That was a one-time thing," Del said.

"Still," she said. "Don't you think we should discuss it? Talk about it, go over it in detail? Really work it out? Isn't that what we're supposed to do? I'm supposed to feel something about her, right? I'm the girlfriend, and you were sleeping with her, or whatever. I don't have the whole story."

"You do," he said. "You do."

"I'm supposed to feel something about that. Maybe it's supposed to excite me. Is that what it's supposed to do? I can't quite get a bead on what it's supposed to do. Maybe I need some help on this from, like, an older man, like you."

"You're ready to go, is that what you're saying?" Del said. "Put an end to this panty situation over here?"

"Look at that," she said. "You get smarter when you get older, don't you?"

20

AT TWO IN THE MORNING Del was wondering how Karen looked sleeping in whatever bed she was sleeping in, off in Oregon or wherever, and thinking about Jen, who was asleep in his bed inside, and about Margaret and the mess they'd gotten into—she'd told him in a phone call that evening that she and Bud hadn't "quite got back on track since the summer." He was on the balcony, and the Gulf was like standing water, and what struck him was that romance wasn't a movie, the music never swells, the sun does not sink, the lone saxophone isn't around the corner. He was middle-aged, with a young woman who probably wasn't going to stay around in his bed and a dime-store job at Audio Instincts. He could quit or not; it didn't matter. He had no reason to do it either way, other than to keep them in sandwiches. He could get back into PR in Biloxi, maybe start a little company, or he might just as well be a flounder man. None of it mattered much; it was downhill, dripping away from the center: things were getting stranger.

There were blinking lights out over the dark water, and there was an almost-full moon, so that the sky at the horizon was lighter than the water. A shooting star shot by. A helicopter came into view on the western horizon, moved slowly across his field of vision until he could just begin to hear the thucking of its blades. It was like the movies, or it would have been if he'd been a CIA man, a private eye, an architect with some very nasty habits, a boxer, a newspaper guy with just a piece of the story. Then the helicopter spun around and shot its lights directly toward shore, toward where he was sitting, kept them trained there for nearly a minute without moving, then turned again and headed back the way it had come. He liked that, the way it seemed mysterious, no matter what it really was.

Jen was good for him. Quick and easy, she had ideas of her own, even if they were a little frayed around the edges. She had things she wanted. Not big things, not things to change the world—they were intimate, personal things. That fit his construction. She wanted to go to the store and put up posters about someone's thumb discovered in a pond, or some cabbie who discovered a box of human heads, or forty kittens that vanished in Carrington, New Jersey, because somebody liked to put them one by one in gallon-size Ziploc heavy-duty freezer bags. Small things that asserted her Jen-ness, that drew attention to her particular brand of news. He liked her because she was light on her feet, because she wore her skin as if it fit—satiny, unmarked, pale. And she was young and sexy, and so made him enviable when they went down the street together, when they walked through the mall, when they stood on the beach, when they sat together at a restaurant. That produced a feeling of power, inescapably, and if he wasn't proud of the exchange, he wasn't unwilling to accept it, either.

It was pleasure to be with her, to look at her, to talk to her, to wonder what she was thinking or what would come out next. Surprise was part of her draw; it had been a while since surprise was a factor in his relationships. He'd spent years with Karen, who was his age, and they lost their fresh-

ness together, and now he was using Jen to refresh himself, to
make up for things he couldn't see new because he'd already
seen them, to make tired questions interesting again. Jen made
age less a terminal disease, more an accident. And it wasn't
just her generation—she was a soldier in no army, bought no
belief system but her own. She was as disconnected in her way
as he was in his.

A green light at the edge of a rock jetty blinked in a steady
two-step. This was a lovely little light, frail and unfocused,
like something alive. It was there to keep people from smacking into the rocks, but from a distance it was more beautiful
than it could have been effective. Two hot-rodders went by on
Highway 90, their exhausts cranked up to thunder. One was
a black Chevrolet, about 1958. He leaned up to the rail, trying
to catch a glimpse of the strange little taillights that he remembered from hot rod magazines. His mother owned a later
model Chevrolet, blue, that he had somehow persuaded his
father to buy with certain performance-enhancing options.
How he had persuaded his father, what argument he had used,
he could not now imagine, but the reason he wanted it was to
race against his high school friends, which he had done, win-
ning more often than not. He didn't kill anybody, either,
though he'd come close once.

A small boat with a spotlight on it rode out through the
channel in front of Dog Island, out toward the jetty light. Another boat with a spotlight was two hundred yards behind the
first. He wondered if that's what he'd do if he were a
fisherman—rock out on a little boat in the middle of the night
and catch something he could sell to somebody. He wondered
if that would be more fun than selling stereo equipment, but
decided it would be harder, and less profitable. But then, as
the boats passed the green blinking light and turned out away
from him, heading southeast, shining spots into the water
ahead of them, he wondered if it wouldn't be more satisfying.

The moon was so bright on the still water that the Gulf seemed like a vast glassy rock, flat and untouched, with these two boat silhouettes inching along the horizon right on the top.

Jen came to the balcony door and stuck her head out. "What're you doing out here?" she said.

"I'm keeping an eye on our property," Del said, waving out at the Gulf.

"What do you see out there?" she said.

"The usual," Del said. "Do you want to come out and sit down? Are you dressed?"

"No, but I don't see how that matters," she said. She came a little way out onto the balcony, pulled a chair half through the open door so its back legs were inside. She sat in that chair and they watched car lights crawl down the highway.

After a few minutes Del said, "I'm glad you're here with me. I'm glad we're together."

"Me too," she said. "This condo is much better than the van I was living in."

He couldn't tell if that was a joke or if she meant him to take it straight.

Then she said, "Joke."

"How'd you know what I was thinking?"

"Well, you're almost fifty, and when you're fifty you don't have many things to think. You pretty much think the same thing over and over again, don't you? I learned that from my father."

"Gee, thanks," Del said. "You're a sweetheart, you're a pal, you're the one. You take the dark out of the nighttime."

"Moody Blues," she said.

"I don't think so," Del said.

"They were dead before I was born, anyway," she said. "Whoever it was."

"You couldn't sleep?"

"I didn't want to. I was thinking of what you were doing out here. I was wondering about you and this priest guy. I don't know about this priest."

"Priests bother you?" Del said.

"They don't make me feel good. I don't want to fall down and whisper every dirty thought I ever had."

"That'd take too long," Del said. "But without confession you don't get the bliss of contrition, the bliss of absolution, the bliss of acknowledged guilt."

"What if I go to confession to you, right here, right now?" she said. "I'll get on my knees and you can give me that sign of the cross thing, and then I'll tell you all the terrible things I've done. We could do that right here on the balcony. It'll be great. I'll tell you everything." She inched out of her chair and knelt down on the wood slats of the balcony, pressing up against the glass so she wouldn't be scared. "What am I supposed to say?" she said.

"You're supposed to get up."

"No, tell me what I say," she said. "Bless me something."

"Bless me, Father, for I have sinned," Del said.

"O.K. Bless me, Father, for I have sinned. Here's my list of sins—you ready?"

"That's enough," Del said, sighing, tugging on her arm trying to get her up.

"Don't yank on my arm," she said. "You'll tump me over the rail."

"I don't want to hear any more," he said.

"Guys always want more," she said. "It's just we're not in the kitchen or in bed after we've screwed for four hours. We're doing the balcony scene. We're doing it like in church when you were a kid."

In moonlight the vertical steel rods in the balustrade cast

shadows across her T-shirt, across her bare legs. Del put his arm around her and let his hand slip down her back over her bare butt.

"Bless me, Father, for I have sinned," she said again. "I have fucked a lot of people. I lost count ages ago. I counted the first forty, and then I stopped counting." She hesitated a second, then went on. "O.K., that's a lie. I didn't really stop counting; I just forgot to count some, and then it didn't seem important to count the rest of them, and I assumed a few that I didn't actually remember, and then the number started seeming outrageous for a person my age, and then I just quit."

"Forty's not so many," Del said.

"How many have you fucked?" she said.

"Not that many," Del said.

"Come on, let's get specific," she said.

"Who remembers?" Del said.

"Yeah, sure. Wanker. See, I came up in the Me Generation," she said. "We were encouraged to fuck a lot of people, so that's what we did, that's what we were supposed to do."

"Get up off your knees, will you?" Del said.

"I just started my confessional," she said.

"Get back in your chair," Del said.

"I really loved my parents," she said, "but I never told them. I acted like I hated them. God knows why I did that— that was a sin. I acted like they bored me. They did bore me, sort of, but I didn't have to act that way. They were kind of goofy; maybe they were nice. They still are. But I wasn't a good daughter. I ran away, and made fun of them, and said stuff just to piss them off."

"I don't think you're the Me Generation," Del said. "You're too young for the Me Generation."

"So what generation am I?" she said.

"I don't know what they call the generation after the Me Generation," Del said.

"When was the Me Generation?" she said.

"I forget," Del said. "But you're too young."

"I saw some photographs of my mother and father naked," she said. "That was a sin. I saw my father's erection. Once I went by their door while they were screwing, and my mother was talking to him about the big forest, and about the big tree in the big forest."

"This is too disgusting," Del said. "I've had enough. I'm going to jump." He stood up and pretended to start going for the rail.

"Quit!" she screamed, pressing herself back into the glass. "Don't even play about that. Jesus."

"Sorry," he said.

She motioned him back into his chair. "So one night I went through my mother's closet, and way up at the top was a shoe box, just like always, and there were photographs, Polaroids. My mother in red high heels. My mother touching her pubic hair. My mother offering her breasts. And this one photo of my father taken from the foot of the bed, up between his legs, his penis in full flight, his testicles tight and round like a small fleshy wrinkled thing. He leaned his head up to look at the camera, and he had this stupid smile on his face. He looked like a pathetic jerk. I don't know how my mother ever screwed him if he looked like that."

Jen was off her knees, sitting on the deck with her legs stretched out toward the railing, her back against the glass. "They're dead," she said. "That's why I feel bad. They died in air crashes, both of them. Two different air crashes." She shook her head, staring at the moon. "That's a lie," she said.

"God, I'd never have known," Del said.

"You should see this place where they live. I told you Baton Rouge, right? But it's this place somebody just built over there, kind of a Stepford World, all the houses with these real nice paint jobs, real careful contrasting paint on the trim, and the colors are all slightly off, like the greens aren't really green but more like blue-green, and the pinks veer toward salmon. I guess they're pretty colors, but in a brutally tasteful way. And all the lawns are manicured, and all the hedges are cut real carefully into boxes, and balls, and a couple into tasteful small animals—what do you call that? I don't remember, and it doesn't matter. This place is sort of a retirement community, I guess. They've got a lot of house hygiene people working for them, the people who run the subdivision do, so there are always people out scrubbing the fences, combing the roofs, straightening the mailboxes. It's like all of these houses have bibs. My mother and father really like it there, and I don't blame them. They say it's real clean. They say they don't have to worry about a thing. There aren't any African-American people who live there, there aren't any Mexican people or any Asian people, there's nobody there outside their own personal socioeconomic group, no strange religions are allowed, no hot rods, no unwashed anything—it's a golf place, you know?"

"Sounds great," Del said.

"You wouldn't think that if you were there," she said. "It's the kind of place where you only have to print the newspaper once, because nothing ever happens. Everything is cookie-cuttered. In the police report section of the newspaper they say things like 'A male subject was wearing a black hat with a silver brim at Charter Foods yesterday.' Or 'A pumpkin was maliciously placed in a mailbox on Booth Avenue.' That's my favorite."

"Empty World," Del said. "Let's go tonight. Can we stay with them?"

"They'd hate you. Besides, you're as old as they are."

"That's where we're headed, don't you know? You and me. Bud and Margaret. All of us, even Father D'Lo."

"Oh, God. Father D'Lo," she said. "You actually told that guy stuff you did when you were a kid?"

"Yeah, sure," Del said.

"Did you tell him you masturbated and stuff like that?" she said.

"Sure," Del said.

"What else did you tell him?" she said. "Did you tell him you screwed somebody? Did you screw this woman he married?"

"Yes," Del said. "I think so."

"What do you mean, you think so?" she said.

"I don't remember," Del said.

"That's hard to believe," she said.

"It's true," Del said. "I know we fooled around, but I don't remember what we did."

"You could probably remember if you tried hard enough, couldn't you? But it's probably better not to, now that I think about it," she said. "He had the look of a man who'd be coming back."

At the horizon there was a string of very pale, very tiny, shadowy yellow lights. "Those are fishing boats?" he said.

"You're changing the subject," she said.

The lights seemed tall and thin, the way their reflections shined in the water and the sky. Each flickered like a tiny star. But they didn't change color the way starlight does on a clear night. They just sat on the horizon.

"What do you suppose those people are doing out there?" he said, trying to imagine what it would be like to be out that far at that time of night, surrounded by dark water and sky, only moonlight and running lights to see by.

"Screwing," Jen said. "And drinking."

"Probably families," he said. "Fathers and sons, brothers, drinking buddies. I wonder what it smells like out there."

"Briny," she said, yawning.

"I'm not much of a seafarer," he said.

"You're not much of a landfarer," she said. "But I still love you."

"Thanks," Del said.

She reached up and ran her hand over his leg. "Do you want to, like, fuck or anything?" she said.

"I don't know," Del said.

"Yeah, neither do I," she said. "I've had my sex for the year. Let's forget it. You want to watch TV? You want a sandwich? You want to play Crazy Eights?"

21

DEL MET BUD at the Faculty Club for a beer on Friday afternoon, the weekly high season for faculty who frequented the place the better to mimic the workingman. Del didn't want to go but figured he had to because Bud wanted to talk about the college, about Del's future there.

When he delivered the invitation Bud had said, "There's something fundamentally wrong with you being in the stereo business. It lacks something."

"What would that be?" Del asked. "A future? Dignity?"

"Neither of those," Bud said. "The future's just another word for nothing left to lose, and dignity these days is Billy C. biting his lip—parody."

"Maybe it just changed its shape," Del said.

"Think pregnancy problems," Bud said. "Or burst condoms, or people seeking the best of everything by looking it up in books. If you have to look it up— Well, you get the idea."

"O.K., so I'm not missing much," Del said.

"No. When I'm talking about teaching, I'm not talking about a big step up. You face a class of hot-water bottles and you look the other way while they slip through college, something they don't want to do but think they'd better. They wouldn't get through without you and thousands like you averting your eyes. They want the degree so they can get the easier jobs and easier money, so they can buy the expensive gas grills, go to more ball games, burp and fart through their dwarfy lives trying to get horny, trying to fuck each other's wives and daughters."

"Gosh, you make it sound so great," Del said. "Makes me want to rush right over."

"You did already," Bud said.

THE FACULTY CLUB was an old house the school had received from some poor woman who couldn't quite figure out what was going on when she was on her deathbed, so she turned her home over to the professor who'd been assigned to be sweet to her. He'd done marvelous work.

It was a good house, in the fifties way. When the school took it over, they refurbished. They waxed the wood-veneer floors, shampooed the shag carpets, shined the paneling, installed a rollaway bar on the porch, and converted the bedrooms to meeting rooms. This was done by the addition of brown metal folding tables with laundered white tablecloths, and a supply of brown metal folding chairs with padded brown seats. Cardboard nameplates were put on the hollow-core doors to the rooms—The Jasmine Room, The Hibiscus Room, The Peony Room. Art students had been engaged to rub down Letraset type on the pebbleboard nameplates and then to rubber-cement the cardboard to the doors. They did it very tastefully, dark-blue type on cream-colored board. Fancier rooms had hand-applied black-ink borders around their names.

Bud was in the Hibiscus Room when Del got there, talking to a stringy guy with skin that looked as if it had been dealt through a grinder once or twice. It had the look of hammered veal. Bud introduced this guy as Fauntleroy Trophy. Del shook his hand; the guy smiled and made a pun about stereos, something about giving Del a hi-fi.

"So, Fauntleroy, what is it you teach here?" Del said.

"I teach these children to dance on the heads of pins," Fauntleroy said, waving his glass. "I teach them the fandango, a lively Spanish-American jig in triple time, performed by a man and a woman exercising castanets."

"Fauntleroy's in black-hole science," Bud said.

"No kidding?" Del said.

"You got it. You said it," Fauntleroy Trophy said. "The blacker the hole, the more scientific I get."

"So how are you fixed for loudspeakers?" Del said.

"That's my brother," Bud said. "Always working, always toughing it out. Always selling. You want a beer? I'll get you a beer." Bud waved at the lovely Vietnamese girl who was waiting tables, a student, probably, picking up four dollars an hour for carrying beer ten feet from the cheesy bar to the toilet-seat-size tables in the Faculty Club. She came over and took the order.

There were a lot of people at the Faculty Club, and they were all having a real good time. They were talking loud and laughing. The Hibiscus Room looked to have been one of the children's rooms, and it was so small that when anybody had an opinion, everybody had it. One real thick guy was talking about the Knicks, the basketball team, arguing with a real short guy who was talking about the Blazers. The only big man in the room seemed to be talking about microcephalic rats with a young girl wearing jean cutoffs and a black tube top with four straps racing over her shoulders. Several of the men had paunches, and the women were defiantly homely. It was not a room for the gifted and distinguished.

"These people aren't as bad as they look," Bud said, after

he'd gotten rid of Fauntleroy Trophy. "They just work too hard at being in the game."

"In teaching, you mean?" Del said.

"No, the culture. In the culture. They want to be part of it, make it. They want to be on *Nightline*. They're dying to answer all Ted's questions."

"So why are they talking about sports?"

Bud gave him a stupid look. "Del, this little room is bursting with dweebs. Weasels. Sports is what they *aren't*. They're trying to de-dweeb."

"I get it," Del said.

"Now, me," Bud said, "I'm sports neutral. But here at college we will talk about anything we can read up on in the newspaper. We get deeply thoughtful hockey men and professors of baseball, and everyone knows his stuff, numbers at the fingertips, opinions honed to a razor's edge. A disproportionate number of us were stats nerds when we were kids."

Del got his beer, and they sat down at one of the tiny tables.

Bud took a drink and shook his head. "But forget all that—here's the deal. I talked to Rudy, and he's willing to give you a visiting lectureship, let you teach a couple of courses next semester, a couple in the summer. Then we'll look at it longer term."

"Is this what I want to do?" Del said.

"You need to try it," Bud said. "You need to enter the world in a solid way. Even when you were working for the mayor over there you were sort of on the edge. There was something half-cooked about it. You were slipping by."

"I was making a living. What's this, your life's work? A divine call?"

"There's something about it that's different. I guess I believe it, finally."

"C'mon, Bud. We both know better than that."

"No, I do," he said. "I don't believe in it *much*, but there's some left. Every once in a while a kid comes along and I think, Maybe I can help this one. So I give it a try, and it works, and that makes the rest of it worth doing. It's a tiny percentage. Two percent. Less. It's very personal—they take me with them, something of me, what I see in the world. It's not about what you teach, the courses. It's about looking, telling somebody what you see, having them get it."

"I know the feeling," Del said. "I get people buying junk equipment to play crap from their glory days. Then somebody comes in and *hears* things. You say a tweeter is cloudy, and he listens. It's different."

"It's like a hobby," Bud said.

"That's right," Del said. "I'm saying I know what you mean, and I don't have to teach at the college to get that."

"It's such a tiny thing," Bud said. "Isn't it a tiny thing? Don't you wish it were less tiny?"

"I do," Del said.

The Vietnamese girl was back to check about refills. Del ordered another beer. Bud was having some kind of mixed drink. She brought a bowl of peanuts. They both went after the peanuts. Across the room Rudy was talking to an administrative type. They were laughing in an ugly way, the two of them. "It's odd how you can tell from how they laugh what kind of people they are," Del said.

Bud turned to see who Del was talking about. "You don't have to see Rudy laugh to get him," Bud said.

Rudy was laughing hawkishly, head jerking up and down, eyes darting around, checking the perimeter, on the lookout.

There was a sliding glass door in one wall of the Hibiscus Room. Outside was the modest and carefully manicured yard. Del thought he saw somebody dodging around out there, some shadow, some person jumping from behind a pile of bricks on the right over to a place behind a bush where there was a big, eight-foot, black-mesh satellite dish. He elbowed Bud and said, "Did you see this?"

"What?" he said.

"There's somebody out there hanging around the satellite dish," Del said.

"No, I didn't see it," Bud said.

"Well, look," Del said. He pointed out the back window, then he tossed peanuts from his hand into his mouth, watching the clearing where the dish was. Then a very fat guy with a beard jumped up onto the dish and spread-eagled himself across it, rocking it.

"What's the deal with him?" Del said.

"That's Igor," Bud said. "Igor's one of my students. A wonderful kid, very funny, very gentle."

"His name is Igor?" Del said.

"Yes, it is," Bud said. "He's one of the ones I was talking about. He's a decent kid. Talented. Maybe he's a sad kid. He loves television and satellite dishes. He loves the sweeping gesture."

"So that's what he's jumping on it for?" Del said.

"I guess. He does that. Sometimes he does it right in the middle of some big TV show to interrupt the reception, shake a fist at the moon. One of those things," Bud said.

"I didn't think anybody had shaken a fist at the moon since 1952," Del said.

"Yeah, yeah, sure," Bud said. "Like you haven't."

"I didn't call it that, anyway," Del said.

"That's what I'm saying," Bud said. "There's plenty of reason for doing it out there. I mean, you read *USA Today,* don't you?"

"Sure," Del said. "I look at it."

"And you think it's O.K.?"

"What, to look at *USA Today?*"

"No, I mean everything's wrong and *USA Today* partici-pates, takes part in it. Encourages it, in a way. People who are supposed to be removed from what's going on, well, they're all part of it now. Everything that could possibly go wrong has al-ready gone wrong, and now it's going wrong even more."

"I don't know. I feel all right. I'm O.K."

"I'm not talking about you, Del. I'm talking about every-thing else. There was a time when Peter Jennings didn't seem like a noxious, self-righteous, stupidly biased, holier-than-thou, moderate prick. When he was just a reporter."

"Oh," Del said. "*That's* what you mean. Right. That's about my view."

"And you're going to live with that?" he said.

"What do you want me to do, hang myself with my belt in some hotel room in Florida?" Del said.

"Wait a minute," Bud said, squinting, as if trying to place the reference.

"It was that Band guy. I forget his name," Del said.

"It was Donald Droll or Roy Leaf," Bud said. "O.K., it wasn't. Anyway, we've got to do something. Margaret wants you to come teach at the school. Margaret has a special feeling about you."

Just at that moment the Vietnamese girl arrived with their drinks, so Del had some time, while he took a swallow of his and Bud took a drink of his, to look at Bud carefully to see if there was anything other than what was apparent in this re-mark about Margaret.

"Yeah, well, what do you want me to teach?" he said. "What can I teach? Introduction to Communications?"

"Yep," Bud said. "That would be for now, but later maybe you could go anywhere. Who knows what you could teach. It's such a small dump, we teach across all lines. No experience necessary."

"Maybe I could try it. Maybe try it and stay at Audio Instincts part time."

"I thought you were quitting," Bud said.

"I'm always quitting. I quit and then I unquit. I need the money."

"I thought you had money stashed away."

"I have some," Del said. "Not enough."

"The condo was a piece of luck."

"Yes, it was."

"This is a stupid little school," Bud said. "You know that. Still, I'd rather have you there with us than not. Unless you've got something better."

"I've been thinking about starting a desktop publishing business with Jen," Del said.

"You need to have some people around you, some people to bump into now and again."

"I bump into Jen."

"I like Jen," Bud said, finishing his drink. "Anyway, teaching's O.K. After a while you develop an amazing capacity for diddling around. For days at a time I diddle. Teaching has done that for me."

"And you love diddling," Del said.

"Yeah," he said. "But you know."

"Teaching's not bad either, right?"

"Right." He waved for another drink. "The neighbors, the ones who got the kid Bobo and everybody thought it was going to work out? Remember? Hilary? Right now Bobo looks like a mistake. They put him back in the state school," Bud said. "They didn't want to do that, but that's what it came to. The doctors said. Finally Hilary figured there was nothing to do but believe them."

"Do they go see him?" Del said.

"Yeah," Bud said. "Hilary used to, anyway. She went out every week, sometimes twice a week. Apparently Bobo doesn't quite know who she is anymore. He just had a little burst of lucidity when they first brought him, and then it went away. Living in that pipe, whatever it was, had its effect."

"They never found his parents?" Del said.

"No," Bud said. "Somebody claimed him. A woman, I think. Bobo started cutting on himself with a knife, finally. He had cuts in his arms, on the backs of his hands, some on his ankles. That was it. He wasn't too fond of himself. In a way, being with the Jakeses made him less fond of himself. He wouldn't talk after a while. He would talk to Margaret across the fence, but he wouldn't talk to them."

Fauntleroy Trophy came to their table and squeezed in on the tufted bench beside Bud. "So what are you two guys talking about?" he said.

"Adoption," Del said.

Fauntleroy gave him a funny look. "What about it?" he said. "What are you saying about it?"

"We were saying it's a hard thing," Del said.

"I'll bet," he said. Then he started talking about the college baseball team. The Quail, they were called. He made a lot of quail jokes. He talked about the Quail pitching, about some kid they'd gotten from a local high school all-star team who was bound to go to the "show" after his sophomore year, after his junior year for sure. According to Trophy, he just needed another pitch, this kid. He and Bud talked about what pitch it should be.

Del tuned it out and watched a short woman with straight blond hair and a "hurt me" look on her face. She couldn't decide whether she wanted to be a plain tart or a daring new-wave tart, or what the difference was, so she missed both by half a mile. She had the tiny miniskirt and the Crosley pumps, and she was the center of some controversy over by the television set, which was tuned to a basketball game. Not a local game, a pro game, with two teams whose uniforms Del didn't recognize. She was pretending to box with this skinny guy who was pretending to be some old-time boxer, some Marquis of Queensberry rules boxer, a gentleman boxer: arms extended, hands curled upward into fists. When they finished that, he put his arm around her and she put her arm around him, and Del watched her squeeze his butt. She squeezed it, then rubbed it, then patted it, then squeezed it again. Then she rubbed it and patted it, and then she squeezed it again, then she poked it and rubbed it and patted it. Then she traced its curve with her palm. When she had done all that, she let her hand come to rest softly around this guy's ass, like a constant, ongoing, motionless caress.

Del nodded at this, chuckling a little, and, when Bud looked at him, jerked his eyes at the two in the corner.

Bud said, "They're ours. They're the newest additions to our faculty," he said. "They come from different corners of the country, and they're already in love."

WALKING ACROSS the deep gravel in the Faculty Club parking lot, Del had his arm over Bud's shoulders. Bud said, "I just want you to think about it. It's not that bad, and besides, I'm lonely out there. I need somebody like you around to keep me straight, to keep my eye on the ball. I need your help."

"You've never needed my help," Del said.

"If I haven't, I do now. And if I don't, I'd like to," Bud said. "Right now I've got Rudy to deal with, Trophy here, and the Love Gobs—who have I got?"

"Mr. Marco D'Lo," Del said. "Don't leave him out."

"You," Bud said.

"Maybe if I had a project," Del said. "I could write down every thought that runs through my mind, maybe make up a few extra thoughts so it looks like more run through than actually do."

"One of my exceedingly competent colleagues has already done that," Bud said. "Published the cadaver with Garland, I believe. One of the very fine do-it-yourself shops. And was advanced to full professor on its strength."

They were standing by Del's car. The air was filled with the scent of field corn, something Del remembered from the farm his aunt and uncle had owned, and there was perfume out there too, drifting along, probably carried by some woman in the club. Crickets roared around, and the moon was haloed by mist, and the street lights were mustard yellow. The weather felt as if it was going to change. His car creaked.

"I'm thinking hard," Del said, shaking his head and patting Bud's shoulder. "I just don't know what to say sometimes."

Then he pulled Bud to him. They held on to each other for a minute, and he could feel the gravel underneath the soles of his feet, feel it right through his shoes, and when Bud stepped back Del felt the pulling away, and they waved at each other from three feet apart, each of them doing the same wave, a little flip with the right hand, waist high, and then Del got into his car and shut the door, stuck the key in the ignition, and cranked the motor. Bud stood still right there, close to the glass.

DEL DID A LONG STINT at the store on Saturday, sold a couple of high-end systems, and a set of expensive five-foot-high junky speakers to a guy who thought they were good because they had a lot of bass. He didn't remind the guy that speakers were the penises of the seventies, that they'd replaced cars back then.

He was exhausted when he went home. He got to the condo a little after ten. It was raining lightly outside, and he was looking forward to putting his feet up and opening the doors out onto the balcony. But when he got upstairs, Jen was there with Father D'Lo.

Del said hello, then excused himself and pulled Jen into the bedroom.

"What's he doing here?" Del said.

"I don't know," she said. "He showed up about a half hour ago. He said he wanted to talk to you."

"Why didn't you tell him to come by the shop?" Del said.

"I did, but he seemed all right. I showed him some of the stories—the box of heads story and a couple of others."

"What's the box of heads story?" Del said.

"You remember. The cabdriver who found the box of heads in New York. Somebody was transporting heads from a hospital to some university lab, a kind of research center, and the car was stolen. The guy stopped to get a pizza, car stolen, thieves started tearing the car apart and found this box of heads, so they split, leaving the box of heads on the sidewalk. The cabbie comes along and finds them."

"Is this a true story?" Del said.

"Of course it is," she said. "It's AP or UPI, one of those. Reuters. Probably Reuters. They seem to have a lot of the gory stuff."

Just then Marco knocked on the bedroom door. "Excuse me," he said, pushing the door open a little bit. They were all standing awkwardly there by the door, between the bed and the door. "Excuse me. I don't mean to butt in, but I think I'll just go ahead and leave now. I just wanted to tell you that I'm heading back in a couple days."

"Heading back where? You don't have to leave if you don't want to," Del said.

"I think it would be better," he said. "I probably shouldn't have come over in the first place. I was just in the area, and I thought we would just talk a little bit. It looks like my gambling plan isn't working. I may start a small business of some kind back in Beaumont."

"What kind?" Del said.

"I don't know. I haven't decided that yet. Just something simple, maybe some kind of service thing. Something everybody needs."

"Therapy's a good idea," Del said. "The world is full of ex-priests making a killing in therapy."

"I don't really want to do that," he said. "I don't want to hear about other people. I heard about other people for years, and I don't want to hear about them anymore. I don't want to hear what they think. I don't want to hear what they feel. I don't want to hear about their hopes and dreams. I don't want to hear their ideas about themselves and about other people and about God knows what else. I don't mind saying hello, shaking their hands, talking about the weather, but that's it."

Del rubbed his face. "Does he remind you of my brother Bud?" he said to Jen, pointing at Father D'Lo.

"Look, I'll just go on and, you know, maybe we'll get together for dinner some other time."

"He wants us to introduce him to some women," Jen said. She looked at Marco, and Marco looked at the floor. "That's what he told me before you got home. Didn't you tell me that, Marco?"

"Something like that," he said.

"His thing with Sandra is kind of on the fritz," Jen said.

"We aren't actually married," Marco said. "We talked about getting married, talked about it a lot, but we never did it. I was always a day late."

"You're not married to Sandra Romano?" Del said. "Is she here or not?"

"She was," he said. "She was here until a couple days ago, and then she left."

"We could set him up with Mimi," Jen said. "You remember Mimi?"

"Wait a minute," Del said. He looked from Jen to Marco and back. "Mimi. She had a lot of opinions, didn't she?"

"You mean you think she had more than were absolutely necessary?"

"I don't mind a woman with opinions," Marco said. "I can work around them."

"You don't understand: this woman has *opinions*. You see?" Del said.

"I didn't think she was that bad," Jen said. "Del thinks everybody has too many opinions. He thinks it's a kind of disease, a kind of cultural thing. He gets it from Bud. He thinks people watch TV and then ape it, as if they know what they're talking about. Or they read *The New York Times* or *Newsweek* or *Sports Illustrated* or *The Nation*. He reads 'em too, of course, but for some reason his opinions are his own."

"It's not just that," Del said. "Mimi is Rudy's girlfriend, isn't she?"

"Rudy and Mimi broke up right after Alabama."

"Oh, yeah?" Del said. "Why? How do you know that?"

"Margaret," Jen said, giving him a look like it was obvious.

"She sounds interesting to me," Marco said.

"I'm beginning to think a bucket of peanut butter would sound interesting to you," Del said.

"Oh, Del," Jen said.

"What would you think about an alternative newspaper published right here on the coast?" Marco said. "Something like *The Village Voice* or the *Berkeley Barb*? I hear you're interested in desktop publishing."

"I think that's about the worst idea I ever heard in my entire life," Del said.

"Yeah, you're right," Marco said. He looked at the ceiling

thoughtfully. Then he said, "Things aren't going so well for us, are they?"

"I've already called Margaret," Jen said. "About Mimi."

"So why bring it up? Congrats to all. Good luck." Del was tired. He put his hands over his face, wishing Marco would disappear. Then he said, "Are you a priest or not a priest? Are you really out, or are you just saying that?"

"I'm out in a manner of speaking," Marco said.

"What manner is that?"

"It's kind of a temporary trial furlough arrangement," he said. "Something new. Been out three months."

"Why didn't you just say that in the first place?" Del asked.

Marco sighed. "I wanted to see what it was like to see people—if they, you know, thought I was just a regular person. It was a bad idea. I'd better go." He left the bedroom, and Del followed him out.

"You know," Jen said, trailing after them, "first you said you didn't want to hear what people thought, and then you said that you liked a woman with opinions. You recognize that's a contradiction?"

"I thought about that," he said. "I thought about it when I said I liked a woman with opinions. The only thing I can figure out is that I was lying. I wasn't intentionally lying, but I was just saying what I was supposed to say. A problem of vocation. That's what we do, you know. That's what I do, anyway. I'm in a conversation and somebody says something and I don't actually pay attention; I try to figure what I'm supposed to say. Then I say that. It's very strange. I end up saying stuff I have no idea about whatsoever."

"Thanks for coming by," Del said, steering Marco out of the bedroom and toward the front door. "Give us a call. Keep us posted."

"Right," he said. "Maybe I'll get with Jen about Mimi—that O.K.?"

"That's great," Jen said.

At the door he shook Del's hand and stood out on the corridor-like balcony that fed all the condos at Tropic Breeze. He said, "I envy all the guys who stayed in. When you're in there you think there's a whole world out here, a whole range of experiences, a fabulous array of things to do, ideas to have, women to meet. It's all bullshit. You get out, and there's nothing out here."

Del nodded. "So why don't you go back in?" he said. "There's a life for you in there. Do that contemplative business. There's nothing wrong with that."

"Maybe," Marco said. "They'll let me try it if I want to, but sometimes I think it wouldn't be fair to Jesus, because of Sandra and everything. Plus I'd probably get in there and then out here might start looking real sharp again."

22

DEL WALKED ALONG the beach a short distance, seeing a lot of small dead fish. It was midnight, but there was plenty of light from the beach highway, not to mention the moon. A bird nearly four feet tall was hopping along, picking up the fish and swallowing them. Del watched it swallow three. When the bird was getting ready to swallow, it would hold the fish crosswise for a minute, change its grip, suddenly shake its head, and let the fish fall lengthwise into its beak. Then the bird would jack its head back and swallow the fish, which might be eight inches long, in one gulp. The fish would lodge in the bird's throat; he could see the fish outline in the bird's neck.

He had come out for a walk after talking to Jen about joining the faculty at the college. She'd said it wouldn't be so bad, visiting lecturer; he might find it more pleasant than selling stereos, and it would leave him more time. The pay was likely to be bad, but with no mortgage, that wasn't a problem.

A sour-looking woman was sitting at the edge of the sand in a drugstore beach chair, watching a second bird about ten yards away, standing on one foot. She had a flashlight, which she turned on the bird. Its other foot was broken and hung at the end of its leg. Still another bird had a stump. There were a couple of two-footed birds around, kicking up their heels.

Del crossed the sand, light from the street fading as he got farther away. He climbed up on a big rock on the jetty and stood there in near-complete darkness, with whitecaps breaking broadly, water churning on both sides. He high-wire-walked a few more rocks, out into the water. It was hot for October, sticky and overcast. The few stars appeared and disappeared as haze moved across the sky. Half a mile to his right there were lights from a cluster of hotels, and to his left it was closet dark.

The rocks in this jetty were as small as coffee tables and as large as half-refrigerators, piled in a clumsy line that ran a quarter mile into the Gulf. It was darker out on the rocks— he could barely see twenty feet away. He listened to the breakers lap the sand. He didn't want to climb too much; the rocks were wet and sandy, oddly shaped, and sometimes they tipped when he stepped on them. Finally he sat and faced the Gulf, listening to the water, smelling the thick scent of decaying fish and of the stale water that ran under and around the big rocks.

Bud and Margaret worried him. Wasn't Bud likely to blow up one of these days? Del's flirtation with Margaret, which was no more than that by now, and mostly harmless besides, should have been old news, but he wasn't sure that it was. Neither was he sure if he actually thought it should be or only *needed* to think that, but in any case he was certain that Bud had another view. Bud hadn't let it slide, exactly, but he hadn't finished it, he'd kept it alive; it came up in glances and gestures and jokes, in bits of business that went on between them. There were doubts in every double take, every hand over a shoulder or resting on a forearm, every cocked eyebrow. When they tried to talk about it they skittered around it, elaborating the avoidance.

Maybe Bud was trying to do justice to what he felt, and

maybe he felt that if he talked about his brother and his wife he'd be settling for a cartoon, that nothing could do justice to those feelings. Or maybe in the pantheon of Bud's angers and bitternesses, his depressions and distastes, the performance of his wife and his brother together was not such a potent or striking thing.

Suddenly a man in a dive suit, rubbered head to foot, holding flippers, a tank on his back, a spear gun in his hand, was standing twenty feet away at the edge of the water. Del could barely see him against the sand and the little whitecaps. The guy stood facing the water for a long time. He seemed quite large, remarkably large, and he didn't notice Del. The equipment was banging and clanking. The man stepped into the water and got his feet wet, bent over and wet his flippers, backed up and cocked a foot to put a flipper on, then put that foot down and cocked the other. This was all in silhouette, the black suit against the lighter bars of beach and breaker and highway. The diver cut on a flashlight for a few seconds, a narrow bright beam that he kept pointed at the ground. He rinsed his mask, then shut off the light.

It was spooky to think this guy was only twenty feet away and had no idea Del was there, that Del, or the diver, could be that close to the other and go unnoticed.

The diver pulled the mask over his head, then straightened himself, turned around so he was facing the highway, and backed into the surf. Slowly, deliberately, in almost complete darkness, this silhouette dissolved into a slightly less black surface split by white breakers. He backed in until he was knee-high, maybe a little more, then turned, bent forward at the waist and wagged his hand over the water in front of him as if in incantation. He was dodging back and forth. It looked as if he was trying to stare under the water.

Finally, when the diver was a little more than waist deep, he fell forward into the water and flipped on his light, which was bright green under the surf. He did a three-hundred-sixty-degree circle in the water, then swam out along the jetty, dodging this way and that, his light seeming to surround him, brighter in front, duller behind. The light spread out underwater like a fan. Soon the angle of vision was cut so shallow that the diver was just a lozenge of green light in the water.

Del couldn't get over the eeriness of the guy coming out of nowhere, appearing suddenly so close, then vanishing into the surf, a navy frogman out of a World War II spy movie.

WHEN HE GOT BACK to the condo, Bud was there. He and Jen were jumping around in the living room, laughing as Jen tried to show him some Cajun dance steps she'd learned. "It's big in New Orleans," she said to Del. "People go to festivals and do this for hours."

Bud grabbed his beer off the Arvaratum-box coffee table.

"They must be darned healthy," Del said.

"Oh, wait!" Jen said. "Big news! You don't have to worry about Marco D'Lo anymore. He called while you were out there, and he's going back into the priesthood. He said that you persuaded him, that you were right all along."

"I thought he was married to Sandra Romano," Bud said. "Didn't you tell me that? How is he going back in if he's married? Or do they allow that now in the Church?"

"They weren't really really married," Jen said, sighing. "They were just an item, is what he said. In fact, they were having trouble, and we were just getting ready to set him up with some chicks over here. Mimi, maybe."

"Yeah, like he doesn't have enough problems, anyway," Bud said. "I don't remember going to confession to this guy, but I must have. I think he arrived the year before I left for high school. I probably confessed my early conquests, my early

would-be conquests, told him all my dirty thoughts. If only I'd
had the dirty thoughts then that I have now."

"Watch out," Jen said, going into the kitchen for a new
beer. She called back to see if either Bud or Del wanted one.
They both said they did. "Why didn't you bring Margaret
tonight?" Jen asked.

Bud gave Del a slow look, then shook his head. "She's
sleeping," he said. "It's after ten. Margaret always sleeps
after ten."

"Oh, that's not true," Jen said.

"It seems like it," Bud said.

"Bud's feeling his oats," Jen said to Del. "He feels he needs
to get out more, see some people, see some things. He's worried about being too isolated over at the college."

"He is that," Del said. "Of course, he's got Wally, or Bea-
ver, or whatever his name is, to help him out."

"Fauntleroy," Bud said.

"Is he dirt froth or what?" Del said.

"Yeah, I guess he is kind of scummy," Bud said. "But then
who isn't these days?"

"You," Del said. "Me."

"What about me?" Jen said.

"Wait—what is this, the purity of the family?" Bud said.
"Triumph of the beloved? Are we pure?"

"We are pure," Jen said, lifting her fist.

"Your pal screwed my wife," Bud said. "How pure was
that?"

Del shook his head. "No," he said. "Just no."

Bud raised his hands. "O.K. Sorry. So I agree this particular guy isn't a guy I'd want eyeing my daughter."

"You have a daughter?" Jen said.

Del stared at her. "Hey, Jen," he said, waving at her as if
she'd had too much beer and he was trying to get her atten-

tion. "He means this is the last guy he'd want looking over his daughter if he had one. The guy's triple pond scum."

"You'd be surprised what daughters can handle," Jen said. "I've had my father's friends come after me, so I know what I'm talking about. They're easy to deal with, usually. Unless you want them to come after you and they have the morality thing. Jeez, is that a mess. Otherwise you old guys are easy to control." She plopped down onto the sofa and draped her legs over the arm. "That's how I deal with Del mostly, I just control the shit out of him."

"That's great," Del said. "I feel better. I feel deeply under control. You're a take-charge gal, and you've taken charge of me. I like it too. I'll just do whatever you say from here on out, and we'll have a splendid life."

"Deal," Jen said.

AFTER BUD WENT HOME, Del and Jen went into the bathroom together to get ready for bed. Jen wanted to bathe, so Del started the tub. He asked her what she and Bud had talked about while he was out walking.

"Uh, school, the job, some about you and Margaret. They haven't got over it yet, I guess. That's not all that's pissing him off, though. You know how Margaret says he gets upset about the school? Well, that's happening again. He talked about the kid the neighbors tried to adopt, that spooky kid? He misses seeing that kid."

"What about me and Margaret?"

"The same stuff," she said, stepping into the tub. "He doesn't get it. You shouldn't have touched her. She shouldn't have. I can't imagine what made you screw her."

He looked at Jen. Just stared.

"What?" she said.

"I didn't screw her. I almost screwed her."

"Whatever," she said. "Almost. Same difference."

"If it were the same, we'd *all* feel cheated, wouldn't we?"

"Fuck you completely," Jen said. "Don't touch that razor now, O.K.? Not with you feeling so cheated and all."

"I'm feeling lucky that I didn't fuck up all the way. There's some grace in that."

"Maybe he understands," Jen said.

"He said so?"

"No," she said. "But it sort of came up, in a guarded way. We were talking about lying and stuff. I said I didn't think you were lying, either one of you."

"He agree with that?" Del said.

"Yeah, sort of. He said he wants you to stay and teach and all that, be here, and this other stuff is in the way. I don't think he ever thought you were lying. I think he was just protecting himself."

Del was cross-legged on the bath mat, facing the tub. Jen had her feet on the hot and cold water knobs. "Maybe they were better off when I wasn't here," he said.

"He seems crazy about you, for some reason." She twisted her left foot and shot a stream of hot water into the tub.

"I don't know," Del said. "We weren't that close when we were growing up. We got closer later."

"Margaret's younger, right?"

"Than him? Yes. Than me too. By a margin."

"She's lovely," Jen said. "So steady. That's what makes it odd. You wouldn't think of it. To look at her you wouldn't think of it."

"Bud wants to act as if it didn't happen, and then he does his little things, makes these moves, you know, like he did coming back from Alabama, or smacking me up."

"That's just like horsing around, isn't it? A kind of mean play, punishing both of you at the same time? He didn't really try to hurt you, did he?"

"It's hard to say," Del said. "He didn't keep beating on me, so I guess he was under control."

"Psycho brothers," she said. "What is it, some pesky little deal since childhood, driving you insanely into the waiting arms of your brother's wife?"

"If you just think affection, maybe gone a little wild, then it's not crazy at all."

She got up in the tub and took a towel off the rack and started drying her face. "Give me a minute, will you?" she said.

He went into the living room, looked out the window. There were four divers he could see out there, working in twos on different sides of the jetty, their lights either just above or just below the water. Above, the light was a straight, narrow beam, but the water spread the light as soon as the diver went under, so there was a splash of illumination. The color changed too—yellow above, green below.

Jen came up behind him. "Are you going to teach there? Are you going to take the job?"

"Probably," Del said. "You could waste a life there, but I'm probably going to waste it anyway."

"Woe is us," she said. She folded the tissue she was carrying and blew her nose, then said, "Excuse me. I'm having a nasal interlude."

"Bless you," he said. "I don't want to end up thinking nothing is something, and that seems the rule out at the college. They do this dinky stuff and call it groundbreaking; they lie. There should be a reward for trying to stay honest."

"Whoa," she said. "It's Deepman. The Deepman in the window."

"I know," Del said, getting up. "Sorry. But you should have met this guy Trophy. You wouldn't believe it. What a guy. He's here in the middle of nowhere, doing nothing for nobody, knowing nothing and calling it everything. He's here thinking highly of himself. He's utterly lost. He's fly leavings."

"You didn't like him, huh?" Jen said.

"Maybe he's not that bad; I don't know. But if teaching is like when I went to school, it's piss. You need time and intimacy, and they don't allow that at college. Maybe that's O.K.—they're kids, after all. They've got to learn it for themselves. But the teachers believe *they* are the center of things, and that's the worst."

"That hasn't happened to Bud," she said.

"Not yet, maybe, but it could. You never know what's going to happen with Bud. He started off way ahead of the game, so it may not happen. He's got a plenty bad attitude, and that helps. But these are college professors, remember; they have a strong sense of orthodoxy. A guy over there told Bud he was setting a bad example wearing bright-yellow pants. Can you believe that?"

"I can't believe Bud was wearing yellow pants," she said.

"It's like life for robots."

"There's always *Organ Meats*," Jen said. "You could throw in with me on that. I don't believe in big stuff, though. I'm warning you. It's all small for me. Putting stuff on telephone poles, helping people one at a time."

"I thought you changed the name," Del said.

"Went back," she said.

23

RUDY CALLED the following week and formally offered Del the lecturer job for the spring semester. "I don't want you to think of it as a trial," Rudy said. "It is a trial in a way, of course, but I don't want you to think of it like that. You're going to have to make up your mind pretty quick, though, because I have to turn in a schedule."

"I've talked to Bud about this," Del said. "It's his idea, right? He leaned on you?"

"No. Bud never leans on me. It was my idea. I talked to Bud, of course. To see how he felt about it, so maybe it was kind of a joint effort."

"You and Bud?" Del said.

"Stranger things have happened," Rudy said. "But look, if you don't want to do it, just say no. Or if you're not sure, take the job anyway and worry about it later. That's the way we do things down here."

"Kind of easygoing, huh?" Del said.

"Whatever," Rudy said. "Listen, I want you and Jen to come for dinner, and we'll talk it over, go into the details. I got your vita from Bud, of course, so I know the background.

You could come Sunday, and we'll have some steaks or hamburgers—you eat meat, don't you?"

"Yes," Del said.

"So we'll have dinner, the four of us—Sonya and Jen and you and me—and we'll get it settled. How's that?"

"You know that I've never taught," Del said. "I have no reason to think I can do it."

"Yeah, but you worked in the field," Rudy said. "That counts. Most of my bozos couldn't get a job in the washroom out there. And you're Bud's brother—in spite of everything, Bud's pretty good at this. It ain't Harvard, you know. We don't get the fast horses. I have to use my imagination sometimes."

"That's what you're doing?" Del said.

"Yes. Besides, you're available. I need somebody, and you're here," he said. "So I'll see you Sunday?"

RUDY WAS WEARING a striped Polo shirt and real small shorts when Del and Jen got there Sunday night. The shorts were much too small for a guy his size. He met them at the door and showed them into his house, which was cramped and full of bric-a-brac, some of it more elegant than Del had expected—an old daybed, a pair of art prints that had been popular in the seventies, some attractively brown cardboard boxes that were stacked in his living room. He was especially proud of the boxes. "This is my new sculpture," he said, pointing them out. "It's a Duchamp, Don Judd, Robert Morris thing. Maybe it's a little late, but it would have been good in the sixties."

"Looks like an Al Del Greco thing to me," Del said.

"I missed the sixties," Jen said. "Most of them. I guess you two were both alive back then? Probably demonstrating up a storm. Peace and love."

"That's us," Del said.

Rudy introduced Sonya, who was short and skinny and wore a black body stocking and a torn-neck T-shirt that had MY BUTT'S ON FIRE in half-inch letters across the chest. Del goggled his eyes at the T-shirt, and Sonya laughed. "Not really," she said.

"Who's for beer?" Rudy said, herding them into the living room, which, apart from the cardboard box sculpture, looked like a miniature stage set for some far too strange drama—artfully placed black-leafed plants, droll mantel objects, a squat theater-style sofa, goofy curtains with cows and mice on them. In a minute Rudy was passing around beer in plain bottles.

"Where's the label?" Del said, studying the green bottle.

"I took it off," Rudy said. "It's just Grolsch, but it's the best we can get. It's not Stelzig's Wheat Beer, but what is?"

"Boy, I was wondering that too," Sonya said. "Sort of the Korbel of the pretentious set."

"O.K., Sonya," he said. "Thank you for your help." He turned to Del. "She's always attacking me for things. She feels if she attacks me it relieves her of responsibility somehow. Don't let it bother you."

"O.K., I won't," Del said.

"I don't either attack you," Sonya said. "I was just trying to help you out, remind you of what we talked about with all the top ten stuff."

"Sonya thinks maybe we spend too much time putting things in rank order around here. She says I'm compensating for various things—that's an attack, isn't it, Del?"

"It depends," Del said.

"What things?" Jen said.

"I'm just man's best friend," Sonya said. "I'm just sitting here thumping my tail."

"This stuff tastes fine," Jen said. "Whatever it is. Don't worry."

"It *is* pretty good, isn't it?" Rudy said to her, happy that somebody seemed to approve. "It has some special flavor, doesn't it? Some little spin?"

"Yeah, sure," Sonya said. "Like you drink enough of it and you fall over and start puking."

"I get a headache," Del said.

"I piss wildly," Jen said.

Rudy made a face and pointed at the three of them, one after another. "O.K., I'm outnumbered now. I surrender, I apologize. I'm going to the store to get a six-pack of Really Ordinary Lite, so you won't think I'm putting on airs."

"I don't think you need to apologize just for being a little bit showy," Sonya said, giving him a way-too-earnest look. Then, sweetly, she said, "Are you still mad at me?"

"You're fine. It's these two causing the problem," Rudy said, pointing to Del and Jen. "They're acting like his brother."

"Why are you hiring him, then?" she said.

"She's plainspoken, isn't she?" Del said.

"I guess she is," Rudy said. "I wanted you to feel at home."

"That's mighty white of you," Del said. "Isn't that white of him, Jen?"

Rudy got up and pointed to the kitchen. "Let's just move along here, what do you say? I guess I'll fix the burgers. Maybe that'll help settle things down."

"I want another of these double-good beers," Jen said. "I'll go with you."

The four of them went to the kitchen. The hamburger patties were already made and sitting on a cookie sheet, each one topped with a square of waxed paper. The patties were two inches thick and as big around as CDs. Del looked at Jen and

gestured to the patties as they followed Rudy and Sonya out
the back door, where they were going to check the coals. Jen
popped him on the back of the neck and hushed him.

They watched as Rudy got ready to grill. He was in and
out of the kitchen several times. There were six burgers to be
cooked. The fire was hot, the coals were red and gray. It
smelled smoky out there. Rudy put the big patties on the grill
in a circle. Then the four of them stood there watching the
burgers sizzle.

"They look delicious," Jen said.

Smoke curled off the grill, following Rudy as he moved
around the fire. Del waved smoke away from his face. "These
are really big guys, aren't they?" Del said.

Rudy polished off his beer and clapped the bottle down on
a redwood table he had out there. "Are you saying that they're
too big?"

"They look right to me," Jen said.

Sonya was off by the garden, poking at some flowers that
were wilting. "There's no tomorrow for these," she said.

Rudy pressed the pancake flipper hard on top of each of
the patties, causing big flames and lots more smoke. Then he
turned to Del. "One thing we need to do is talk about Bud. I
think he's getting ready to have another crisis, you know?"
He wiggled the flipper in a circle next to his head.

"Why don't you talk to him?" Del said.

"He doesn't like for me to talk to him," Rudy said. "That's
the last thing he wants me to do. So you want to talk to him?
You could find out what's going on. It's for everybody's
good."

"Rudy's in love with Bud," Sonya said, coming back from
the flower bed. "Rudy talks about almost nothing but Bud.
Twenty-four hours a day—Bud this, Bud that. I wish Bud
would do such and such. If only Bud thus and so. See, we're
way long on Bud. We need you to take a load off."

"I am not in love with Bud," Rudy said.

"She's direct, she's funny," Jen said, nodding at Sonya and tapping Del's arm.

"I'm serious," Rudy said. "Bud's getting loose around the edges. And if he goes to California again, we'll have problems with the dean of studies."

"Oops," Del said. "You've got a dean of studies problem?"

"Yeah. He's an old fart who features himself Mr. Educator. He was in English at some half-good university, and he's never gotten over it. He published a book on a local subject —corruption in city administration, something like that, maybe the college administration—and ever since he's a vital cog in the free press of south Mississippi. But that's not the problem. The problem is he doesn't like anything disturbing the surface of his world. He was upset when Bud left last summer."

"Why? It was summer," Del said.

"Bud was scheduled to teach last summer," Rudy said. "And Bud's security isn't what it was, especially if the dean of studies has him in mind."

"I see," Del said.

"Just chat with him," Rudy said, waving his burger tool at Del. "Don't make a big thing; just see if you can't . . . you know."

"Yeah," Del said.

Rudy waved them away from the grill and then he flipped the hamburgers, one after another, trying to be sure they landed right back where they started.

AFTER DINNER they sat around in the living room making conversation. They didn't do a very good job. Rudy sat in a white wicker chair with a floral-print seat, his knee cocked up and his testicles edging out of his shorts. The testicles were held in white mesh, the kind that's inside a bathing suit as a built-in underpant. Del studied this situation curiously, assuming Rudy was doing it on purpose, though he couldn't quite feature what the purpose might be. Jen gave Del a look like What the fuck is this? and Sonya seemed to be working to signal Rudy, shifting her legs around, but Rudy didn't get the signal or didn't take it if he got it. There was talk about rock 'n' roll, MTV, international affairs, domestic politics, movies, Jen's magazine, Biloxi restaurants, Spike Lee, students, foreign cars, but nobody managed to tell Rudy about the shorts.

Finally, as the conversation was sinking under its own weight, Jen wagged a forefinger at Rudy's crotch and said, "Who're your little friends here?"

Rudy glanced down, saw himself, said, "Oh, shit," then shot up out of the chair, bouncing a couple of times to get everything straightened out, then bounced more, going off into the next room, shouting his goodbyes.

ON THE WAY HOME Jen and Del stopped at a Circle K gas station minigrocery to get Vienna sausages. Jen had an idea that she couldn't last the night without Vienna sausages, so they stopped. Del got a couple of boxes of Chocolate Snaps, a kind of cookie he remembered from childhood and could only seem to find in gas stations. Jen got two cans of Vienna sausages and a loaf of white bread. They got some diet Cokes and a two-pack of Grolsch. There was a kid in the Circle K who looked just like a killer—he was having a bad hair day, there was grease on him, he had skin problems, the big sneer, clothes that looked like they smelled bad, and teeth out of an old David Lynch movie. He was buying lots of gum.

Hidden behind the chip rack, Jen whispered to Del about this guy. He hushed her, got in line behind the kid, and paid for their stuff, then dragged her out to the car.

It was a still night. No breeze. It was one of those nights when the air is like a glove exactly the shape of your body.

"You want to stop on the beach?" he said. "Sit there and take it easy?"

"Sure," she said, but when they got the car pulled over, she didn't want to get out. "It's kind of hot out there. And what are those people out there doing? It looks like they're having some kind of party." She pointed toward the beach, where there was a group of maybe a dozen, maybe fifteen people. They had a small bonfire that had burned away, leaving only embers and an odd flare. Occasionally, Del heard laughter rise like scared birds.

"Take the job," Jen said. "It's good. I don't think Rudy's that bad, except for the balls—Jesus."

"You think he didn't know they were danglers?"

"How could you not know?" she said, shaking her head. "What about Bud and this dean? You think he's in trouble?"

"No. Bud lands on his feet. Bud always does all right."

"If Bud loses his job, Margaret's in trouble, he's in trouble, and you're in trouble."

"You mean, for the job?" Del said.

"No, for him. Your investment in Bud is substantial. You love him."

"I depend on him to bring us large gifts," Del said.

"Yeah," she said. "You're a real tough guy."

HIS MOTHER CALLED at two o'clock. He'd been connected to Compuserve, reading stories for the next day's *Washington Post,* and because he had call waiting, her call knocked him off the network. She was worried about him, she said.

"Are you trying to be quirky mother of the year? You're seventy-seven years old. You're supposed to be asleep."

"I know," his mother said. "I didn't feel like sleeping. Your father's asleep. It seems like that's all your father does now is sleep. He sleeps in the morning after breakfast, he sleeps after lunch, he sleeps after dinner, and he sleeps at night. He's got some kind of narcolepsy."

"I think he's fine," Del said. "He probably just likes to sleep."

"He's trying to escape me," Del's mother said. "I know what he's doing. How's your brother Bud? I'm really worried about him."

"I thought you were worried about me."

"I worry about both my children," she said. "I was sitting here reading this book on Laurence Olivier, you know, the one you sent me—I like this book, by the way—and I was sitting here reading, and I suddenly started thinking about Bud, and I had the feeling Bud was in trouble."

This was typical. Whenever she was bored and wanted to call but had no reason, this was the kind of reason she would give: she had suddenly had the sense that Del was in trouble, or that Bud was in trouble, or that Margaret was in trouble, or that Del's wife was in trouble, when he had a wife.

"No, I think he's fine," Del said. "I'm going over there soon, maybe tomorrow. We're having dinner."

"Are you and Bud getting along?" she said. "Do you think it was a good idea for you to move over there?"

"We always get along," he said.

"You like Bud, don't you?" she said.

"Yes, Mother," Del said.

"If it turns out he's in trouble, I want you to take care of him," she said.

"He's not in trouble," Del said. "He's fine. And why'd you send this guy over here? This semi-priest guy? What's that about?"

"He said he was a friend of yours. He was at Saint Anthony's, wasn't he? What's the harm? You could use a priest."

"He's not a priest anymore, Mother. He's the Antichrist."

"Oh, pish," his mother said. "What's the next book you're sending?"

"I don't remember," Del said. "Maybe a murder mystery. One of those true-life murder mysteries. How would you like that?"

"No," she said. "I don't like murder. Just pick out something and send it. It really doesn't matter. I'll forget it the day after I read it, anyway. Last night I saw a movie on television I thought was wonderful, so I told your father, and he said we'd seen it last week."

"He didn't have to tell you," Del said.

"Oh, you're always attacking your father," she said.

"That's what he thinks," Del said. "You don't think that."

"Sometimes I think it too," she said. "What are you doing up? Are you alone there? Do you have company?"

"Yes," Del said. "I have company."

"Is that the teenager?" his mother said. "With the horror stories?"

"She's twenty-four, Mother," he said.

"Now, her name is Jen, is that right?" His mother wasn't used to Jen yet, wasn't used to him having a new girlfriend instead of Karen. It wasn't that she thought having a new girlfriend was a bad idea; on the contrary, she seemed excited by it, interested, even intrigued. There was wry approval in her jokes. Still, she wasn't sure, and when he first told her about Jen, she suspected it wasn't much of a relationship but was more of a *convenience,* as she called it. But after Jen was around for a while, she warmed to the idea. From time to time they sent her some of Jen's magazines, and she seemed to enjoy those. At least she said she did. Sometimes she clipped grotesque stories out of the Houston papers and sent them over. She was more lively than most mothers at seventy-seven, even though her memory wasn't so good. Sometimes she'd ask something, forget the answer, and ask again before the conversation was over. That bothered her more than him. Sometimes, when she was in a good mood and Jen was in a good mood, he'd put Jen on the phone, and then she and his mother, more than fifty years apart in age, would talk away as if they were old pals. He'd sit across the room and watch, listening to Jen's part of the conversation, wondering where they learned to do that kind of thing.

Del said, "Mother, it's time you went to bed. Say good night."

"Is everything O.K.?" she said.

"Yes, everything is fine, but it's the middle of the night. It's time for you to go to bed."

"You're awake," she said.

"I stay up late," Del said. "I'm a young man, and I can afford to stay up late."

"Did you see the story about the new sins the Church has decided on?" she said.

"No. What story?"

"It was in the paper. There's a new universal catechism that updates the sin list, identifies sins that are products of modern-day society." He heard her rattling the newspaper. "Here it is. Tax evasion, mistreatment of immigrants, financial speculation, environmental abuse, and artificial insemination."

"You're kidding me, aren't you? That's not the list."

"That's it," she said. "Part of it. Holy Mother Church has put some German guy on the case. Drunk driving is a sin, and so is 'having an immoderate taste for speed' in the automotive area. That's you, isn't it?"

Del said, "Send it, will you?"

"Do you want me to wake your father?" she said.

"No. There's no reason to wake him," Del said. "I'll talk to him tomorrow, the next day—sometime when he's between naps."

"Everything O.K. with you and Jen?" she said.

"Peachy," Del said.

"Bud's O.K.?" she said.

"Yes."

"I'm just reading over here," she said.

"I know, Mother. Laurence Olivier," Del said.

"He was good," she said.

"Yes, I know," Del said.

"I guess I'll read a little more," she said.

JEN WAS TRYING ON new white cotton underpants she'd bought earlier in the day. "At least she knows my name," Jen said. "We're making progress."

"Yes, we are," Del said.

"That's good," Jen said. "I like her. You should tell her to send pictures. I'd like to see what she looks like now."

"Maybe you could swap pictures," Del said. "We could get the camera out here tonight and get some pictures of you in this new casual wear. Send those over."

"I'm sure she'd love that," Jen said.

24

A COUPLE OF NIGHTS LATER Jen came over while he was watching the late rerun of *Larry King Live* on CNN. "I have some things I want to put around," Jen said. "Some new things. You want to go out with me to do it?"

"Now?" Del said. "It's the middle of the night, isn't it?"

"Not the middle," she said.

"You know what I meant," Del said. "What do you have?"

"Alligator boy," she said. "I've got the Amazing Alligator Boy, and Men Learning to Be Men." She was riffling through the Day-Glo sheets in her hands. "I've also got A Land of Turtles, and one other one, I don't remember which one it was. Something I just got. Oh, yeah, it's The Most Beautiful Sounds of Life. It's a new thing."

"What is it?"

"It's this ad I found for the Private Moments Prenatal Sound Amplifier," she said. "It says: 'Listen to the very first sounds your baby makes! The miraculous sounds of new life! Feel closer to your baby than you ever thought possible! Hear thumps, hiccups, kicks, even the heartbeat, by the third trimester! Includes external speaker, headphones for personal listening, and outputs for recording.' "

"Hey," Del said, taking that issue from her. "This is a breakthrough, isn't it? A new kind of grotesque."

"Maybe," she said. "I wasn't sure about it."

"No, it's good," he said. "Big step."

"I was just looking around a little," she said. "Trying some stuff. I was thinking of getting them out before I change my mind."

"And you want me to go with you?" Del said.

"You could. It would be nice. You could protect me from the dangers of this vile night, where all wretched and terrifying events are at every moment on the point of happening to a young woman such as myself."

"I could come along and watch, anyway," Del said.

"You could do that," she said. She struck some poses. "Here's me screaming. Here's me with my eyes rolled back in my head. Here's me scratching the cheek of my assailant. Here's me in a high dramatic conflict with my world."

"Are you going dressed like that?" Del said.

"What's wrong with this?" she said.

She appeared to be wearing only a T-shirt. "You seem to be wearing just a T-shirt," he said.

"I have pants on," she said. "You just can't see them."

"What good are pants if you can't see them?" Del said.

"You could see them if you maneuvered into that area," she said. "If you got close enough, you could see them."

"But if we're out there stapling things to telephone poles, it's going to look like you don't have any pants on," Del said.

"Well, what it looks like and what it is are two different things," she said.

"I know that, and you know that, but the raping population is unaware."

"What do you want me to do? Wear a sign that says 'Pants Below'?" she said, waving a finger across the front of her T-shirt.

"Whatever," Del said, getting up, waving away his own objection. "Whatever you say. Maybe you should just take the pants off and we'll go without the pants, since the shirt doesn't say that about the pants being there." He started for the front door.

"That's clever," she said, turning around and heading toward the bedroom.

"Where are you going now?" Del said.

"In here to make you happy," she said. "I'm going to make you love me, make our lives worth living, make my pants visible—all at once."

25

DEL TOOK MONDAY OFF, slept until one, traced some new horror drawings for Jen to look at, then went for a late-afternoon lunch at Mandarin House, the Chinese beachfront spot where they usually got takeout. He stopped to see Bud on the way home. Bud was on the sun porch, sitting by the window in a wicker chair with the cat, Walter, both of them looking out at a bird that was in the tree by the glass.

"What's all this?" Del said, doing a quick inventory of the room. There were about two dozen clock radios on the floor surrounding Bud, all out of their boxes.

"Students," Bud said. The bird Bud was watching shifted around, jumping from one limb to another, rippling its feathers. "See that?" he said, nodding his head toward the window. The bird was standing on a limb of the tree, scratching its beak on the bark, twisting its head back and forth, seeming to stare in at Bud.

"Why are there all these radios here?" Del said. "What're you doing?"

"Right now I'm watching this bird hop around in this tree," Bud said. "It's got something stuck in its mouth. It could be a chinaberry, but it looks like a rock to me. So what makes a bird eat a rock?"

Del realized then that his brother was drunk, but he couldn't tell how drunk. "You had a few drinks, eh?" Del said.

"You think there's more to this rock than meets the eye?" Bud said, his voice turning mechanical. "Does this rock look like a real rock? What about the bird? If the bird is chewing on the rock, why isn't it getting smaller?"

"Oh," Del said. "We've got a problem, is that it?"

Bud grabbed Del's arm and pulled. His grip was solid and tight. "But listen," he said. "Where did that rock come from? What about the bird? How strong are birds' teeth? Is something wrong with that bird? Is something written on the side of that rock? Does this tree look like a real tree?"

Del yanked his arm free. "Well," he said, "it's coming out of the ground and it has leaves, so I'd say yes, tree."

Bud turned back to the glass. The bird was gone. "Hmm," Bud said, looking around in the yard. "It was not a real bird, I guess. Might have been a bird, standing there, displaying human emotion."

"So what is all this junk? Did you take the MasterCard approach? Can we return everything?"

"Sure, I guess. I was at Sam's and Service Merchandise." He stopped and eyed his purchases. "Hey! They're looking at me, see that? How they're all sitting out on their boxes?" He pointed around the room, sweeping his open hand. "They're like devoted little students."

"I'm going to get started on this," Del said, waving at the room. "Maybe I can put it back together before Margaret arrives." He started repackaging the radios. It wasn't that difficult. Bud had just pulled them out and put them on their boxes, as if they were on display. Del put each one in its packing materials, then its box, carefully, trying to make it look as if nothing had even been touched, as if nothing had happened.

When he finished each package he taped it shut with clear package-sealing tape, then stacked the boxes by the door. Bud watched him work. "I'm O.K., you know," Bud said. "I'm not that drunk. I could do this."

"It's fine," Del said. "I don't mind helping."

When the telephone rang Bud dived for it and missed, landing on the floor of the sunroom. Del picked up the receiver and said, "Hello?" He put out a hand to help Bud up. Margaret was on the phone.

"We're having a little bit of a problem over here," Del said. "It looks like Mr. Bud went on a radio expedition."

"What'd he buy?" she said.

"Radios," Del said. "I'm reboxing them now. Is Jen with you?"

"Yes. We've been at school. We were calling to see if Bud wanted dinner. Then we were going to call you too. We were thinking a family thing. We're going to Bob's—do you want to come?"

"Maybe not," Del said. "I think you need to give us a while over here."

"Is this a real problem? Should I come back?"

Bud had gotten up and was sitting on the arm of the sofa, motioning for Del to give him the phone. "Who is it?" Bud said. "Is that Margaret?"

"No, we're fine," Del said. "You go on. Why don't you come by the condo later. That's where we'll be."

"O.K.," Margaret said. "I got it."

WHEN THE REPACKING WAS DONE, they headed for Del's. It was turning dark outside, the way it does in fall, fast, as if the sun suddenly runs out of energy. There was mist coming in—the weather was getting colder. It was chilly already. In the car, Bud was pretending to be a dog, sticking his face out the window, snapping at the retreating light. He laughed at himself doing this.

"Bud," Del said. "Get in the car, will you? C'mon. I'm rolling up the window."

Bud stretched his neck out over the edge of the glass. "Roll it up!" he said. "Roll it up!"

"Oh, Jesus," Del said. "O.K. Let's hear you bark, anyway."

Bud did that, barked, for the rest of the trip through the short lamplit streets to the Tropic Breeze.

Del gave Bud the second bedroom, which was mostly storage and computer setups and a single bed, left over from Pixie's reign. Bud was up and down, going to the bathroom, going to the kitchen for water, looking for snacks. Finally he stayed in the bedroom for forty minutes, quiet the whole time, so Del assumed he was sleeping.

Then, when he came out, he was hung over. The condo was dark except for the reading lamp Del had been using to flip through the new issue of *Windows User*. It was raining lightly outside, and the windows in the living room had condensation on them. There was no thunder or lightning, just a steady, spare drizzle, small bits of water on the glass.

"I feel like shit," Bud said, standing at the edge of the room in his socks. "Why did we come over here? I have to go home, don't I?"

"Don't worry," Del said. "Nobody's there. Jen and Margaret are eating, and then they're coming here. Margaret can take you back to the house after that."

"That's going to be fun," Bud said. He crossed the room and snapped on the TV, fingered the four cassettes that were alongside it, took one out of its sleeve and pushed it into the VCR. He hit the button. There was blue screen while the tape settled itself, and then it was Bud working, the tape Bud had sent back from California. Just the tight frame of Bud ignoring the camera, moving papers around, talking to himself.

"Are you sure you want to watch this?" Del said.

"I put it on," Bud said, leaning back from the TV to watch himself. "See? It's me. Have you got aspirin? I need milk and aspirin."

Del went to get them. He heard Bud crank up the sound on the tape, just the noises in the hotel room, the squeaks in the chair Bud had been sitting in, the click of his ballpoint put down on the plastic tabletop, the rough breathing. Del leaned over the kitchen counter to see if Bud was watching. He was, mimicking what he was doing on-screen—scratching his chin, turning his head, folding his arms.

Del got himself a diet Coke, and the milk and aspirin, and went back to the living room.

"This is strange, isn't it?" Bud said. "Why do you suppose I did this?"

"To give us the pleasure of your company," Del said. "You look a little like Brian Dennehy sometimes in here."

"That's what you think when you look at this?" Bud said. "Look at me here." He grabbed Del's neck and pushed it toward the TV. "What do you see? Trouble, right? What's he doing? You see tiny and delicious lamb chops anywhere in his future? No, you don't."

"You don't like lamb chops," Del said.

"Yes I do," Bud said, dropping into the sofa, wiping his forehead with his hand. He sat there a second looking at his open palm, then showed it to Del, holding it out in front like a Stop sign. "It's wet," Bud said. "Anxiety."

"You want a towel?"

"Hey! Wait a minute," Bud said, sitting up. "Here's a great idea. Have you got a lot of gauze? Tape and stuff?"

"You're going to dry your head with gauze?"

Bud was up and headed for the master bathroom. "Is it back here?" Bud said.

"Yes," Del said, following him. "I guess. In the closet there. The usual."

Bud brought a fresh towel and a handful of first-aid stuff —rolls of gauze, adhesive tape, a pair of scissors.

"What're we doing here?" Del said. "Bud?"

Bud smiled, patted Del's shoulder. "Wait and see." He went into the kitchen.

"What do you want now?" Del trailed after him. "Why don't we come in here and sit and talk, maybe wait for them to come home?"

"That's exactly what we'll do," Bud said. "But while we're waiting we have a program." He came back with aluminum foil, paper towels, a thing of Magic tape.

"I thought you wanted to watch yourself on TV," Del said. "Look here—watch your eyes here, right here."

"I've seen them, Del. Many times." Bud started unraveling the gauze, then stopped. "I want to do my head, you know? Like we used to when we were kids. But first you need to know I'm better. I feel better. Who knows why. It just went away, and now there's this relief."

"Do your head?" Del said.

"Hold this a minute," Bud said, handing Del the gauze. "You're a good brother, Del. I like you. Really. You're even interesting. We had the good, restful sleep. And you repacked all that crap I bought, which was brotherly. I just kind of got taken away there, buying stuff. Sometimes I start something and then I get tired."

"How're you feeling now?" Del said. He was staring at the screen, looking at that version of Bud instead of the one in the room with him. "You know, I've been worried about us since I moved here. I don't know how this happened, honest to God, and it's killing me. How we got messed up."

"It's not you," Bud said. He slapped Del's forehead. "Are you listening? Not you and Margaret. Never was, really. Or maybe it was contributing, but it got confused. But now I know what it is, and it's me. I changed. It's when I'm out there; when I'm going around and I see a woman I'm interested in, I'm not interested anymore. That used to be everything to me, but it changed and I didn't even know it. I must be giving off a new signal too, because they know I'm not a player. I'm dead to them."

"C'mon," Del said. "You're exaggerating."

"No, I'm not. I like to remember what it's like being enchanted by a woman, to have her look at you and to look back, and both of you feel it. You don't even want to follow up, just want that minute when she smiles and means that if it were another life, if the circumstances were different, if the time and place were right, then, unequivocally, *yes*. That, and the scent of her as she passes you in an aisle, the light trace of her skirt grazing your thigh, or her blouse on your forearm as you reach for a magazine. You want to touch her hair as if by accident. That's all."

"It's a mood deal. You're going to be fine," Del said.

"I am fine. I like Margaret. I like you." Bud pointed to the first-aid stuff on the sofa. "Now I want you to help me with my head. Here, I'll show you." He took the gauze and wrapped it around his head a couple of times like a blindfold, then held it with one hand, motioning to Del with the other. "Cut it there, and tape it, please."

When the blindfold was secure, Bud began to wrap the paper towels around his head. He angled them down toward his neck, tighter there so they made a kind of collar, then back up and over the top of his head. When he dropped the roll he said, "Shit. Will you get that? You better take over."

"How much of you are we doing?" Del said, fetching the towels.

"Just the head, maybe the hands," Bud said. "Clothes cover the rest of me. Like the Invisible Man, remember?"

That was a thing they'd done as kids, wrapped each other up like the Claude Rains character in the movie. They'd used old sheets, and pillowcases, even towels sometimes. It had been a staple among the rainy day amusements. One or the other of them would get to play the Invisible Man, would get wrapped up so that his whole head was bandaged, body and arms too, if there was time and the rain was persistent. When the wrapping was complete, whoever was wrapped would stay that way for hours, would stagger around the house and try not to bump into the furniture, would try to eat through the tiny mouth hole, try to talk, try to listen to the TV, or would just sit there and try to be invisible.

"O.K. Here we go," Del said. "Can you see?"

"I can't see anything." Bud stuck his finger into the bandage in the center of his mouth, making sure there was an opening.

Del opened a new roll of gauze and wrapped that around his brother's head, skirting the mouth. Sixty feet of gauze. It covered the paper towels and pressed them into more of a head shape. "Here comes the Reynolds Wrap," he said, covering Bud's head with the foil. When he finished he formed the foil to Bud's head with his hands.

"How's that feel?" Del said.

"Feels O.K.," Bud said, reaching up to peel off some foil by his mouth. "Ready to go." He was sort of mumbling. The mask of foil moved when he talked. He reached up and split the foil a little more.

Bud was a metal head with a ragged hole where his mouth was.

"Just a minute," Del said. He went to the bathroom closet and got out a white sheet, brought it into the living room, started cuts about a foot apart along its short side, then tore the sheet into strips.

The video was still running—Bud at his desk shuffling papers, the sound of the drawer being opened, the chair groaning with Bud's movement.

"What're you doing?" Bud said. It was a little hard to understand him.

"Sheet strips," Del said, wrapping Bud's head again, crisscrossing the strips around the mouth. He could feel the air when Bud breathed out. He held each strip in place as he started the next, and when he finished the last strip he taped the end of that with a few circuits of masking tape. Bud's head was getting quite large.

"You can't see, can you? Not even light? You know that glowing kind of light?"

"I still see the glow," Bud said, shaking his head.

"You want me to keep going?" Del asked. There was no answer, so Del kept going, wrapping Bud's head with a new roll of gauze.

"How about that?" Del said, speaking softly to check Bud's hearing.

There was no response, so he bent over close to Bud's ear, where he figured his ear was, and said, "Is it all right?"

Bud shook his head to say no, then flailed about trying to grab Del's arm, finally getting it. He said, "More." It sounded like a noise a small cow would make.

Del went into the bedroom and found another sheet, white with a pale-green and sand-colored Art Deco print. "This is it," he said, bringing the sheet back into the room.

He wound that sheet without tearing it into strips, and he finished quickly, steering clear of Bud's mouth, tucking the tail of the sheet up under the wraps. Bud's head was huge.

"How about that?" Del said, talking loud.

Bud suddenly tried to stand up, but he was wobbly. He held out his arms as if to catch something, and Del grabbed him.

Bud said, "Window," then pointed where he must have thought the windows were.

"Wait a minute; just stand here, O.K.?" He tapped Bud on the shoulder to be sure Bud understood, then went into the second bedroom and brought out the office armchair that was at his desk. He rolled that over in front of the window, then guided Bud to it and sat him down.

The head was big and elongated, fatter at the top and tapered toward the neck. When he was sitting, Bud rubbed his feet quickly back and forth on the carpeted floor, then held both his legs straight out as if he wanted something to rest them on. Del shoved the Arvaratum box across the room and steered it under Bud's feet.

Then Bud held up his hands. "Hands," he said, his voice muffled.

"The chair is loose," Del said, wrapping each of Bud's hands with a pillowcase and then pulling a clean thick white athletic sock over it to hold it in place. "It's loose, so you'd better be careful, O.K.?" He punched Bud's shoulder with a forefinger.

Then Bud just sat there in front of the glass.

Every couple of minutes Del tapped Bud's shoulder and asked if he was O.K., and Bud made a sound each time to say he was.

Then Del sat down on the couch for a few minutes, watching his brother against the glass. After a while he straightened up the room, made himself a sandwich, got a Coke, then sat back on the sofa, watching Bud. He lowered the volume on Bud's tape so that it was just a calm, open-microphone sound. It was quiet in the room, raining outside. Bud was listing slightly from the weight of the head-wrapping. Bud on TV was working on his papers. Del had always wanted Bud to be a little steadier, a little plainer, but now he knew that wasn't going to happen—it was going in the other direction. He listened to the tick of rain on the glass, on the deck outside. He heard the hiss of tires on Highway 90. He caught a high whistle noise from Bud, saw Bud's breath rippling the loose wrapping around his mouth.

"I guess Margaret and Jen will be here soon," Del said.

Bud waved indifferently, moving his left hand just enough to show he'd heard.

"I think this is probably good, what we're doing. It's going to be fine," Del said. "You look funny like that, but this is a good idea. I remember doing this. I wish I could be wrapped up too. It helps us get things in perspective. All the stuff that has gone on, all the messy business, the way things got fouled up there at first. Who knew that things were going to go like that? I didn't know." He watched Bud on TV, then Bud in the room with his head wrapped up. "There was no way to know. We've got to get beyond it, though, all of us. Go straight out there, into the darkness. What else is there to do?"

Bud rocked forward suddenly, out of the chair, standing uncertainly.

"I like living here," Del said, getting up and crossing the room to see what Bud was doing. "The town's good. I like the people—I even like Rudy, and Father Marco D'Lo, if he ever comes back. The brown water out there—I like it all. It's more like a real place than those tourist deals. Maybe that's just my way of seeing; I don't know. But it's good being here. You're a big factor for me, Bud, you know that? Without you I'd probably have been a lawyer. You said you thought I was all right once, way back. I came to see you in San Diego. That started it all for me. Anyway, everything's going to be O.K. now. I'll take that teaching deal, just to try it out. See how it goes."

Bud hit his hand on the glass door. "Open," he said.

"What? You want to go outside?" Del said. "It's raining."

Bud hit his hand again on the glass. "Open it for me," he mumbled. "C'mon." He was using both hands to get at the lock. Del heard it snap.

"Wait a minute, Bud. What're you doing? You don't need to go out." Del grabbed his brother's arm, but Bud yanked it away and turned, awkwardly, to face him. It was like facing a mummy.

Then Bud felt his way back to the door handle and slid the door open. He forgot the screen, though, and walked right into it, bounced off, and Del had to catch him.

"You hit the screen," Del said.

There was a very high, faint whistle coming out of the wrappings, a tune, like a march. Bud tapped Del's arm with his sock-covered hand. "Screen," Bud said.

So Del opened the screen and led Bud out onto the balcony, guided his hand to the rail, then stacked the chairs that were in Bud's way off in the corner. Bud paced the length of the wood-decked balcony, moving mechanically, holding on to the handrail, then turned and paced back. Del followed him, edging along just behind. The rain was light, mistlike. After two passes Bud stopped, turned to Del, and pointed inside, smacking the glass with his sock-covered hand. "I got it," he said.

Del nodded and said, "O.K.," then slipped past Bud and stepped into the living room. He stayed by the door for two more turns, watching Bud go back and forth unsteadily, then he backed up and sat on the couch, watching his brother through the glass and the open door. Bud's whistle grew more pronounced. He was clearly marching out there, keeping time with his free hand as he swiveled and tilted across the balcony, swinging left and right, rocking back and forth, his sheet-wrapped head bobbing like an enormous Q-Tip against the little black sky.